TRAVELING BEYOND THE SURFACE

To Raelynn —
Wishing you live well lived each
day — thanks for listening to me
as I put this book together

Carol Pru

TRAVELING
Beyond the Surface

CAROL R. PALO

LUMINARE PRESS
WWW.LUMINAREPRESS.COM

Printed in the United States of America

Luminare Press
442 Charnelton St.
Eugene, OR 97401
www.luminarepress.com

LCCN: 2022905473
ISBN: 978-1-64388-932-0

Dedicated to

    My family

    Our beautiful planet

    That which connects us on our journey

Contents

Invitation

This is your invitation to join me on an adventure

A most unusual adventure… and you will note this is not the standard travel agenda and our travels will entail more than suitcases.

I'll be your guide, guest authors will assist, and one of the them will share his story covering all these travels in a most positive way.

We'll start with how I grew into a passion for traveling in its many forms. You'll find a large portion of these travels covers six continents: icebergs, tropical islands, and pandas, as well as people, customs, and our commonalities. Then we will veer off into journeys more personal and inward, followed by the journey of aging. The adventure continues into the turbulence of life's unwanted journeys via illness, the remembrance of a war, an essay on the perils of character deficits, a journal on Pandemic 2020, and interviews with fellow travelers dealing with the pains and difficulties we all face.

You can select a section or particular place of travel that appeals to you, but I hope you will travel the whole distance with me because, in the process, we will be creating a new place that redefines the sense of what traveling is all about. Together we will share the laughs, joys, surprises, triumphs and poignancies of being alive-a fuller richer meaning of the many types of traveling that make us who we are.

Interested? Curious? Then, as in all travels, we take a step into the beginning…

Six Continents

*T*he epiphany came to me while standing in front of the meat counter. I had stopped by the grocery store on the way home from work and realized, with my son and daughter away at college, I could buy any package or cut of meat I wanted. No need to worry about who eats what, their schedules, or my budget. I could eat it at midnight if that seemed like dinner time to me. The revelation was soon muted by the realization I had no idea what I would want to eat. It had been so long since thoughts of what I wanted just for me had occurred, I wasn't sure I knew what to do with this sudden power. I bought a box of cereal and went home.

Eating my cereal, I talked to myself (easier to do when you live alone). "I don't know what I like to eat, if I want to cook, or who I've turned out to be," came out of my mouth. I certainly wasn't the same person I had been twenty years earlier. After some thought, it seemed dinner was only the symbol of a deeper question. Who am I now and how will I choose to live?

Over the next few weeks I found myself stepping outside myself a bit, studying this woman I had become, and wondering what should be done with her. Of course, there were parameters. I was still a mother, had a career, a home, and friends. What else did I want to do with my time, money, and energy?

Traveling had been a part of my life as far back as I could remember. As a child, there had been many road trips from Canada to Mexico. The idea of new places, bright lights and returning home with goodies of various types, was a happy memory. In my wilder late teen years, there had been a great deal of travel crisscrossing the United States with its own set of stories and adventures. It seemed a trip with my children was the way I always chose to spend any extra money that came my way. The idea of actually seeing the world, just picking a spot on the map and going, was very exciting. With my fiftieth birthday approaching, I decided to celebrate with a trip to someplace in Europe.

Europe seemed less exotic and less scary than many other parts of the world, which was important to me, since I wanted to go by myself.

I pulled out a map of Europe and spent a good deal of time trying to figure out how I would determine which country or countries to visit. The planning took place in 1994, before the average person would be relying on the internet, apps, or much in the way of technology. The telephone, word of mouth, travel agents, AAA (American Automobile Association) or similar organizations, travelogues (short movies about interesting places in the world), maps, and books were the more common tools to determine travel plans. The major sources of communication were the telephone, post office mail, and fax machines. I can hardly believe I am writing this. Technology plays such a vital role in our lives it doesn't seem possible that safety, fun, and worthwhile travel times could have taken place. But they did, and what wasn't available then allowed for a type of travel just as valuable but offering different opportunities.

I decided to start with Italy. It was a country I hadn't experienced yet. The vision of the art, architecture, and diversity of landscape was almost overwhelming. My daughter had lived in Milan as an exchange student and spoke Italian. She was also familiar with the cities most tourists visit their first time to Italy. So I determined I would spend time in Rome, Venice and Florence. I was planning to use all my vacation time on this trip and had limited funds. I made a decision that would prove to be the sound basis for my future travels, and which I recommend. Rather than wait for the perfect amount of time, plenty of money, and the ability to see everything I wanted, I would fit in what I could do with my time, money and wish list. Perhaps there would be the opportunity for future trips to see more, but at least I would have experienced this trip with some of my wishes accomplished. Then came the question of how many days to spend in each city, whether to focus on those cities exclusively, or visit somewhere else. I talked to my daughter and wandered the aisles of book stores scanning through travel books of Italy and their recommendations. Although I could easily have spent the two weeks available in the three cities, I decided to look at my map again and see what other countries surrounded Italy.

Because Italy is adjacent to so many countries I wanted to see, it seemed best to look at what would attract me enough to visit one of them instead of spending the full time in Italy. Jazz sparked my interest, so when I heard there was a jazz festival in Montreux, Switzerland occurring while I would be in Europe, it seemed to be a terrific opportunity. Without internet to check such things, I placed a phone call to the Montreux Chamber of Commerce (phone number provided to me by the phone company's international operator). I asked the lady who answered the phone if there was a jazz festival. Yes, a jazz festival was scheduled. Her English was good and she gave me additional information about which jazz greats would be there, places to stay, and transportation options. When asked who I should talk with to set this up, she told me there was an American company that specialized in jazz festival travel and they handled all the details. She told me they operated out of California and gave me the company's name. After hanging up, I decided to attend the jazz festival in southern Switzerland at Lake Geneva and then travel to Italy.

After ensuring I could take the two weeks in July that I needed for this trip, I contacted the travel agency that specialized in jazz festivals and found out what their tour covered and what I would need to take care of. Then came figuring out travel to and from Europe, how to travel through Switzerland and Italy. There were itineraries, hotels, plus more and more as I thought my way through what these two weeks would entail. As I write this now, it sounds daunting, but I was focused on having a great adventure and celebrating my fiftieth birthday in Italy, so the research and decisions were just part of that adventure.

The whole process got much easier after contacting some airlines and explaining my travel plans and goals (again, using the telephone and dealing directly with people). I selected an airline with travel packages that included setting up hotels, train travel between cities, as well as getting me to Europe and back. My first big solo venture would be flying to Rome. I would transfer to the train station and take the train for a day trip to Assisi, then back to Rome followed by an overnight train ride (with a shared compartment to sleep in) to Montreux. From there I would take a cab to a hotel in easy walking distance of the concert venues and the lake. I got a good tip to ask for a room facing away from the lake because they were half the price of the lake view rooms. After the jazz festival, I would take another night train back to Rome and follow the itinerary set up for me. There would be several days in Rome, followed by time in

Venice, Florence, and finally Milan, where the trip would end with a flight home.

My dream was becoming a reality. I sent in down payments, started checking the exchange rates for the dollar and made lists of what I still needed to do. It was exhilarating, scary, empowering. I purchased a small book of Italian phrases and asked my daughter to help me say some of them accurately. There was no Euro to unify spending money, so I prepared to purchase both Italian and Swiss currency in the USA at a local bank and overseas. I checked my credit card limits too. What should I pack? What about the summer heat? I never even thought about how hauling two very large bags would be for me. Bags didn't come with wheels in 1994.

July came, and with it a bon voyage party at work. I was really going on this great adventure, which felt surreal until the plane actually left the airport.

Now an experienced solo traveler, it seems I'm in the air viewing sunrises on most trips and have written about many of them. But this was the beginning of a new passion: travel, and for this first solo trip, it was a sunset that caught my emotions. Through the airline travel package I flew from Portland, Oregon to Cincinnati and on to JFK in New York. On the flight to Rome I observed in my journal, "The sky is like an ocean frozen motionless in time. Out at a distance, reflecting the pink and lavender of sunset, clouds roll in like every type of wave. Capped tight curls move in crescendos of power and closer in, all is a soft clear blue that goes on and on toward the changing hues."

I realized how much I needed the freedom of adventure and how constrained I slowly became without it. I slept off and on, found myself studying Italian at 5 a.m. between the end of a movie and red orange streaks of sunrise.

Getting from the airport to the train station was simple but I hadn't considered how excitement, too little sleep, hot sticky weather, and a propensity to faint would affect me. Here is why I now pay attention to such things.

The train station was huge. I needed to find the right clerk and window to get my ticket to Assisi, but the signs kept changing and my limited Italian wasn't up to it. I walked back and forth, dragging my luggage, finally standing in the middle of the massive hall to assess what to do. I finally determined to strike out toward a promising open window. Instead I opened my eyes looking up at a crowd of concerned Italians mulling over what to do. I had fainted. They helped to my feet and gathered my bags for me.

Someone who spoke English said, "You probably haven't eaten for a while and need sleep. I'll take you to the café in the station for some breakfast and you'll feel better."

I did feel better, but by then it was too late to go to Assisi and make it back in time for my train to Montreux. I was still feeling a little woozy, so striking out on my own in an unknown city felt beyond my ability. I spent the rest of the day in the train station until it was time to board for Switzerland. Police assigned to look out for irregularities in the station gave me the eye as they passed by me again and again. I wished for the ability to explain why I was there for so long but my carefully practiced phrases didn't cover the situation.

Eventually my train came; what an enjoyable train ride I had. The compartment, actually called a couchette, was cozy and I slept well. It was a shared compartment, also occupied by an Italian couple and a young woman from England. This made for sleep, restful viewing of the changing landscape and pleasurable small talk with my new acquaintances. After a solid breakfast I felt ready to tackle Switzerland. We arrived at 8:30 a.m. As I approached the back of the train station, I was blown away by the beauty of wildflowers and quaint buildings gently rolling down the hill toward glistening Lake Geneva.

I took a cab to the hotel, finding a grander representation of all I had imagined a Swiss hillside hotel might look like. It felt intimate and cozy in spite of many massive arches, shade trees, balconies, and exterior cream-colored stone. Perhaps because I arrived early, very excited to be on my first trip to Switzerland, they placed me in an extra-large room at no extra charge. The room held everything I needed and the location was perfect. It was close to the concert venues and only blocks from the lake. The hotel was mid-hillside. The various music venues formed a zigzag pathway down the hill to the lakeside boardwalk. A late afternoon hot shower had me energized for the welcome party put on by my jazz tour company. Common interests created instant friends. Ironically, in my search to meet people from all over the world, the first person I spoke to was as excited as I, and hadn't been to a European jazz festival either. He was from my home town.

Although this was a jazz festival, other types of music were also honored. Bob Dylan played the first night. There were no chairs in the large hall for good reason. The room was packed with standing room only and the crowd was predominately in their early twenties. Dylan performed with a small band and played drums incredibly well. At the end of his set there was silence and then, almost in unison, everyone pulled out a cigarette lighter, held it up and flicked it on. The tribute to his longevity as an artist and the crowds' respect for him was physically tangible.

Jazz has always felt like the sunshine to my soul, and during my stay, I was privileged to be present for Bela and the Flecktones, Cassandra Wilson, Herbie Hancock, Roy Hargrove, Randy Weston, Betty Carter and Shirley Horn. I had heard Betty Carter in New York, when I took the A Train to Birdland at age eighteen. It felt very full circle to hear her again at another pivotal point in my life. Hearing the name of the hotel where she might be staying, I tore a blank page out of my journal and sent a note to her through the concierge. I wanted her to know of my early trip to Birdland to hear her and how thrilled I was to hear her again in this amazing locale. I hope she got the note. Being such a jazz fan, I kept a journal of my impressions of the festival experience. There were several halls with performances scheduled at the same time, so we had to determine whether to hear one for their entire set, move from room to room to catch more performances, or hope to catch them at the impromptu after-hours sets. I heard Cassandra Wilson for the first time and was stricken by her style and sensual voice. I stayed for a full set by Roy Hargrove and his group playing amazing straight ahead jazz. Next up was Herbie Hancock. This is a musician who over the years keeps coming up with new techniques and ways of expressing his music. I know he was tired by the time I saw him in the lobby of one of the halls, but he was gracious enough to pose with me for a photo I still have. In the Miles Davis Hall later that night, I heard Randy Weston who unbelievably turned the piano into all kinds of things with his textured performance. The dynamite show with Betty Carter and Shirley Horn ended around 2:30 a.m., and was followed by a visit to Duke's for a rock and roll band, people watching, and some flirtation.

My routine goal became seeing as many venues as possible and then hitting the after hour joints. I slept in until the last breakfast call. Being on a very limited budget I filled up with muesili and fruit, a new taste experience for me, as well as an array of cheeses, meats, eggs and rolls, and walked down to the lake. I wandered along the boardwalk, eventually stopping at a stand selling ham and cheese crepes. That would be my early dinner. Then back to the hotel for rest, change of clothes and opportunity to catch as much music as I could handle into the wee hours.

AS GREAT AS THE MUSIC WAS, THERE WERE OTHER GREAT experiences to be had in Montreux. I had two impromptu day excursions. I had taken a risk, gambling that traveling by myself would equate to being more spontaneous than my normal life had allowed. It would also force me to connect with new people if I wanted someone to talk to and be more present through each day, since it was just me responsible for my wellbeing. All of this proved to be true.

While walking along the boardwalk one early afternoon, I saw a beautiful white ship out in the lake. The water was incredibly blue and sparkling with no clouds in the beaming sky. The ship seemed to be moving closer to my side of the lake. I watched, transfixed, until it became clear the ship would land almost in front of me. I spotted a ticket booth and asked about the ship. Turned out to be a tour boat and not only could I get on, but because I had a Europass rail ticket, I could get on board free. I couldn't believe my good luck. I got on, paid a small amount to go up to the top deck, and rented a deck chair. It was so beautiful and peaceful that time disappeared. We stopped in several picturesque communities going outward. There were no stops heading back but we passed a charming little town that created an unexpected and superb moment. People on shore were waving to us. We saw small sail boats bobbing close to the shore and a lone figure sitting on a bench was playing "Let a Smile Be Your Umbrella" on the horn. During the cruise, I kicked back in my deck chair enjoying the light breeze, unblinking sun and flawless lake. Wow! I was one of those fortunate people on a gleaming boat in the middle of Lake Geneva for others to look at. I had a grin on my face that felt like it would never come off. That afternoon, life was very, very good. Nobody knew where I was. No plans had been made. This was just a spontaneous reaction to "I want to do that now." For someone who had been a single mom raising two children and trying to build a career, this was the most exotic thing I had done in a really long time. On my way back to the hotel, the sun slid behind some clouds as I purchased my customary ham and cheese crepe, and readied myself for an afternoon nap. I woke up to massive rain, thunder and lightning. I was up quickly since I'd forgotten to close the window and the rain had ready access to me and my belongings. A little rain wasn't going to slow me down on my quest for adventures!

The next daytime adventure was a tour of Chateau Chillon. I had never been to a castle before and the ethereal beauty of the place along with its history and architecture made for a most amazing afternoon. I took a local bus to the castle and picked up the self-guide brochure. There were twenty-eight points of interest to see and learn about including the dungeon Lord Byron was held in, gallows, and eight flights up to the watch tower. Chillon was erected in the thirteenth century on Roman foundations. The castle was the residence of the Counts of Savoy throughout the Middle Ages. It underwent many transformations over those years as a fortress and for the vanity and embellishments of its owners. Many prominent figures of history, such as popes, princes and emperors were guests. In the 16th century, Lord Byron was imprisoned and during his lengthy stay composed his famous "Prisoner of Chillon." Not hard to feel the damp, gloom and sense of abandonment a prisoner would feel in the bowels of that castle. Post cards paint a stunning and brightly colored view of the castle but the real interior is faded and ancient, which makes it easy to imagine earlier times. I was moved.

I found the perfect balance point to the music and crowds another day via a steep one and one half hour train ride into the hills above Montreux. The village of Caux provided sunlit meadows and train stops allowing ample time to step out and experience the sweet smells of the grass and flowers as well as panoramic views of the valley and lake. This was my last afternoon in Switzerland and I knew packing and catching a train that evening were intruding on my attempt to savor just a little more time here. This first part of my trip had been a wonderful experience, so different from my regular life. I lived on big breakfasts (normally skipping breakfast at home), dined by a lake on crepes, and filled myself with Kit Kat bars and Sprite in the evenings. My hotel had been clean, gracious and close to every place I wanted to see. Having contacts with the jazz tour group gave me time to myself yet was never alone unless I wanted to be. The music, venues, and crowds impacted me in such a positive and powerful way. I found Montreux to be friendly, honest, clean, and most beautiful. These were my thoughts in Caux as I settled onto a bench in the shade. The very hot sun blazed down on the local chickens, finally causing them to stop cackling and focus on looking for their own shade. Eventually I saw it was late in the afternoon and time to move from the Swiss part of my trip toward Italy. Little did I know what an interesting trek that would be.

After checking out of my hotel and trudging up the hill to Montreux's train station, I double checked the time my train was leaving and settled down for final looks and thoughts of this first half of my trip. I got to the station one and one half hours early to relax and enjoy the last of my Swiss adventure but also to make sure I caught the right train. It was hard to imagine Italy to be as sublime as Montreux but I knew that was just due to my limited knowledge of Italy. Anything might be possible and the overnight sleeping compartment would ensure I would be rested for Rome. Trains seemed to arrive every ten to twenty minutes and one came for a very brief stop at the time my train was supposed to arrive. But the heading on it read Geneva Airport so I let it go by assuming mine would be the next. But it wasn't, and before long it was dark and the station master came by.

He told me, "No more direct trains till tomorrow morning. You'll have to leave."

I was stunned and told him, "I've been here for several hours. My train has not come yet!"

"Let me see your ticket. Yes, that train came right on time," was his annoyed response.

"That train said Geneva Airport not Rome on it. How could that have been my train?" I demanded.

He looked at me wearily and explained, "It doesn't matter what the train header says. When it's time, you get on the train that arrives. You're supposed to know the airport is in the same direction as Italy. You missed your train."

What to do? I'm a pretty calm, nondramatic kind of person, but I'd always wanted to throw a major dramatic temper tantrum and this seemed like the perfect time for one. So I did. It was very satisfying.

"This is not possible!", I bellowed. "I have to be in Rome in the morning. I implore you. You must help me get to Rome. There must be a way." I think I was sobbing by then.

The station master looked alarmed. It turns out one last train, no nice sleeping compartments, a simple train stopping at every single town and headed for Milan. Yes, in Milan I would have to change trains around four AM and there might be another change as well. I'd be standing and maybe sitting all night but arriving in Rome in the morning.

"Oh, you are saving me!" I gushed, "and I assume I can use my ticket. You'll see to that?"

With his shoulders drooping in resignation he refunded me my couchette fare and issued the ticket that might ultimately drop me in Rome. Because I'm sure he wanted to be rid of me, he waited with me and made sure I got on the train, the right train. We slowly wound our way through the darkness as I settled in, sitting on one of my bags and hoping someone seated would get off at the next stop. Actually there were some very interesting people to talk to on the long ride. After changing trains in Milan, we headed toward Venice and a last train change to the correct station brought me to Rome. I managed to find a seat several times and actually dozed for an hour or two. "Finally in Roma," I thought smugly to myself and with much relief, caught a cab to my hotel.

Apparently, the airline flights, cities to visit, trains and hotels on my agenda were just as attractive to many other people. There was a small group of people in the hotel lobby wearing the same little badges I had just put on. We would come across each other so often, we wound up making plans and all sharing the trip together, including an impromptu goodbye dinner in Milan on our last night. But that first morning in Rome was the introduction. The package we all seemed to have purchased had us starting in Rome and proceeding by train to Florence, Venice and Milan. In each city there were choices for tours of museums or half-day city tours. We were encouraged to use all the free time to find and enjoy the aspects of each city that spoke to us. Knowing this prior to the trip allowed us all the opportunity to do a little research or just plan on improvising. I chose a half-day tour of Rome, just to get a feel of its architectural dense wonder, and a tour of the Coliseum. I had also been in touch with the Chamber of Commerce and Tourism for Rome and received several detailed walking maps of the Seven Hills of Rome with what to look for along the way of each.

The half-day bus tour was so helpful I have incorporated such a tour into many other trips since then. A glimpse of an area or specific attraction made it easier to decide whether I truly wanted to spend more of the short time there to explore that particular site. Getting a sense of how close or far apart these locations were guided me to get maximum sightseeing each day. We had four days in Rome. I carried my English to Italian to English dictionary at all times. Often, when I was attempting to speak Italian, many natives were willing to meet me half way with whatever English they could speak.

On one of my walking tours, while looking for the buildings and statues my printed guide was pointing out, I discovered the former house of the Russian author, Nikolai Gogol. As a fan of Russian authors, spotting this plaque was very exciting. I think I spent at least an hour with my dictionary translating the plaque and I learned finding unexpected treasure in a new city is extremely satisfying. On my walking tours with maps, I could make as many impromptu stops as I liked. High points of these ventures included: coffee and people watching from a café at Piazza Navona, which is a huge public square of cafes, and often concerts and big screens for sporting events; viewing the incredible statue of Moses; Trevi Fountain, where I honored tradition and threw a coin into the fountain for good luck. It is said if you throw a coin into this fountain, you'll return to Rome someday. Of course, it would be hard to say I'd been to Rome and not taken a tour of the Vatican. The artwork, opulence, sense of history, and religious piety filled every surface and even the air. It felt very private even though my small tour group was just one of many that day.

The third day in Rome was my birthday. As I promised some friends from work, I walked to the center of a bridge over Rome's famous Tiber River and opened my birthday card from them. Out blew a large quantity of multicolored, metallic tiny figures of fifty. As they blew around me, eventually floating away on the river, it made me smile to realize fifty could feel and be whatever I wanted it to be. The day was also a big day for Italy. The Soccer World Cup was playing that evening. The games weren't in Italy, but Italy was in the final match playing their fierce rival, Brazil. If Italy won, there would be much celebrating which I would borrow for my fiftieth birthday but it was not to be. Rome was uncharacteristically quiet that night.

Just as I was becoming comfortable moving around the city it was time to board a train and head for Florence. Firenze, as the lovely city is called in Italy, is so different from Rome it is almost impossible to compare them. Where

Rome felt angular, historic, traditional, Florence had a sense of leisure, balancing nature, art, architecture and gelato. Yes, the gelato was a most sublime counterpoint to the heat of July. My "must-go-to museum", the Uffizi, was worth the one hour wait in line. So many incredibly crafted marble statues and seeing Bellini's paintings for the first time was unexpectedly moving to me. I became quite emotional. It seemed to me, these feelings came because he was able to capture the emotion of each character he painted, catching their expressions of body and face in a deep and personal way. I was also surprised to see a drawing by Henry Moore, the sculptor, in what seemed to me the only Brit in a sea of Italians and a rare opportunity for me to see an actual drawing of pre sculpting ideas and analysis. Totally exhausted that first day, I had dinner at my hotel's restaurant. It was set up as a first class cafeteria of the world and I had the delicious Florentine steak the staff suggested for me.

The next morning I joined a tour group. We crossed the Arno River and drove up through luscious gardens and opulent housing to the Piazza of Michelangelo. At the top of the winding road is the piazza, a plaza with a copy of the marble statue of David and a breathtaking and expansive view containing all of Florence. It turns out many models of this statue he started were also there as well as other sculptures and paintings of that time. I compared David, the copies and original to the Moses I'd seen in Rome. The Moses affected me more deeply. In sorting out why that was, I thought of preconceived ideas I'd had of what would move me, but then how lovingly each fold of Moses' marble cloth had been carved. Making my way through the city later, I entered the San Marco museum. This was a drastic change, as few tourists were present and it was a monastic maze of cells, steep stairs and all types of pious artwork from the early fifteenth century.

By this time the skies had clouded over and it was raining with dashes of thunder and lightning. Not prepared, I was grateful for a plastic bag given to me; which I stretched out above my head. The rain didn't last long. Even though some in my initial group of travelers left that night, I hadn't had enough of Florence and opted to stay through the next day. This was the day to explore the shops built on a bridge crossing the Arno. Oh my goodness, the quality of leather goods, creative household wares, the meld of tourists, artistic graffiti, and one last Florentine gelato. By late afternoon I was waiting for my train to Venice.

The wonderful thing about train travel is the stitching together of these large and famous cities with the countryside villages, farms, and forests. This, when traveling, is what makes a country multi-dimensional. On these rides I wished I could spend weeks in Italy, riding the trains and getting off to explore whenever a location looked appealing. Maybe someday, but not on this first trip.

The train moved us through lush forests, scattered towns and then onto tracks surrounded by water. In the distance, something appeared on the horizon, water expanding everywhere. Slowly towers, buildings and bits of land appeared. The sun came out sending out a dazzling burst of light onto the multi planes of the skyline, and with a thrilling heartbeat I found myself saying aloud, "Wow, this is Venice!"

After Rome, the train station in Venice was a miniature struck with color. Colors primarily from computer machines placed to assist with train timetables, places of interest and maps. In 1994, this was somewhat of a novelty.

My hotel, just steps away, had been a small palace in the prior century. Its deep pink stucco finish opened into a cozy, elegant space with palatial rooms now divided up into shoe box size accommodations for the many guests staying there. I didn't mind the small space at all. My whole ceiling was taken up by one enormous, ornate, crystalled chandelier. I had a damask bedspread, satin wallpaper and shuttered windows that, when opened, allowed the sound of bells and view of tiled rooftops.

Venice was such a departure from both Rome and Florence and most immersive in its own way. It is a ridiculously beautiful blend of buildings in winding mazes around opaque canals, all slowly sinking with the tide tables. The canals are the roadways and while tourists might take gondolas, most everyday business and living was handled by the vaporetti (the plural of a single vaporetto), water buses as a means of public transportation. I enjoyed a gondola ride, because I was a tourist and it's something you'd just want to do while in Italy. But the joy of the vaporetto was for me. I had a great time just wandering and getting lost riding the waterways, and walking the tiny bridges and paths to discover shops and the most delicious espresso and biscotti for breakfast and scampi for an evening meal. A major highlight for me was a visit to the Peggy Guggenheim Museum on the banks of a canal. Peggy had come to Venice and after settling in, opened her home to the artist community when so many now famous artists were just getting started. Today that home, Palazzo Venier dei Leoni, has been opened up to the public as a museum and the array of modern paintings and sculpture had me feeling I would like to move in and see them every day. Early works of Picasso, Klee, Leger, Kandinsky and my super favorite,

Magritte, graced the walls of her home. Both indoors and outside held an array of sculpture. Sculptures by Brancusi are featured as well as a particularly startling outdoor statue of a man on a horse. If you are familiar with these, you can imagine how satisfying this experience was and if you are not, perhaps you are now curious enough to check them out.

I also took part in tours to the islands of Murano and Burano, and walked through St. Mark's Square on my own. The Square, or La Piazza as it's called by Venetians, is the principal square in Venice; home to the Basilica and Doge's palace, one a religious and the other a political historical home. My first impression was marble ornateness and beauty covered in tourists and pigeons. I left with this impression, rather than wade through the cooing, wing-flapping, and more mumbling pushing tourists than I wanted to come into contact with. Motor boats to the islands proved to be a delight as the cool water sprays, breezes, sun and water brought viewpoints of both Venice and the approaching islands. Burano is an island of brightly painted houses and centuries of finely-honed artistic skills in the making of lace. The intricate patterns stood on their own as works of art as well as attachments to dresses, table cloths and handkerchiefs as a means of creating unique looks. In watching a demonstration of this rare intricate hand work, I was so impressed, especially since doing small repetitive tasks with my hands makes me crazy. Murano is the island noted worldwide for its hand blown glass foundries and the glass art that comes from them. We watched demonstrations of the techniques used to create large vases, intricate miniatures, flowers, shapes to put together for jewelry and whatever the artist felt like making next. It was very much performance art. The audience oohing and applauding at the completion of each piece as the creator smiled and bowed. I think I heard someone yell "Encore!" at the completion of a large multi colored vase. I had to have a souvenir, and purchased a small vase and an assortment of glass candies that look exactly like the fancy kind in their wrappers. I've had to stop people in my home on occasion who reached for the candies saying, "Oh, candy. I'll have one."

The following year I stopped by an art shop in my home town that is dedicated to the works of local artists and spotted a beautiful necklace that looked just like the Murano glass I had seen in Italy. I asked the owner how this clearly Murano piece could be local. He told me, "I met the artist when she brought in her glass pieces and told me her story. As a young woman she went to Italy to study to be an opera singer. When she saw the Murano glass and its creative potential she fell in love with it. She stopped studying opera and took classes and eventually gained an apprenticeship to become a glass artist." The world may have lost a fine opera singer, but I am selfishly grateful she changed careers. Of course, I bought the necklace.

There is truly no place like Venice. It is seductively easy to be led into the bliss of a little too much heat, dampness overridden by a vaporetto ride and its cool breezes. The stately buildings stand less like preserved historic sites and more like its home and heart. The food… beyond sublime in its freshness and flavors. Last dinner in Venice included antipasto of fresh tomatoes and mozzarella, fettucine Bolognese with meat sauce and, of course, a fish course. The incredible scampi, lighter than lobster, less fishy than crab, just so perfect I felt I would never be able to eat it again unless I was back in Venice. Being a dessert person, there was no way I could pass up the house-made tiramisu. Layers of cake soaked in coffee filled with a fine vanilla cream, all powered by dark chocolate and espresso. No way to move after such a meal, so I took the opportunity to ride a vaporetto in the full circle of its route. This took an hour and I could finally find my way back to the hotel to pack and prepare for a train ride to Milan where my Italian travels would end.

The train to Milan was quite empty leaving time to write, with windows open for the cool breeze. After stopping briefly in Verona, the train slowly pulled out and headed to its final destination. I supposed there were three gentlemen on the train. Milan, at a first glance, appeared very cosmopolitan and clearly business oriented. The hotel was quite beautiful and upscale and my room was large. The stay in Milan was short, and I wanted to maximize it, so I quickly showered, changed clothes, and headed out to the Duomo. The Duomo is a symbol of Milan, a unique Gothic structure and a must see. I got directions at the front desk to catch the "underground" but still located by the letter "M" for metro. I must have been getting comfortable getting around in Italy because on my way I was stopped by a couple with two children who asked me for directions in Italian. I chuckled and shared my map with them.

Aaah, the unexpected beauty of coming up the stairs, not knowing what awaits! First, there is the sign and then Piazza del Duomo appears. Directly in front of me, I caught my breath seeing the huge fragile castle like Duomo. To the left is the quad, a huge glass dome housing an exclusive shopping and restaurant area. I wandered through, peering, sometimes just gawking in the windows at the elegant timeless styles. Branching off were side streets housing more modern and casual shops full of creativity, fun items, and musical instruments.

Getting a feel for this dynamic city by walking around, seemed a good way to start the winding down of my travels.

The highlight was to be a dinner our loosely formed group decided to hold on our farewell night. A couple volunteered to make reservations at a ristorante recommended by our hotel. We met at the hotel bar over drinks and a sampling of nuts, dates, and some yellow orange fruit I couldn't identify. I was glad the nine of us walked to dinner together. On the way we encountered lots of state police, armored trucks with machine guns, a bit of a parade containing a loud rough-looking group. I was told this sort of protesting was quite common in many European cities. It was a special last evening to eat such delicious food and share our adventures. Too soon, we dispersed to pack and be ready for what we thought would be early morning flights.

Also more common, I found out, were workers striking for what they felt were inequities. This time it was air traffic controllers in France. This meant no flights could travel through French air space. Flights were being rerouted and after approximately five hours flights started taking off. I didn't mind the wait, just hoping to not miss my connections in New York. I took this time to appreciate how much these fellow travelers I'd met enriched the trip for me because of their joy of traveling and sharing the experience. I marveled at what an interesting collection of people made up our group. We had no whiners and no rudeness. I had dinner one night with a couple from Connecticut at a family style non tourist restaurant on a side street. They were my age with two children away at college like me. There was a grandfather taking his granddaughter to start a cycling trip that would wind through Switzerland as their next phase of travels. We had a few much younger folks who we saw less of. Some came for the museums, some to shop, a couple from Kentucky celebrating their twenty fifth wedding anniversary. One couple had their luggage stolen in an earlier part of their trip but they were still smiling and determined to enjoy the trip. Interesting people: a dress designer, an attorney, a doctor, business people, homemakers, and students all witty, open and having come with a mindset to have a good time. I didn't know if I had just been very lucky or if this was the norm for traveling overseas in the 1990s but whichever, I was grateful.

On the flight between Milan and New York, I was seated next to an Italian gentleman. The time passed quickly as we tried to carry on a conversation with my English, his Italian, and a bit of French we had each taken years ago in our respective high schools. Of course, the late flight caught up with us all and my flight home was long gone. I was one of many trying to find the hotel where my airline had us staying until the first flight of the day. Still, a chance for a shower and a couple hours of sleep felt good.

On the plane, during the last leg of my journey home, my thoughts went along the lines of "what a great passage of space and time. I have crossed the demarcation into fifty! I hope to now celebrate all future birthdays with joy and anticipation. Also, when traveling, don't underestimate the beating your kidneys are likely to take-either you can't find the bathrooms or there's no time to use them. Not just when traveling but in everyday life, I vow to make the first move, more often, to smile, speak to, and get to know people. From this first international trip on my own, I'm returning a stripped-down version of myself and the bonus payoff is the ability to be spontaneous.

On my first day back at work, I wandered around the office a bit thinking "Hmm, so this is my real life, this is what I do every day... a whole year till another vacation... wow." It actually took me several months to integrate all the elements and the effect of the trip with the life I normally lead. But I knew that first day back, I would soon start planning the next summer vacation - probably to see more of Europe.

A few weeks later, I received a great life lesson from this trip that has influenced me since then wherever I am. Back then, it took a while to have camera film developed. When my film came back, I went through my Swiss/Italian trip photos with relish. There was one photo of a beautiful floral meadow that I was having trouble placing. Then it dawned on me. There was a bit of unused film when I got home so I just took some random pictures before sending it in. The lovely florals were my backyard. I had to laugh and acknowledge how I took my local scenes for granted while being mindful and vigilant to miss nothing when traveling. Now, I make a point of pausing to be awestruck by a decadent sunset, perfect branch of blossoms or floral meadow even in my home town.

My Real First Trip to Europe

arly in 1980, my husband and I were getting a divorce. He wanted to keep the house. The kids and I were moving to a community ten miles away for a new home and change of perspective. I was talking to my nine year old daughter and twelve year old son about perhaps going to the beach when school let out. "We can't do that" was my daughter's response. I asked her why not and she said, "Mommy, we don't have a man to take care of us." I was stunned and told her so. I was not a weak willed timid soul, but had to admit the thought of parenting and being financially responsible for the household seemed daunting. Some people might have just accepted that as the reality. Some people would have gone to the beach anyhow. Not me. I recalled the open invitation from the family of an exchange student who had lived with us for a year. I decided to contact them to see if the offer still stood. It did and with that, I informed the kids we were going to Europe, starting in the Netherlands.

This trip in June of 1980 was my first actual trip out of the country except for Canada and Mexico. The plan was to start in the Netherlands as a safe place, since we would be staying with people we kind of knew. We would move on to Belgium, France, Germany, and finally Denmark. I come from a very small family. In fact, except for my parents, my only known relative was an aunt I had never met who lived in Denmark, was widowed and had a son and grandchildren. It seemed fitting to finally meet them. I thought this three week trip would either end with feeling we were a strong, capable unit and set the stage for our new home and schools, or we would all need therapy when we returned to the States. I was hoping it would be the former since, after a down payment on a house, I was spending all the extra money I had on this adventure.

This was also the spring Mt. St. Helens, in southwestern Washington, erupted. Even at a distance away, the air was thick with ash, leaving everything touched with a grey gritty covering. There was loss of lives and property closer to the site and for months afterwards the mountain shook , relieving itself periodically and creating a great deal of restlessness in the area. Even in June, the mountain was spewing out ash, and our flight out of the country was one of the last to be allowed to fly that day. During our trip, even people who hadn't heard of Oregon, nodded in acknowledgement when we told them, "close to Mt. St. Helens."

Without internet, cell phones or satellite-connected news services everywhere, foreign countries were largely unknown quantities unless you knew someone from there, saw a country being used as a backdrop in a movie, or watched a travelogue. Being met at the airport and whisked away to a safe haven was a good call and sane way to start adjusting to the newness of everything about to happen.

It's hard to describe the awareness that descends as you realize for the first time, you are in a large city, and can neither read the street signs nor understand what any of the people on the busy streets are saying. I was so intent on just taking everything in during our first ride on the local bus to shop, that I didn't even realize my wallet had been taken from my purse. I felt someone bump me. The bus was crowded. A moment later I saw my purse open and the damage done. Fortunately, my passport and some money were at our hosts' home. Unfortunately, some money and my only credit card had been taken. My bank and credit card company seemed to have nothing to do but miss my calls and wade through paperwork. No credit card was available to me until a week or so after the trip ended. We managed pretty well through most of the trip and then were gifted in the nicest way. But first came getting to see how the average family in Rotterdam lived, cobblestone streets in the old town area, and so much sightseeing my mind was boggled. I could not tell you how many windmilled, tulipped canals and lowlands we traveled through. Eventually, I got the hang of being in such a different part of the world and looked forward to my kids and I venturing out on our own.

Our trip occurred prior to the United Europe, so each country had its own currency and borders that might require a passport check and possible visa. After talking to other travelers, the plan I came up with was to find an open bank first in each country to change our money into the local currency. Next, we took a family vote from the list of "to-dos" for each city and would attempt to find them in the order of importance to us. We took the trains everywhere and first stop was Belgium. We wandered through the streets of Brussels poking in shops, cathedrals and parks. I remember one very rainy afternoon getting completely lost. We were hungry and wet when suddenly rounding a corner the sun came out, shooting daggers of light everywhere and specifically pointing to a cozy looking restaurant. We couldn't read the menu. A matronly waitress sat down with us and helped us come up with a grand meal. We had chicken with dates, rice and some other exotic seeming ingredients. It was divine.

Two conveniences we now have when traveling through Europe are the Euro, taking the place of changing money in every country and not having to find and pay to use toilets. Some of these toilets were little more than holes in the floor. Both activities took so much more time and attention than we had expected.

Of course we had to see Paris. Even my son, who voted "no" on a visit to Notre Dame, was impressed. We made it almost all the way to the top of the Eiffel Tower and marveled at the more modernistic museums. I thought the Louvre would be a little stuffy for my kids, but that was not the case. One could spend days at the Louvre in an attempt to see everything and we were only there for a couple of hours. Both children found paintings that spoke to them and we bought one in the gift shop mounted on particle board. It was a painting of a painting being painted in a painting being painted, etc. We rode the Metro everywhere. Again, using even a little French was met with friendliness and assistance. I noticed when we made no attempt to speak French, no one understood or had time for us. But after all, we were in France, and English is not their national language. I'd heard the Metro was notorious for pickpockets so I asked my son to see if that was true. He put tissues in his back pockets whenever we used this public transportation. Even though he seldom felt anything, every time his pockets proved to be empty as we climbed the stairs to the city sidewalks. We stayed on the Left Bank, colorful with lots of little shops versus the supermarkets my kids had grown up with. The weather was warm and we attacked our list with zeal, knowing we had only a few days before leaving for Berlin, Germany.

In 1980, Berlin was still a divided city between the east and the west. We stayed a long walk from the train station. In this huge international city, I wanted to be sure we would be secure in our low-end hotel. I was assured, as the staff person handed me two keys, that the buildings and all floors were completely secured. We took in some sights and, exhausted, headed back to our room. We had passed an American hamburger restaurant on the way back and were all ready for some simple fast food. My son, as any restless twelve year old would be, volunteered to get hamburgers for us. After he left I determined not to think about the possibility that he might make a wrong turn, and how would I find him in this massive German speaking place? The sound of footsteps and smell of hamburgers told me before too long, that his mission was accomplished. Just before bedtime, as we were discussing plans for the next day, we could hear the stomping and drunken singing of one or two German men. The sounds got close and I hoped they weren't in the room next to ours. Suddenly I heard a key turning in our door lock and in tumbled two very drunk and startled men. My kids froze in their tracks and I jumped in front of them screaming, "Get out!" as loud as I could. As soon as they regained their balance they backed out, apparently apologizing and looking almost as alarmed as us. After they left, we piled as much furniture in front of the door as we could and attempted to get some sleep. The next morning, I found out at the front desk that all guests had one key to let them into the building itself and another to access their floor. It seemed, after reaching your floor you were supposed to remember your room number as all the keys for that floor were the same. I had never heard of such a thing before and haven't encountered it since.

On our last day in West Berlin, we scheduled a tour of East Berlin. The unique opportunity and history of the Wall couldn't be passed up. We were quite a variety of tourists, and as we approached the wall, were warned to be quiet, make no sudden moves, and obey the armed soldiers that would soon be boarding the bus. The soldiers, machine guns in hand, walked through slowly, peering under seats, scrutinizing some tourist and pointing to items for inspection. My son, not realizing in the moment how serious this all was, whispered, "Don't come out" as he bent under his seat. Visions of arrest, separation, who knows what, immediately filled my head. Fortunately, the nearest soldier turned to see who had said those words and perhaps remembered what it's like to be twelve. He turned back to accompany the rest of the men as they left the bus. Driving through East Berlin was like stepping onto a different planet... planet 1948. We kept circling the same six or seven blocks. They looked solid and functional with occasional plants in front. But all you had to do was look down any of the side streets to see buildings bombed and broken, people in long lines all dressed shabbily in dark colors, and potholes covering what was left of roads. It was such a sobering sight. I couldn't wait to get back to the West. I quietly pointed this out to my kids and it had the same effect on them.

Next stop was at my son's request, the Olympic stadium in Munich. The stadium was impressive and we had it all to ourselves since we arrived in the middle of a mighty rain storm. We were travel hardy by then and knew clothing would dry and we would too. Whatever notes I had from that time are long gone so there is not much else I remember about how we spent the remaining day there. The plan was to board a train and travel overnight through East Germany, arcing back to Copenhagen. We had reserved an economy sleeper and found we were sharing the six berths with adult strangers. This was clearly not a big deal to them, probably a common occurrence in train travel. It was all new to us. I just looked at my kids' looks of concern and said, "This is how they do it in Europe. It's going to be fine."

And it was, until the conductor and a military person came into our roomette later that night. We had all settled down in our berths efficiently, and after seeing my son and daughter were asleep and our roommates were settled in too, I let my guard down and also drifted off to sleep. Some hours later, we must have been at some border crossing because there was a brief rap on our cabin door and in stepped the conductor and a soldier. They woke us quietly and demanded to see both our tickets and passports. I had not expected this and half asleep pulled out my bag and frantically searched for both. I handed the conductor the tickets and he returned them. However, when it came to our passports, the military person wanted to verify and take them until we arrived at the West Germany border. My mind was racing with the possibility of my children and I being stuck in Eastern Germany with no passports and at the mercy of who knows who! I showed them the passports but would not let go of them. Voices were raised at me but I wasn't having any of it. My fellow sleepers were all waking up from the noise and I didn't want to scare my son and daughter but I knew I wasn't going to hand over those passports. I hoped I wasn't going to jail. I was so scared. I think they decided the interaction wasn't worth the effort as they shrugged and left. What a relief I felt upon finally seeing a sign out the train window indicating we had passed into West Germany. The whole concept of freedom hit me emotionally in a way I had never considered before. How easy it is to take what we have for granted. Finally, our train arrived at the station in Copenhagen, Denmark and we stepped off to complete this final adventure in Europe.

The inexpensive hotel in the downtown area turned out to be close to the Tivoli Amusement Park, which was very good news. It was also in a very rough part of town. Our room was pleasant enough with a shared bath down the hall. The hotel served breakfasts as part of the daily charge. That first night we went to the park and were dazzled and happy, staying until the park closed at midnight. On our walk back to our hotel, I could see how rough the area truly was. People were fighting, getting mugged, some were drunk and yelling and we saw car break-ins in progress. I tucked each of my kids in close to me and said, "We will just walk with purpose and not look at anyone." That is what we did each night we attended the park and had no problem. I suspect more good luck than assertiveness helped us out.

At our first breakfast I spoke to the hotel manager, who wore many hats and was taking breakfast orders that morning.

I chuckled while explaining, "Good thing the breakfast comes with the room. I wouldn't be able to pay for it otherwise. Being on our first trip overseas, I was lax when it came to watching my purse and my credit card was stolen. We've got just enough cash for a few meals and meeting with my Danish aunt whom I have never met before and, of course, our room here."

"You are not getting the impression of Europe we want you to have as visitors, and especially Denmark." replied the manager and he went on to add, "Save your money for what you want to do or buy souvenirs. You can have all your meals here and if you want to have your aunt meet here for a late breakfast we will do that too. You can send me the money when you get home."

I was stunned and so grateful at his generous offer and immediately took him up on it.

We ventured out into Copenhagen for little adventures and visited the Tivoli gardens each night. My aunt Margot and my cousin Peter and his wife came by our hotel and joined us for a light breakfast. It was gratifying to meet my relatives and share that experience with my son and daughter. Peter and his wife drove us all through the countryside and we arrived at their home for a first-rate Danish smorgasbord they had prepared for us. The youngest of their children was there as well. Peter's English was minimal but his wife, who worked in a bank, spoke English fairly well. This felt like a magical moment to me. My mom had told me her sister was prone to holding long-time grudges and had not approved of the girl her son married. She had actually never met her grandchildren or been to their home before. We seemed to be the catalyst for a change of heart. Everyone got along very well, and I envisioned a future where our visit had reunited this branch of our family. That might have happened, but my mom reported to me later, how correspondence with Margot related a return to her prior stance. At least they all got together that one lovely day and we were able to share in their rare family event.

We arrived home a few days later and I promptly sent payment and thanks to the hotel manager in Copenhagen. Coming home was not returning to our old haunts. Home now meant a new house, the rest of summer vacation pointing toward new schools, and a job search for me. But there were no qualms about us moving forward as a unit and individually. The familiarity of our furnishings, reuniting with the family dog, and having our own space were powerful anchors in contrast to navigating through new languages, cultures and having no sense of where we truly belonged.

Back to My Commitment to Travel Large Each Year— Trip Two

My first trip to Europe convinced me I could successfully travel wherever I wanted, and I wanted more. For my second trip, I planned to go to the North Sea Jazz Festival in The Hague, Netherlands. I was still in touch with the exchange student who had stayed with us. He was now married with three children and working as a professional athlete. I was invited to stay with them for a few days at their home in Belgium. This combination had the makings of a fine trip. As it turned out, this was not a solo trip for me. I had a friend at work who had never traveled out of the country, was a little intimidated by the idea, but wanted to. She talked about it a lot. One day at work I told her to write me a check for a specific amount of money. I insisted on it. She did, asking what it was for. I told her she was going to Europe with me and this was the down payment for the jazz festival. A bonus for me was realizing the savings from not paying single traveler supplements meant I had more money to travel. We decided to add Paris to the trip. I hadn't been to Paris since the trip fifteen years prior with my kids and was thrilled to have the opportunity again. As a bonus, this jazz festival's timing was also accommodating to my birthday.

The evening of July 7, 1995 found us changing planes in Chicago. The exhilaration of traveling returned to me as the plane rose and leveled off for our final destination.

Out the window, almost obscured by the wing, I saw a flag of bright blue with a canary yellow strip and a thin salmon stripe below it… no nation's flag but belonging to the sky. Warm lemony towelettes, a nice little luxury, along with sleep, food, movies, and finally continental breakfast prepared us for landing in Brussels, Belgium.

The exchange student, all grown up but in my mind still our exchange student, picked us up at the airport and soon we were at the sumptuous home he and his wife had designed. They had agreed to my friend joining in the visit and we all had such an enjoyable and insightful time. The student remains a dear family member and it was gratifying to see him doing so well. It was also bizarre to have someone I'd known so well be famous enough to have people stop him on the streets for autographs. He and his wife were such gracious hosts. We spent time in their home and yard relaxing and telling stories of the time since we last saw each other. The weather was hot and humid and their swimming pool was a big bonus. I remember it being the season of fresh mussels, a big eating occasion in Belgium. We sat with many others out of doors, at simple tables and chairs consuming buckets of mussels prepared in so many ways. Of course they were served with pomme frites, the Belgium version of French fries. And it seems fries are the basis of jokes between several countries in this area. We all toured the towns of Ghent and Brugge. Brugge is the town more visited by tourists of the two, full of gingerbread architecture, canals and generally a very pretty place. Ghent is more of a working town, gritty, working class, with intensity in its architecture. I preferred Ghent and its energy versus the leisurely sunniness of Brugge. It's entirely possible, so many years later, the cities are much changed. But in my mind they stay as they were then.

The next afternoon we all went to Antwerp. This is a very old center of commerce and architecture. We wandered the maritime museum, viewed the luscious artwork of the painter Rubens and ventured to the waterfront where we found great breezes to dispel some of the one hundred degree temperature. Our generous host treated us to a sumptuous lunch at a simple but posh restaurant. We dined on slivers of salmon, interspersed with caviar, onions, sauce and more.

The following day we were dropped off in Brussels to explore on our own. We were duly teased about wearing white sneakers, which pegged us immediately to all as American tourists. We started off at the Grand-Place, which I recognized as the spot my kids and I had stumbled onto with shafts of sunlight fifteen years prior. We continued on to great food, a few museums not closed on Mondays, St. Nicholas church, and the magnificent fountains at Brussels Park. This was a very tall fountain and the breeze was blowing light sprays of water onto all of us who stood at the fountains edge. In the heat it was pure bliss. Of course, we found many fine chocolate shops and sampled some we proclaimed had to be the best in the world. We picked up little gifts for friends and family back home and were more than ready by early evening when we were picked up and could return to the backyard swimming pool. Our visit ended with hugs and promises to stay in touch. They gave us a ride to the Brussels train station and two hours later we arrived at The Hague for jazz festival partying. After checking in to our hotel, we took a local train to a very posh hotel on the beach for the jazz group's introductory cocktail party. Like the year before, I mixed and mingled so there would be lots of familiar faces through the festival. I was surprised some people had also been to Montreux the previous year and even remembered my name. When we got back to our hotel we were treated to a pleasant surprise. In their restaurant we were brought very fancy and delicious hors d'oeuvres, Italian bread and truffles with our coffee, compliments of the hotel. The actual entrée, a great seafood salad, hit the spot and we were ready to roll. The festival involved different venues of music across the town at night and day tours you could sign up with as well. We tried to balance both. We split up each night because our music tastes were different, each taking a different train and returning whenever we were ready.

This intense venture was an exercise in burning the candle at both ends. Each day was spent in pursuit of museums, history, general wandering; each night was spent in a variety of music venues. There were trips and tours into Amsterdam, the downtown area and local museums of The Hague and seaside beaches of Scheveningen, a town name so difficult to pronounce correctly it was used as a test in World War II to distinguish the Germans from actual Dutch citizens. Amsterdam's Rijksmuseum featured major works by the master, Rembrandt. But there were also works by Willem van de Velde, who was new to me, and I really liked his black and white sea scenes. In The Hague, we visited a museum featuring an exquisite exhibit titled Modern Glass by diverse and specialized glass artists. My favorite piece was a packet, bound with string and entirely fashioned out of clear and light green glass. There was a renowned sculpture by Rodin and the works of more recent artists, Kandinsky and Van der Leck, all located in the Gemeente Museum. This museum also featured the architectural building by Berlage, whose masterful skills inspired many great artists of the De Stijl collections. Throughout the museums I saw works of several artists I had never heard of or knew only vaguely by name. It was invigorating to discover their works and techniques. We were wowed by the panorama of Scheveningen's beaches and historical depth. We marveled that The Hague, all commerce and politics by day, could be this wild diverse place by night.

Of course our main reason for being in the Netherlands was the North Sea Jazz festival. A sheet of venues, times and performing artists was available for planning for each evening. Here is an example of what each of these evenings offered from 6pm to 2am: Each evening there were fifteen venues. One venue offered Oscar Peterson and his trio starting at 6 p.m., Manhattan Transfer 9 p.m., George Shearing Quintet 11 p.m., Count Basie & the New York Voices 12:30 a.m.. Another venue announced Yellow Jackets, starting 6:30 p.m., followed in order till after 2 a.m. The Brecker Brothers Band, B.B. King, Chuck Berry, and wrapping up with George Clinton. A third offering showcased Charles Haden Quartet West, Christian McBride Quartet, Ray Brown Trio and winding down with super-talented Ernst Reijseger. You can carry this through for twelve additional venues. Over the course of the three nights we both attended Neneh Cherry, Roy Hargrove, The Robert Cray Band and the Jazz Crusaders plus many amazing and talented Dutch Jazz groups. The diversity of music... jazz, R&B, and the blues was matched by a variety of venues: some air conditioned, some posh with reclining seats, moving to the music body to body and by midnight, many a venue where we're all dancing on the tables. We were on the street in bleachers, on roof tops, wherever the music and our good- natured crowd could follow the beat.

In the basement of one of the venues was an informal spot selling related souvenirs, CDs, and artwork. I was able to buy a limited edition print of a self-portrait done by Miles Davis, whose music I adored but didn't know was such a talented painter.

My birthday was the transition day from jazz festival to Paris. It started at midnight rocking in the aisles to George Benson and ended at the top of the tallest Ferris wheel in France. Not one single minute was wasted on this vacation. I felt for my friend on her first trip to Europe. She looked quite shell-shocked but also pretty happy. We were up early to catch our train, and the excitement of upcoming Paris kept us awake until we checked into our hotel and collapsed for a quick nap before sightseeing. That evening we met up with friends we had made at the jazz festival and all went out on an illuminated night tour of the city. This is how we reached the well-lit and decorated Ferris wheel. The next morning we were up early to beat the crowds to the Eiffel Tower. It is incredibly large, making the Seattle Space Needle look like a tinker toy. We went all the way to the top and also stopped at the second level on the way down. The view was spectacular. We strolled down the Champs-Elysees. How easy and pleasurable to explore all the little shops and cafes, finally finding our way to the Musee D'Orsay, a converted train station. I was awestruck by so many of the artists. I had not seen so many different paintings and techniques on display from Degas, Monet, Cezanne and Rouault. There was too much art for my mind to absorb at one time. The next day we went through the very abstract Pompidou museum, where I drooled over the cool sleek looks of the Brancusi sculptures, the Braques and actual structure of the building that was a great example of form, function and creativity. For the perfect change of pace midday, we visited Notre Dame. We entered and just sat, feeling the silence of the ages, seeing the columns like tall shoots /trees of bamboo's density. The columns to the side had a modern art sculptural look about them. In all, the sense of continuity was restful and very pleasing to my soul.

That afternoon my friend wanted to spend time at the Louvre and I wanted to explore L'Orangerie Museum. I told her it was time for her to solo in Paris and we talked in detail how she would travel to the Louvre and back to the hotel. She was not pleased, but I left her anyhow. I needed my own space for a while and more importantly, I knew she was ready and this trek on her own would give her the freedom to trust herself and enjoy new opportunities that would come her way.

L'Orangerie is a round, dome-topped building just off the Place de la Concorde. Each of the round rooms featured a most famous artist, starting with their earliest painting techniques and moving through to their most well-known styles and skills. It was delightful and I found I liked some of these artists' earlier works better. The whole lower level is made up of floor to ceiling murals by Monet of his gardens. Benches are placed in the center of the room and sitting there, I felt much immersed in the play of light and shadow of those gardens. A few minutes after I returned to the hotel, my friend showed up grinning and exclaiming there was nothing to this getting around Paris.

A tour out of Paris to the Palace at Versailles marked our last day in France. It was easy to see why the peasants had revolted. The opulence, gardens and culture were so vast, experiencing them almost made us forget the persistent heat of July. The ride to Versailles gave us the opportunity to see some of the suburbs and countryside. The Palace appeared just in time to rouse us to our feet. Each room was more extravagant than the next with special themes, jewels, art with intricate columns and arches. The Hall of Mirrors was breathtaking. It is noted as one of the most famous rooms in the world, containing seventeen mirror clad arches that reflect seventeen arcaded windows overlooking the gardens. The rest of the time was spent enjoying the vast gardens and fountains. I had a small second-hand 35 mm camera in those years and it had a panorama option I used in the gardens. I had one of my favorite views of garden and water enlarged and framed. As time went on in my career, I hung that picture in my office as a focal point to remind me to relax and turn off every busy thing for a moment. Today it hangs in my home and still makes me smile.

The flight home was like decompressing from the intense experience of art, music, foreign languages, adventure. When I went back to work, both my friend and I would knowingly nod when we ran into each other acknowledging the shock of being just mere mortals back in the workplace.

Two trips to Europe had me celebrating the diversity of traveling both solo and with a friend. The spontaneity of traveling solo is sacrificed when traveling with someone else. But in exchange there is someone to watch your back, your luggage, and share a moment, offering their interpretation and view of everything. Both trips were terrific and both trips were taken from different perspectives.

After Two Great Trips an Interesting Interlude

1996

After the second trip to Europe, travels in the United States sounded good for a change of pace. Local opportunities came along with trips to visit family in Utah and Central California and were followed by a trip to San Diego with a friend later in the year. In between, came summer and a desire for an adventuresome way to celebrate my birthday. This is why I found myself watching movies of people falling out of the sky and not surviving due to lack of preparation. They make you watch these films and sign all kinds of waivers before you can go up in a small plane and skydive.

This is how I wound up in a jumpsuit with a microphone in my face being asked "Why are you going skydiving in Las Vegas this morning?" This was part of the video the skydiving company was making for me that would include being tethered to a skydiving instructor. There would also be a totally crazy skydiver who would fly with us and jump out first, so he could turn and video me as I jumped out, experienced my sky adventure, and landed. All this was, of course, set to music. There were musical choices and even today I still think of this great experience whenever I hear Tom Petty.

I saved the VHS tape of my flight along with pictures and my notes written the evening directly after skydiving. Sharing those immediate thoughts is probably the best way to share the experience with you.

What a spectacular birthday! This is three great birthdays in a row and I can't even imagine what 1997 will bring! Tropical birds, pirates on a blazing ship, a street light show, lots of fun small jack pots in the casinos, an Egyptian exhibit, comedy, music, people watching, dolphins, and more sunshine and heat than anyone needs. All surround the primary purpose of the trip… skydiving over Las Vegas.

Woke up at four thirty a.m., adrenaline pumping, eyes wide open. Lay there never really sleeping till the alarm went off at six thirty a.m.. I arrived at Boulder City just after eight. Once there, I began the viewing of warning videos, signed a million waivers, got into a jumpsuit and knee pads and waited my turn. Not too scared, really feeling ready to go. That adrenaline push is powerful. After a few practice walkthroughs, five of us are crammed into the little plane. There were the pilot, me, Chris, the trainer I will be hooked to and tandem jump with, Kurt the video guy, and another guy who I guess came to close the plane door after we've all jumped out. As soon as the plane took off I was fine. It was a very calm beautiful smooth ride climbing upward two miles. The sky held a little haze with some semi fluffy gauze like white clouds. Kurt passed around a roll of lifesaver candies. He must have known how dry my mouth had become. When Chris put on his helmet and goggles I had my only moment of fear. Then, as we get into action, there is only remembering what to do. This sequence is indelible in my mind and senses. It is breathtaking magic. Kurt opens the door. The wind is cool and makes a crunchy whooshing sound. The clouds are now white and grey surrounding us as Kurt backs out onto the step and I move forward on my knees to where he has just been. Left knee against the boards, right leg stretched to step as Kurt films and jumps. Chris and I are hooked together now. I feel the pull of the wind and our bodies swaying as he says one, two, a moment of wonder-am I really doing this? And then 'go'.

Suddenly I am face down to the earth, kicking my legs back and up as I spread my arms-this is exhilarating! We turn right, left, and then shoot upwards (the force is hard enough to bruise my shoulders) as the parachute opens. Then it is quiet and slow. The view is amazing. Chris pulls both cords and we stand still in the middle of the sky. Soft quietness suddenly interrupted by looking down and seeing the ground coming up at me so quickly. Too soon I have to bend my knees and land on my heels. It takes a few minutes to get my land legs back. I talk to some of the other jumpers and there is that same smile and unity, a shared vision fulfilled. When I get back to my car I don't know what I feel. The adrenaline is gone. Am I tired, hungry, nauseous, energized? It doesn't matter. Forty nine seconds of free fall, five to seven minutes floating under the parachute, a video-taped to music, and I am invincible.

Falling asleep that night I thought of how what I expected to be the best part of an adventure, winds up being pretty great. Yet there is actually a different best part I never anticipated. I had imagined the highlight of skydiving would be floating in space. While that was a wondrous experience, the really best part for me was the forty nine seconds of flying

49

at breakneck speed. I don't have enough wows or other adjectives to define that sensation.

Another unexpected bonus took place a few weeks later, at the dentist's office, when I was told I needed a filling repaired. They drilled a bit and poked around and then offered a numbing shot for the pain about to occur. But the drill sound reminded me of the propeller and wind from my trip and I told them to just fix the tooth. I was lost in a replay of all the sounds and textures of my sky dive and soon the tooth was fixed and I left smiling.

Greenland

The joys of Europe and skydiving left me excited and wondering what grand adventure might be available next. Neither of these foreshadowed the quiet, yet insistent feeling late that winter of something internal, not physical but maybe in my psyche that needed tuning. I still don't know how this came to be, but I knew I needed to go somewhere to consider the relationship between the sea, the sky and my insides. Eventually I realized I should travel to Greenland and the mass of icebergs there would somehow fit in the equation too.

It's so interesting how once my mind is open to a possibility, opportunities seem to appear. I don't know if they suddenly appear or if they are always there, but I am not always open to seeing them. Early in spring I attended an IMAX show that included a large and popular upcoming trip to somewhere and highlights of another upcoming smaller voyage to Greenland. A representative was on hand to answer questions on the larger trip.

After the crowd thinned, I handed him my credit card and said, "I want to go to Greenland. Can I sign up now?"

He looked startled and handing me his business card answered, "I can't sign you up, but contact the number on this card and they will take your reservation and answer your questions. Tell them you talked to me and you might get a better deal."

He smiled and gathered up his things. Later I found out he was one of the owners. I did get a discount and the story of how he and his group took a chance, buying old ice cutter spy ships from the Russians and leading these trips of open spaces with no other tourists.

The trip was scheduled for the middle of July. I had started a new job the previous year but hadn't accrued enough days off to take the two weeks I needed. I pleaded my case to the boss, promising I just wouldn't miss work for the following year and really needed to take this trip. It was easy to see him wondering how I would pull this off, but he agreed. I was at the Baltimore airport boarding an Icelandic Air flight on July 11. The flight was uneventful, but two hours out of Reykjavik I noticed the sky changing dramatically. Dark clouds hung differently in the sky. Grey, black, fuzzy blurs were sliced with a slit of yellow sky soon shot through with streaks of pink, hot orange and a strange shade of blue. I was definitely heading for a place different than any other I'd been to.

Our itinerary told us we would arrive at Keflavik Airport in Iceland, and after clearing customs and immigration, we would start our expedition with a tour of its capital, Reykjavik. That evening we would board the ship and be briefed by the expedition leader. We started our Iceland day at a European style coffee shop. I realized there had been only five hours of sleep for me over the prior thirty hours so what is remembered of the tour is minimal. We visited the local zoo. It held captive geese, cows and horses and many other common animals from where I'm from, it's just that none of them were native to Iceland and needed extra care and protection. I learned the early visitors and settlers cut down the trees they found, assuming they would grow back quickly as in their countries of origin. Not true... it had taken centuries for the scrubby trees to grow as tall as they had and centuries since to be noticeable at all. I heard about the Blue Lagoon and its magical waters as well as volcanos, Northern Lights, and landscapes worth seeing-hopefully another trip in the future.

I slept well on the ship. The rocking motion of our small ship had me sleeping well every night of our journey. I had wondered what a week without television, radio, phones, music, or entertainment would be like. Surprisingly I never missed any of them. I simply couldn't get enough of the circular skies, play of the water and unearthly sound and sight of giant icebergs calving all around us. I penciled detailed drawings of many icebergs adding information about their size and coloring. Some comments were: "sleek look, all white with aqua blue detail, maybe one hundred feet long; Iceberg maybe forty feet in height, white, blue grey soft markings; like castles in the distance, a study in light and dark; and stark screaming textured white with grey markings on top and sides, aqua blue towards the bottom and center perhaps one hundred fifty feet long and at its peak probably sixty five feet tall."

I think we were told our ship held seventy seven passengers, an all Russian crew, plus the expedition team. Our expedition team included experts in ornithology, a Celtic and Viking historian, a marine specialist, and our cruise director. Of course there was the captain and Russian head chef. The food was interesting and one our pastimes was trying to identify what we had just eaten. We agreed that everything pink was dessert. It was just amusing because none of us were on this trip for fine dining, it was all about the adventure of ice and discovery.

A tremendous amount of information was made available to us prior to the trip and our on board experts provided lectures and discussions that set each day's scene for us in every sense of the word. Prior to the trip we received a small booklet covering all that we would need to pack and why. This was so detailed they even explained how to protect our cameras from condensation problems and the effects of such cold weather. Even in 1997, ecology and respect for all places were noted in their travelers code. For example, "must nots" included no dumping of plastics or other non-biodegradable garbage, no violation of personal space of birds or wildlife, no taking of souvenirs. We learned a few basic words in Icelandic for the more modern words of that time. Airplanes were called thotas for zoomers. Pocket beepers (forerunners of cell phones) were insightfully called Fridthjofurs or thieves of peace. We learned there are no abstractions in the Inuit language, only concrete images, like the word "mi-kse" for reality that translates exactly as "the thing turned towards you." History, geology, which birds we might see and how to identify them, Viking, and Inuit cultures, flora and fauna, all were covered in written materials, in discussion and all through the trip as our guides shared with us. It was truly an immersion experience.

We saw the humor of Iceland being green and Greenland being white and icy. Puffins with their bright red orange beaks clung to cliff sides while terns of all types soared and dove in the chilled air. This was a time when natives saw tourists only on rare occasions. On one excursion through an area with some houses we saw handmade purses of seal skin, knife holders from animal hides and other objects sitting by the road on boards. Our guide told us that the previous year, their first trip, passengers knocked on people's doors asking if they could purchase anything as a souvenir. There were no stores. Apparently, these boards with handmade goods were the natives' response this year. Ruefully our guide mused, "Probably next year they'll have a booth built and actually start tourist trade." At another stop we were told to wear swim suits under our layers of clothing. Sure enough, we came across a hot springs with natives and their children soaking and frolicking. We were invited to jump in and enjoy with them and we did. There were days when the midday temperature was up to sixty degrees. Other times, when sunning on the ship's deck the illusion of warmth was dispelled by seeing our breath as we talked.

On our first outing, I was gifted with a graphic education of what people look for on vacation. When there aren't many diversions, it's so clear to see what people are actually hungry for and that included me. As we wandered the hillsides and meadow, some people went looking for houses and people, others pulled out binoculars searching for details in the sky and hills. Two couples, who had traveled together, were on their hands and knees cataloguing the tiny greens and flowers. Many folks started to climb to the highest point they could reach, probably to command the best overview of the area and perhaps bragging rights for the climb. Lots of people stopped to take photos of everything and everyone, and some hadn't brought a camera and didn't care. I found myself content to be on my own, in slow motion so as to take in the experience in a most sensory way. I walked over spongy peat bogs, so soft and smelling so sweetly it was easy to understand the references from books I'd read about making a bed of peat rather than straw. By slowing down, it was easier to catch the tiny but profuse variety of flowers popping up wherever their roots would hold. The colors seemed extra bright and the sun and cold winds seemed to bring out their fragrances as well. I thought about these flowers, their pluckiness and will to survive regardless of circumstances and how hopeful it made me feel.

Another day we pulled into a bay, and because the weather was exceptionally warm, were told there would be a barbeque later in the day. The flies were also pleased about the extra warmth. We were warned to wear netting or sunglasses, hats and scarves over our faces as the flies would be all over us. 'All over us' took on a new meaning. The warm moisture of our noses, mouths and eyes were their targets. Luckily, it wasn't too hard to find areas where the flies were less bothersome. It was on this outing I noticed how clear the water was. Standing up to the tops of my boots in water by the ship I could see clearly to the bottom sands and every feature of fish, seaweed and stone. Hiking a ways up, I saw a stream in the distance where a bear was dipping its face in to the rushing water as it moved down the hill. His objective was a salmon and they were literally jumping out of the stream. I'd seen pictures like that before but never witnessed the wonder of it. We were led on a walk through a village. All the houses were painted bright colors. Some native children were playing around their homes and paused shyly on noticing us. The brightness of these buildings, aside from being cheerful and attractive, had a more practical reason. Vivid colors made these houses more visible in winter's snow. I could imagine living there, being out hunting on a wintry day, and scanning the horizon longingly for the red house, my home. We heard a polar bear had been in the village recently and harpooned before it could cause damage or injury. The hide was hanging on a wooden frame to dry. The rest of the animal had been used already, and nothing was wasted. By the time we found our way back to the ship we were tired, hungry and mesmerized by the smell of ready to eat barbeque. The food was delicious and the crew improvised rhythmic sounds and sang.

Most everywhere we stopped were wooden racks of fish drying in the wind. Even when it looked like no one could possibly live nearby, we were assured these homemade dryers were on someone's path between fishing and home. We also came across skeletal remains of a whale that hunters in a village had caught the previous year. This was a case of seeing, but finding it hard to believe. If we had all lined up along side of the spine, that would have matched the length of the spine. The size of each bone and disc made me feel tiny and fragile. The villagers made use of the blubber, hide, teeth, and every bit else just as their ancestors had done. We were warned many birds were territorial and shining anything was taken as an intruder to be dealt with. A big oops to a gentleman in our group who forgot his hat and had the sunlight bouncing off his bald head. A couple of birds took turns dive bombing him and only quick thinking and a borrowed scarf saved him from taking home souvenir scars.

We hiked as a group quite a distance up a hill until we were overlooking the bay and our now fist sized ship. On this bluff stood an old mortarless stone house. Those of us who wanted to remain behind and catch up could check it out in more detail. The roof was thatched and built up against the hillside. Inside, one wall was wood and lined with seal hides. I could tell some people had been making use of this cabin more recently because another wooden wall was lined with relatively new funny papers for insulation. I stared out the large square window at the bay and ship, realizing this was the view early Vikings had as they scanned the horizon for friend or foe one thousand years before me. This entirely new experience caught me with nothing to compare it with except the satisfaction of being entranced.

Zodiac excursions were interspersed into the days as weather opportunities presented themselves. This meant the crew checking for wind, fog, waves, land ice and the gorgeous but lethal icebergs. The extra heavy duty large rubber raft Zodiac crafts were like riding in a rodeo, as we embarked over the grey ocean waves. Seeing the ice up close had a surreal quality. Clearly the same winds, water and time that etched out the Grand Canyon had created intricate designs in those icebergs. We were told the many shades of white, greys and blue were produced by the age of the ice, which made me think of the stories told about the rings of tree trunk. Relationship patterns are everywhere. No wonder I hungered to feel a greater part of it all.

Not all the icebergs were giants. Some of those bergs floating by us were desk-sized, circular, trapezoidal, the size of an easy chair. We had been placed in areas where the giant bergs weren't. Still the land ice was not static and several times we heard "paddle hard away from the land" as groans and cracking sounds foretold of ice about to break off or, as it is called, calving. So chunks came thundering down into the sea in varying shapes and sizes too.

We were all presented with certificates stating we had completed an Arctic Circle crossing, with our names, the date, and ship at Sondre Stromfjord, Greenland. That day I sat in a Zodiac craft which was tied down on the third deck (being in the craft broke the wind a little). I was stretched out wearing sunglasses, a knitted cap, my jacket over my shoulders, jeans, and wool socks as I sketched in the light spray from the waves.

Surrealistic scenes on the ocean at what appeared to be sunrises and sunsets were disorienting in a pleasant way.

One day in particular, I was out on deck and noted the ocean as calm and reflecting the sky of pink and yellow with lavender and light blue highlights. Perched on this pastel flowing out as far as the eye could see was an assortment of icebergs appearing as every imaginable shape and object... a turtle, castle, a blue picnic table upended and sinking in a pink lawn, a giant fish, a ship passing, and a huge slab of ice with actual birds riding along its top.

One of my favorite remembrances of our sea journey in this most northern part of the world was nighttime close to the Arctic Circle in July, which is the all daylight time of the year. The sky never gets completely dark. It was the only time I'd ever been someplace where I could see the sky and still couldn't clearly tell which way was east or west or where the sun set or rose because the whole process was circular. Every evening we had discussions on where we had been with lectures on the history, wild life, or any other features to be aware of for the next day's adventure. One evening after all this, around 10:30, I went up to the bridge. We were always welcome there as long as we were quiet. I spent time just watching a sky with the sun setting, along with a silently hanging white half-moon. Large streaks of pink combined with white and yellow moved through a slowly darkening sky as the pale blue water below moved in gentle waves. Gradually, all darkened in a circular motion and the darkening clouds formed glaciers, mesas, cities and streaks of rain in some distant city. Nothing existed except sea and sky.

An unexpected event occurred as we were all enjoying the initial sunset sprays of color over the mountains, and icebergs. That night a streak of mist rode through and, like a window shade being slowly lowered, rolled down into a thick grey green fog that engulfed everything. We knew the ship was always guided by radar but this was first time, we, as passengers, realized our lives depended on how accurately the crew and radar could navigate through the narrow channels and icebergs with no visual cues. We were in the heart of massive icebergs. We took turns standing near the back of the bridge quietly, spellbound by the grey greenness and the radar screen. Blips and shapes, as we slowly made our way, were all we could see and hear except for the sound of an occasional distant iceberg calving.

After leaving the bridge I went out on deck and experienced it all differently. I was then only aware of how amazing to see the sea and the sky completely taken over by the fog. I wrote the following:

> Out of nowhere comes a streak of mist, then a broader streak becoming a haze. In a matter of minutes the sea and the sky are rolled together in fog. To my insides, it is wonderful.
>
> The sea grey green, like gathered satin, rolls outward from the ship smoother until seamlessly it extends into what you know must be the landscape or sky or something beyond the sea.
>
> It is like the inner side of sleep
> The mathematical absolute zero
> It is rhythmic peace of grey green solitude.

So this is what I came for.

ON THE FLIGHT HOME I ALSO EXPLORED MORE DEEPLY the effect of this trip and what I learned.

I now know:

- My affinity for the motion of a ship at sea
- How great it is to lose east, west, north and south when a yellow, pink, blue sky wraps around your ship in a great circle.
- The combinations of white, grey, aqua and cobalt blue will always remind me of icebergs
- What clean water, clean air and fresh peat bogs really look and smell like
- While I love music, the sound of silence, when out in nature, can completely fill my head
- I will always look at large bodies of water expecting to see ice bergs
- What a blessing it is to be a part of such a beautiful planet.

And then I felt a sense of something missing, an incompletion. This comparison, relationship of the water, sky and my insides felt like a locket with two separate parts that fit together to create the intended object. I had achieved only one half. By the time I reached home, I knew I would need to travel to China, the Yangtze River specifically.

Mainland China, Hong Kong and Taiwan

I've chosen to share my four trips to this area together, rather than in sequence with my other travels. This allows me to share the sense of continuity they hold for me. The first trip was in 1998 and the fourth trip was in 2018. You'll read about many trips in between these trips, beginning with one to Morocco and the Canary Islands right after the trip to Taiwan has been finished.

FIRST TRIP TO CHINA

On the Fjords of Greenland, I realized there was some sort of parallel connection to the Yangtze River. I thought, just as that inner voice telling me to go to Greenland had been justified, so would this unexpected thought of China. So, in November of 1998, I boarded an airplane bound for Beijing.

In the months between July of 1997 and November of 1998, I prepared for this new adventure. I took a class in beginner's Chinese. I planned to do the reading and writing portion of homework during my lunch break at work but worried it would be exhausting. Interestingly, it turned out to be very relaxing. It seems the English language was using one part of my brain; but the Chinese language concepts in picture as characters, used a different part of the brain. So I never left lunch Chinese too mentally exhausted to resume work. I also studied on the light rail ride home from work. One day the person next to me said something to me in Chinese. He probably saw the book I was completely focused on reading. When I looked up at him, he turned out to be a tall, young blond man. He must have seen the look of confusion on my face. He explained he had just returned from a northern province in China where he'd been teaching English as a second language for a year. He had also picked up a lot of Chinese slang that doesn't show up in the text books. He was gracious enough to help me with my Chinese and amped up my street vocabulary which was very helpful during that trip. I also photocopied pictures of important words, like "rest room" and carried them on the trip in case my minimal Chinese or English wasn't understood. A small dictionary with translations of English to Chinese and Chinese to English, both in Chinese characters and phonetically sounded out, served me well and gave me confidence.

Travel has helped me learn to stay open to opportunity, so when I was on a work related tour in my home town, my ears perked up upon hearing someone in the group talk about a nephew in China. Turns out, the nephew was a student at the University of Peking (Beijing) and looking for opportunities to speak English. I introduced myself to his aunt and mentioned I would be in Beijing that fall and would love to correspond with her nephew and perhaps meet him there. This was quickly set up, and after a few letters, we agreed to meet on a specific day and time at the Western gate to the University. I also checked out travel agencies and found one with reasonable pricing and the flexibility for me to be part of tours but also have days to be on my own. After explaining the main purpose of my trip was to travel on the Yangtze River, the travel agent suggested starting in Beijing, departing onto the river in Wuhan and traveling close to Shanghai, where the trip would end. It sounded good to me. I would have a day to myself in Beijing and then have other Americans around for two days of touring in Beijing and the river cruise. The last two days of my time in China, I would be on my own in Shanghai.

I had flown eastward to Europe twice and once again to Greenland and Iceland, but this was my first venture traveling to Asia. I flew from Seattle to Narita Airport in Japan and then onto Beijing. Most of the flight was eerily dark inside, although outside displayed a flawless blue sky with fluffy clouds. People wandered the aisles with matted hair and dulled eyes… like a zombie village in the sky or skid row minus the shopping carts. It was a long flight. On the plus side, no little bags of crackers for us. We enjoyed Luigi's lemon ice and almond cookies as well as some first-rate meals. Economy class flying was a different experience in those days. I arrived around midnight in Beijing and my arranged ride whisked me to my hotel. At the hotel, someone who spoke English was located and showed me to my room explaining that all drinking water had to be bottled or boiled. My room had the equipment for boiling water. I was grateful to have a real bed and passed out until the daylight opened my eyes and beckoned me to begin my adventure.

Breakfast was included with my room and it was buffet style. There were some eastern interpretations of western breakfast food and what I now know to be the traditional Chinese soup, congee, and its variations. I wasn't brave enough for the soup that first day so I worked on the western style foods. Seems the Chinese thought we would want corn with most everything and were very creative with it.

That first day in China, mid-November, sunny and chilly and truly amazing in scope, was the morning I bundled up to be a part of it. Strolling the streets, I stopped in a large department store to just look and perhaps buy souvenirs for friends and family back home. A young woman showed me some miniature tea cups that were lovely and affordable. I used my Chinese to ask how much they cost. She told me and I started to pay but she looked alarmed. Trying to speak a little English with a little Chinese to me, she explained I needed to barter with her, even in this fancy department store. So I did and told her they were gifts. "Oh", she said, presenting boxes to put them in. The cups were nice but the boxes were covered in red velvet and lined with intricately patterned fabric. They were more beautiful than the actual gifts. I dropped the gifts back at the hotel and looked longingly at the bed. The long flight and time zone changes were bothering me but I couldn't pass up more exploring.

I walked a ways to a lane with little shops and entered one that looked like locals might shop there. I had worked up a sweat walking there and the shop was very warm. Lack of sleep, too warm; I suddenly felt very dizzy and found myself sliding down to the floor. Soon I was surrounded by the very concerned shop girls. I wanted to get up but just couldn't. What I had learned from previous travels was to always carry the business card of the hotel where I was staying with me, so I pulled it out of my pocket and waved it at them. They took the card and soon a man joined them. They helped me up and all of us left the shop as they helped me into the man's car. We ALL got in the car. I can't tell you how crowded it was. We ALL got out and they walked me into the hotel and to the registration desk. I tried to tell them I was feeling better, thanks for the ride, but they didn't speak

English. We ALL went to my room and all went into it. They motioned me to sit down and started to take my shoes off. I was now getting alarmed. They motioned to the bed and it was clear they wanted to be sure I was safely laying in my bed and safe before they left. I stood by the bed smiling and nodding and pointing at the bed and they finally decided I would be okay and left. I thanked them in Chinese and English a lot. I can't imagine any shop that I knew of that would close its doors to assist someone from another country; someone who had just wandered in, taking care of them as though they were a close friend or family.

I was very impressed with this first morning's encounters and did take a quick rest before heading out to meet my new friend at the university. Making sure I had a card from my hotel with me, I asked the doorman to help me get a cab and explain to the cab driver exactly where to drop me off. At that time, I could not expect people outside of education or hospitality to speak and understand English.

Back in 1998 the circular grids of Beijing were already in place but the traffic that morning consisted of about 20% cars, 10% carts and the balance in bicycles. Bicycles were not just for individuals or delivery people. Whole families and sometimes their belongings were precariously perched as they lurched through the maze of vehicles and hapless pedestrians. I was overwhelmed by the sheer number of people, the maze of Chinese characters and unfamiliar sounds. All this made me grateful for the new student friend I was about to meet, and the upcoming tour group that would help me around the sights and history of this amazing city.

I got out of the cab and paid what the hotel man had indicated the charge would probably be for me. The gate and its architecture were just what I imagined it would be, but very open and without any authorities or check-in points. Before I could think of this further, a young man and woman waved at me and came over introducing themselves. Here, finally, was the nephew, Alan, and his girlfriend ready to show me their university. We were only a few steps from the city center, but the grounds were beautiful and rural in appearance. We came across a beautiful lake, dormitories, and the student store where I purchased a sweatshirt proclaiming Peking University in English and Chinese. They talked about the strenuous studies and how fortunate they were to have done well on entry exams to be allowed this track to better living. They took me off campus for afternoon tea. The teas available were not anything I had seen before, so I took their lead and soon had a cup full of dried flowers and plants in front of me as well as small plates of beef and pickled sliced hard boiled eggs. The server came back and, standing across the room, produced a sort of kettle/teapot of hot water. The spout on it was at least two feet long. She didn't move and simply poured into each of our cups from where she stood. I was dumbfounded, never having seen anything like that either, and it certainly amused my two guides. With both English and Chinese, we shared information about our lives and finally headed back to the university. This time we approached from a different side and so found ourselves at what now seemed surely to be the main gate. There was a check in-gate, guards, the works. Alan walked over and chatted with them. When he returned, he sheepishly said that apparently, visitors were supposed to have prior and written permission to enter the campus and most of the university was restricted. Oops. I was grateful for the opportunity and Alan, with his girlfriend, walked me back to the west gate where they helped me flag down a cab before returning to their student lives. I gave the hotel card to the cab driver and soon I was back at my hotel. I knew what a lucky break it had been for me to see the students' perspective of life and China's future, to experience the care of a shop full of people looking out for a tourist in trouble, and the lesson in bartering at the swanky department store. This was an amazing first full day in China... yet I wasn't done. The hotel registration desk informed me that there was a bowling alley in the basement, and how could l not finish such a diverse day without bowling? Lastly, a big bowl of Singapore pork chop medicine soup. The sublime meat on bone, broth, dates and vegetables warmed me so completely I returned to my room, got into bed and slept immediately and soundly until my travel alarm woke me the following morning.

My first day had been sunny but cold and now the cold became bitter. I knew the winter snows would be right on my heels. This was all overshadowed by the next leg of my journey. I was picked up at my hotel by a van that held seven English speaking tourists and my time as part of a small guided group began. My companions were a couple from Puerto Rico, he a real estate person and she an attorney; two women from Minnesota who had farms and herds of horses. It seems their husbands preferred to stay home, no interest in travels, but these women were traveling to Mongolia to see about the renowned horses from that area. Another couple, whose information I can no longer recall, turned out to have an itinerary also including Shanghai. We were joined by our Chinese guide who spoke English quite well, and was quite passionate and knowledgeable about his country's plans and growth.

The touring was an interesting mix of amazing sights, visits to the Friendship stores, which are the authorized shopping stops set up for tourists, and outright "opportunities" to learn and buy with a high degree of "not required to purchase but…" On a stop at a Chinese medical clinic, we were told patients see the doctors regularly and pay for their visits, the herbs, and potions to stay healthy. If they become ill, they don't pay for treatment since the doctor was supposed to keep them well.

In that long interesting day we visited the Forbidden City, the Heavenly Temple and Summer Palace. Crisp and clear, the sense of approaching snow, architecture and the stories of the centuries kept us enthralled despite hours of walking. But in between locations, there was much gratitude for the warmth of our van.

The Heavenly Temple was meant for the emperor, not average people such as our group. There, he alone would petition the sun god for blessing and good weather to embrace his kingdom. This day, I stood on that spot, arms outstretched and head back to see the sky as I thanked whatever cosmic grace was available for the opportunity to be in China and at this astonishing temple. The Forbidden City was named so to indicate this place only was for the emperor, his family and those favored for service and entertainment. Family meant the formal family as well as many concubines since that was the custom of the day. The City had a gift shop and I bought a large umbrella with a beautiful wooden handle and fabric covered in Chinese characters. I hoped the characters were for arts' sake and not some type of propaganda. Although it was bone-chilling cold, it was easy to see how the Summer Palace would have been a wonderful breezy retreat in warmer weather. In the lake, connected with this palace, sat a large beautiful boat, appearing to be made of white marble. But that would make no sense since a boat of that size made of marble would never be a useful watercraft. The story goes that a concubine of the emperor gave birth to his only son. When the emperor and empress died soon and suddenly, their son became emperor. Of course his mother, the concubine, actually called the shots. The military was incensed and continually tried to take power away from her. One attempt involved stating the young emperor was not able to look out for his domain since funds had been made available for a proper naval fleet, but there was not even one ship. The clever concubine appeased them by promising to provide a ship costing a great deal of money. The ship was expensive, but constructed of marble making it completely unsuitable. But she had kept her promise. For the enjoyment of all those fortunate enough to spend the summers at the summer palace, throughout the grounds were pathways with canopies that covered them. Paths were covered with stones and twigs designed to depict people, birds, nature, while the canopies' upper walls and ceilings unfolded the stories with children and adults, going about activities of home, travel and war. Easy to see how this would allow a pleasant stroll and take the place of reading or watching television. We finished the day with dinner together of much proclaimed roasted duck. It was okay. On future trips I ate roasted duck and found out, when cooked with crispy skin and tender meat, it is always considered a must try. But this day, it was just fine to be fed, discuss the interesting day and get all toasty warm.

The next day would involve a visit to the Ming Tombs and the Great Wall. As it turned out, we also got a passionate history lesson and excellent prophesy of what the next generation of Chinese could expect.

Up early, breakfast and a quiet drive finally revealed a view of the Ming Tombs through the mist. It was an eerie scene, with incense burners atop the tombs, a layer of trees and Beijing in the distance.

On the way to the Great Wall, we passed blocks of multistoried concrete buildings, grey and ugly amid the colorful and artful shops we had been seeing. When asked, our guide stated these were the new homes to many who had migrated to the city and also those who had been living in the cluster of 'Hutongs', traditional housing.

One of our travelers commented, "What a shame those beautiful dwellings are being replaced by such ugly housing. They are hardly attractive and not anything a visitor would want to see."

Our guide was clearly angry and passionate in his response:

Those lovely buildings, the hutongs around a court-yard, each have one large room for the whole family: cooking, heating, sleeping, with charcoal bricks as the only source of fuel and heat. Perhaps there is one central spot for water, dumping of human refuse, cleaning... a hard way to live. In these 'ugly buildings' is heat, electricity, running water. They are not ugly to the Chinese. We are a country striving to create better living for millions of people, in large steps, for each generation. My father felt he would be wealthy if he could attain a pocket watch and know what time it was. I am fortunate to have modern housing and a bicycle to give me real mobility. Next we will have automobiles for all. Our growth, not tourist opinions, are what matters to us.

I appreciated his candor and the group was quiet, reflecting on his statements until we reached the Great Wall.

One thousand miles of wall, much in disrepair, were approachable from many locations and with so much history it felt like I was slipping into the past. We parked and walked a ways to the stairway of this government approved approach to the wall. There was much climbing, so many steps to reach the top for spectacular views of wall, sky and mountainous terrain. There weren't many people on this crystal cold afternoon. We each seemed to need to find our own space to walk and inhale the centuries and the present all silently represented.

What could break such a spell? Telling what happened next is funny today but felt horrific at the time. Breaking the silence came a brief mechanical stuttering sound. Reverie broken, I looked around and realized there were speakers attached to many of the wall's columns. Suddenly, and most likely meant as a welcoming tip of the hat to visiting westerners, came music. And it was a particularly scratched and poorly done instrumental rendition of "Feelings." This was a song that had seen some popularity several years back, but was now reduced to general elevator music. This is what my notes, taken at the time say. Interestingly, I've been telling people for years, when I share this story, that the song was 'Tie a Yellow Ribbon Round the Old Oak Tree." Did I hear both songs or just remember wrong? I'll probably never know but the effect was still my mind shrieking, "No, no! Not canned music!" And now I was aware of how cold it was, how far I would have to walk back to the van, how my feet hurt and how ridiculous and fragile was my illusion of historic grandeur. Looking back, my last memory was the sense of unspeakable beauty. Before long we were back at our hotel and for some of our group, that meant joining me for attendance at a novel event.

I'd heard there was a Hard Rock Café in Beijing and thought it would be fun to see how it compared to those in the United States. Perhaps I'd pick up a souvenir. This was a point in time where people in my age group wore a lot of Hard Rock gear: hats and t-shirts, so I had been to several, just not any out of my country. Turns out, for our last night in Beijing, it was the perfect evening. This particular night Hard Rock was rocking! A guy from Singapore helped us get our drinks. I ordered a Sprite and noted to myself that every country I'd ever been to always knew what Sprite was and had it on hand. The café had three huge stained glass windows, one each of Jerry Lee Lewis, Elvis, and someone I couldn't identify. As if that wasn't enough, music was rolling in waves, and on a runway in the middle of the place, a fashion show was just beginning. The fashions were bizarre enough to have just come from fashion week in Paris. The place was packed and we were swept up in its vibrating energy.

The next morning we all stepped out into our separate journeys and futures. The couple from Puerto Rico was also headed to the Yangtze River cruise, so we headed to the airport together. I made arrangements to meet up with another couple later when we would both be in Shanghai for a couple of days. I often thought about the two women, brave enough to travel to Mongolia, certain that their love and knowledge of horses would carry them through their wild adventure.

The flight was uneventful and on exiting the plane, we spotted a young woman holding up a sign with our names.

She would be accompanying us for a brief tour of Wuhan on the way to our cruise ship. She smiled and waved, greeting us in what she clearly assumed was nice and clear English. She was oblivious to the blank and curious looks on our faces as we tried to make out what she was trying to tell us. Clearly someone who didn't speak English well had taught her. We didn't want to hurt her feelings or jeopardize her job. But as attempts to communicate continued, we did gently let her know her pronunciations were a little off and she might need to work on them. Our drive to the river reminded us of the vastness and variances of China. Wuhan was a city of one million people at that time, yet all along the main roads were water buffalo pulling carts. As the river came into view I decided this was, after all, going to be a trip of enjoyment. My earlier thoughts of some spiritual meaning didn't seem to be materializing. Maybe the trip was just a reward for showing up in Greenland. With that thought, luggage in our hands, we wove our way down a muddy pathway towards the porters waiting below to take our bags and help us board the Victoria II.

We were told Victoria Cruise Lines trips on the Yangtze River were set up as a joint venture between a Canadian company and the Chinese government (although the daily ship newsletters had a New York address printed on them). This was a means of introducing western style accommodations, meals and venues to the area... a good learning tool for the Chinese, a means of adding new clients to the cruise line and a new profit opportunity for both. The midsized ship was modern and well appointed, and our table of six independent travelers was surrounded by a large number of American tourists traveling with a large tour company.

Each day we received a notice under our cabin doors describing the day's activities and options. Here is an example, the day we stopped at Yueyang-Yichang on our way down the Yangtze toward Shanghai. Starting at 6:30 a.m. early coffee or tea followed by breakfast at 7 a.m.. 8 a.m. had us disembarking to visit the famous Yueyang tower. Return to the ship at 10:30 allowed for time to listen to Dr. Yang talk about Chinese medicine. After lunch, an informative talk called The Heart of China, would tell of the Yangtze River and three gorges. Prior to dinner, one could learn Taiqi, the art of Chinese shadow boxing. A captain's reception followed by dinner led to the evening's entertainment consisting of a fashion show where members of the crew would model costumes from the Qing dynasty to the present. After the show, passengers were invited to music, dancing and cocktails. In-house films were also showing throughout the day and evening.

Each day's schedule sheet ended with a quote from a famous Chinese person. This day's quote was from Li Bao, a famous poet from centuries gone by. His descriptive poem of the perilous paths carved into the mountains on either side of the river as well as the might of the river portended how my day in Yueyang would be.

Yeuyang, situated at the south bank of the Yangtze, was also at the mouth of Dongting Lake. Dongting had once been the largest fresh water lake in China, but over time had been shrinking. Every summer in flood season silt poured into the lake from the river and historically parts of the lake had been filled in for farm land. The November of our visit found the river in this area brown and low, preventing our ship from reaching the dock. Planks were laid between our boat and the next closest boat and so on until we could reach the actual muddy shore and difficult hike up the hill to reach the tower. Aside from my personal quest, a good reason for cruising on the Yangtze was knowledge of massive change coming to the river and all of its inhabitants. I'd heard a large dam was about to be built, displacing a million people. Some were ordered to dismantle their homes and move far up the hillsides to rebuild and continue there. Many would be ordered to restart in cities and countrysides far away. As we reached the temple, we were told the temple too, would have to be dismantled and rebuilt further up the hill. Climbing many stairs inside to the top of the temple, we found in one chamber, a famous poem by Fan ZhongYan. On either side were famous Chinese sayings and poems. I was unfamiliar with any Chinese poetry until this trip and was quite entranced by the clarity and beauty. One of those poems was by Li Bao speaking of the Chinese beauty of grey water and sky as one. Suddenly I thought of the poem I wrote in Greenland. As the fog rolled into a grey green wholeness and I sensed a gate between the Greenland fjords and Yangtze. Could the poem I wrote in current time Greenland be the same poem as a centuries old Chinese poem? I felt a powerful spiritual/emotional connection to that space in Yeuyang; and through timelessness, Li Bao. I wept and could not stop. It felt like pieces of me internally were being rearranged. I was so moved and had never felt like that before. What did it mean? What had happened to me? Would something about me or my life change as a result? I had someone take a picture of me to commemorate the experience and just in case something did happen to me. I only knew a profound spiritual experience had just occurred on the south bank of the Yangtze River at the mouth of Dongting Lake in the Tower of Yeuyang.

Back on the ship, normal life continued. We made other stops along the way and our daily schedule sheet suggested such things as a discussion on the wall of stone, advantages and disadvantages of the Three Gorges Dam Project, assorted films and opportunity to "buy dam lottery tickets". That is, a chance to guess what precise hour, minute, second the approaching Gezhouba Dam front gates would crack open.

One of the daily tours I enjoyed the most, had us leaving the ship and embarking on motorized sampans to sail through the Lesser Gorges on the Dansing River. First we were motor coached through Wushan, an amazing city of about 36,000 people. Crowded honking narrow streets, alleys going in every direction filled with stalls. Little hovels, stalls or cubicles selling food, motorcycle repairs, bags of rice and modern sneakers all side by side. We experienced a bustling, ramshackle, garbage piled city of smiling people soon to be under water because of the dam. Not much time to ponder how that could be, before we were at the river where we could see fishermen, their homes and families along the shore. Children played on the river bank, laundry was hung to dry next to a house. All of this would be deeply under water before too long too. I wondered how life would be for all these people.

Sampans of tourists were now common and the children were quick to capitalize on the opportunity to get money or objects not found locally. They swam up to the boat with homemade items to trade. I noticed one small boy who had nothing to trade and was looking for something, anything to barter with. He ducked down in the shoulder high waters and came up with rocks. These he pantomimed as very valuable. Actually they were valuable to me as beautiful and unique souvenirs. They were smooth and grey blue with lightly colored stripes and I gladly gave him Chinese coins and a pencil. He looked at me as if I was crazy, then shrugged, smiled, and was off to find more rocks and another sucker.

I ATTENDED THE DISCUSSION ABOUT THE THREE GORGES Dam. As people were already being displaced and the finish was forecast for ten years out, I knew I would want to travel this river after the dam was completed to see what could only be major differences from the current landscape. I also spent a great deal of time at the back of the boat watching where we had been. My eyes kept moving to the roiling waters behind and felt as though I was looking for something without knowing what it was. Today I would call this a meditation activity, but I remember then it seemed like being awake but dreaming at the same time. In the white foam I noticed something that looked like a small boat though no actual boat that small was in the water. In this meditative state, the small boat seemed to be in peril as it was tossed in the rough waters. My interest and concern for the boat grew. By the time we arrived in Chongqing, our last day of the cruise, I knew this small boat represented someone I cared about who was in trouble, and it was probably my mom. I would return home knowing I would be called on to be of greater help to her for some reason soon.

Chongqing was a large very urbane city with a major university. The Puerto Rican couple and I toured the city with a visit to the university. Other tours were available but we were more interested in art than shopping and factory tours. We were headed to the Chongqing Museum of Art. It also featured a political and cultural auditorium. Our driver drove at breakneck speed through the streets and barely slowed down to my question, "Why is there a man in a chair behind a large office desk on the sidewalk over there?" In a tone reserved for people not worthy of a response he replied in exasperation, "He's selling insurance, of course." I'd never seen such a sight, but no point in commenting, since we were pulling up to the museum. The architecture, both interior and exterior,r was superb and the tour was informative. The detail on the traditional paintings was exquisite and the modern work so well done. I purchased two paintings, the canvases rolled up for ease of travel. They are now framed and hanging in my home. One is in the traditional *Gombi* style. That is, a simple theme of nature with very precise brushstrokes. The second painting had just been completed by an art professor at the large Sichuan Institute of Art. It was intricate and playful, clearly influenced by Picasso. We must have eaten somewhere along the way. The day moved so quickly. I caught my breath and absorbed the day on the plane headed for Shanghai.

Only one and one half days to see the amazing city of Shanghai. Cranes stood out everywhere I looked and was told so many building were going up the skyline changed every week. As important and enjoyable as it had been to have good company and guides, I was so ready to be on my own to communicate and explore. Having read many tourist guides, I had a list of places to see. After checking into my hotel, I took a cab to the Peace Hotel. This hotel had been around since the 1930s and still had an old time jazz band playing regularly in the bar. I spent the evening enjoying these older than time Chinese jazzmen roll out their era's jazz, also playing their attempt at modern music

-a little Elvis Presley. The people watching was absorbing, as was the reflection of how this city had moved through French, British and American influences, now reclaiming its own space and destiny.

The next morning I headed to the Shanghai Museum in The Peoples Park. It was 9 a.m. when I arrived, and retired Chinese couples were ballroom dancing on the steps of the museum. I was told I'd just missed the Tai Chi which had started earlier that morning. The museum was every bit as incredible as I had imagined, with the history of China displayed in every conceivable art form. Groups of school children were wide-eyed to see a white woman alone right there in their museum. I had brought little souvenirs with me and offered "Seaworld" pencils to them. Many were afraid to come close but some brave students did. They were very excited and we spoke a little. Their English was perfect- my Chinese minimally passable. By this point in my trip, it was clear to me how unusual it was to see a white woman alone in Shanghai. And thanks to the young man who originally taught me some of the more colorful Chinese, I knew I had been pointed out and spoken about, not in a flattering way several times. I was on my own, but knew enough to pay attention to my surroundings and how to be respectful of local customs." Safety first" had me up early each day and not wandering to clubs at night on my own.

Next stop, bargaining for lunch in the open air markets on the way to the serene Yu Yuan Garden, tucked like a little jewel in the heart of the city. When I'm hungry most everything smells good, so it didn't take me long to find my chef of the day. I sat at a rustic table and chairs area enjoying a large plate of vegetables, rice and what I think was snake, the most unusual Thanksgiving meal I'd ever eaten. It was no surprise there were no turkey legs or pumpkin pies in sight, since this November celebration is so very American. I moved through the outdoor markets vowing to attempt to bargain and purchase something to wear on my way back from the Yu Yuan garden.

Built in 1559, this famous Chinese classical garden was originally a private garden during the Ming Dynasty. Information given to me at this first visit informed me it holds forty ancient structures such as the Hall of Jade Magnificence, the nine lion veranda and tower of happiness. The plants were lush and clearly planted with specific intent. Even with many people sharing this experience with me, it was a calming oasis in a vast city sea of sounds, noises and smells. Aaah, breathe and smile. Heading out toward a major street to find a cab, my eyes were drawn to an outdoor stall selling stunning silk blouses. I wanted one badly and between miming, my Chinese, and a good dictionary, I had a red embroidered blouse in my hand. Now to find the right size. I was fairly petite, but still large by Chinese standards. I know I provided a great deal of laughter and entertainment as I tried on progressively larger blouses over my clothing right there on the street. Fortunately, an extra-large red silk blouse with embroidered flowers was in my possession. Feeling very victorious, I presented my hotel card to a taxi and considered the rest of my last day in China as we wove through the streets toward the hotel.

The couple, from earlier in my trip, and I had agreed they would pick up tickets for us to see the renowned Chinese Acrobats. We met at the theater. The Shanghai Acrobatic Theater we viewed is an internationally known large scale combination of circus and acrobatics. The astounding variety of acts and skills kept us entranced and the evening passed too quickly. Examples of unexpected acts included magic flipping of masks, head walking and hoop diving on tables. Still energized from the evening's activities, it was easy to head back and pack my bags for the long journey home.

I thought my Chinese experiences were at an end. After all, I only had to get to the airport and get on the plane for a long and uneventful flight home. But there were surprises.

Morning came so quickly. I had already made arrangement for a car to take me to the airport and thought my planning left plenty of time for last minute packing, breakfast and checking out... however at checkout, the manager said my credit card had been declined. "That's not possible. My credit is great and I don't even have a balance due on it," I retorted. He looked puzzled, reminding me that speaking rapid English was not helping me to be understood. He tried again. Again the card came back as declining payment. My ride to the airport arrived. Almost panic, but I had been told to always carry two credit cards in case of who knows what and this was definitely one of those cases. Fortunately, that second card paid my bill with no problem and I finally was on my way.

The drive to the Shanghai airport allowed me to catch my breath and calm down. This was good because the airport was extremely crowded and chaotic. I was exhausted, and had to carry my luggage (still no wheels on luggage) all over and finally dropped it with a heavy sigh at the correct counter. There, a lovely, poised young Chinese woman looked at my ticket and looked at me. She said softly, "Would you like to fly to the Narita airport in business class"? I was stunned... I had never ridden in business class before and of course said I would be happy to. "Alright," she said smiling and stamping something on my ticket. The next thing I knew, I was pointed to a short line that would take me up carpeted stairs to the sumptuous business class seating, a level above the economy section.

The chairs were massive and cushioned. Beverages were immediately offered along with a menu for lunch so we would have time to consider between mushroomed filet mignon, fish or chicken with udon noodles. I was the only woman in business class. I was surrounded by Japanese business men, all looking a bit confused to see a woman, a white woman, a casually dressed woman in their midst. Conversations with travelers had taught me to carry a tin of small peppermint candies with me. I could offer a mint from the tin, even with just a smile if language was an issue. It seemed accepting a mint also implied a willingness to converse or just acknowledge each other. I offered the tin to the gentlemen near me and most took a mint and then bombarded me with questions in reasonably clear English. This was certainly the first time many of them were experiencing the opportunity to talk to an American woman and I continually had to clarify my comments with, "I can't speak for all Americans," or, "I can't speak for all women," or, "These are only my thoughts on the subject." I let them know I was an American business woman on vacation. It was my first trip to Asia. I had opinions on all sorts of things and would speak about those as well as welcome any thoughts they wanted to share. It was a privilege to be in such comfort and have this extraordinary opportunity to meet these interesting gentlemen and give them a small peek at what a woman's place might be.

This first trip to China was such an intense and rich experience. I wanted to be sure those initial thoughts and feeling were captured, so I wrote them out shortly after I got home.

- In America we have taken pride in ourselves for our Yankee ingenuity since the late 1700s, and were underestimated by most other countries. I saw ingenuity and sensed the same kind of world's underestimation with China. But there are different kinds of ingenuity. A telling difference is that the enormous country of China is all one time zone and that zone is Beijing time.

- Regarding my spiritual experience on the Yangtze River, since that experience, when I am quiet, I feel a tuning fork inside of me that has been struck-a ping that radiates outward. The little boat in the river clearly represented my mom. It was clear, when I returned, that she was on her own journey and I would need to be there to support her.

- The dual trips Greenland and Yangtze marked a sense of passage. The stony cliffs of China along the river and massive icebergs of Greenland both provoked a hold your breath, silent energy movement. Am I to be a guide or be guided? Only time will tell… maybe some of both.

- Remembering a comment I made to a fellow traveler while in the colorful swirl of Wushan, I had said "Wushan reminds me of Morocco." I have never been to Morocco, maybe I was referring to a magazine picture. (I read this statement just before planning my next trip which strangely enough was a trip to the Canary Islands and included a visit to Morocco.)

- Someday everyone will need to understand and speak English, Spanish and Chinese.

SECOND TRIP, 2012

The Three Gorges dam was phased in over three intricate phases. When would I be able to return to China to experience the changes? I returned to China in 2012 but it wasn't until a trip in 2014 that I actually saw the massive changes to the Yangtze River.

I'm not sure now why 2012 rolled in and beckoned me to see more of China instead of focusing only on the Yangtze River. I probably saw a two week opportunity to explore Beijing and Shanghai once again, plus Xian, Guilin, and Suzhou. I would meet with a small group from many parts of the United States in Beijing to get started. This trip also took place in November so I knew the early part of the trip might be in snow, but we would gradually move southward where Suzhou and Shanghai would provide a temperate relief. Since my original trip, fourteen years prior, my life had changed in many ways. A long- term relationship had ended; my health had taken an unexpected bad turn and an extreme spinal surgery followed by a lengthy recovery and rehabilitation period followed. I had retired from my career work. Wanting to ensure the most enjoyable and safe experience, I found a travel agency that was vetted by a reliable source and I came up with an extensive list of questions. I was grateful for the years of improvisation and spontaneity of the past, and would need to accept travel could still be a great part of my life if I was able to accept changes in how I would travel and limitations not considered before.

I needed to know the age range I would be traveling with since there would be no way to keep up with a group in their twenties or thirties. What did 'small group' mean, since being in a group with too many people might mean not enough attention, if needed. It was also important to go over the itinerary to determine if any day's activities might be too strenuous and find if I could do other activities instead. In my earlier trip to China, drinking only boiled or bottled water was the rule and had that changed? That was still the rule per this tour agency and they would provide two bottles of water each day as well as additional water for purchase along the way. The air fare from the U.S. was included with this trip and it was important for me to have an aisle seat because of my back. How could this be set up? As I came to find with most other travels, the tour agency booked a block of seats that were randomly assigned. I could go directly to the airline and request whatever accommodations I needed. Based on the itinerary, U.S. Government travel pages, and information from the agency, I was able to determine what kind of medication and vaccines I would need to get prior to traveling. Most travel agencies have lots of information on what to pack, what to expect, weather, and what expenses are included or excluded. I've learned to ask for all of these if not automatically provided.

Wanting to maximize my chances to participate in as much as possible, I opted to fly to San Francisco the afternoon before leaving for Beijing. That would leave me well-rested and ready for the next day's lengthy flight and whatever the arrival in Beijing would bring. In the last days of October, San Francisco palm trees waving in the warm sun assured me the right decision had been made. Time for a lingering walk, nice dinner and good night's sleep had me ready for adventure and a twelve hour flight.

Checking in at the international terminal was a quick and smooth process. This left me lots of time to people watch. The area was not busy as I sat down near one other waiting traveler. Suddenly her whole tour group appeared and it was clear from their conversations they were all from China. I tried a little Chinese and they were startled. Was this because of mispronouncing their language or that I was trying at all? I didn't know, but one lady helped me with my small dictionary to pronounce some basic words more clearly. The language skills I had acquired for my first trip to China had been unused until this trip and it felt almost like starting over. The group had been traveling in the U.S. and was now headed home. Later, I walked around to stretch my legs prior to the long flight. While in line to go through security, I spotted that lady and she ran up to me as though we were long lost friends to see if we were on the same flight. We weren't but it was a nice vignette for both of us and hopefully an omen of such opportunities in China.

Lucky for me and the young man seated in my row, the middle seat was empty and I had my desired aisle seat while he had the window as he preferred. A Stanford grad now traveling on business, he was conversational and very willing to help me with my Chinese. I had been sure some napping would happen during the lengthy flight but my eyes stayed wide open all the way. We were picked up and delivered to a very upscale hotel and informed there are only nine of us on this tour since a family of seven from the U.S. east coast had been unable to make the flight. This was the year of hurricane Sandy.

We had a guide traveling with us for the entire trip and then a separate local guide in addition for each city. The guides had been given English names although we always asked what their actual names were and would have preferred to at least attempt saying their names correctly. The first day of our tour took us all over Beijing and our guide said because of possible weather changes, they had combined many of the outdoor activities into the first day to make sure we wouldn't miss them. We were told that evening we had walked seven miles. I was proud and surprised at being able to keep up. I hadn't walked seven miles in one day in almost ten years. We spent two full action-packed days in Beijing and I don't remember the exact order of all that we saw but I do remember spending time at the Ming Tombs.

This was a totally different experience from my first visit. All I remember from the first visit is a quick look at the tombs. This time we seemed to come from a different direction and took our time to enjoy the crisp air, bare bending tree branches and massive stone carvings that lined each side of the path leading up to the Tombs. These stone carvings were massive elephants, and creatures both real and mythical, who acted as protective guardians of the grounds and tombs. They were larger than life and amazingly detailed.

In addition to the Ming Tombs, we managed to actually experience (versus drive by) the following in just two and a half days. We walked through Tiananmen Square with a guided historical and architectural lecture. Tiananmen Square had been closed during my first visit. We visited an actual Hutong via rickshaw and had lunch with a family who still lived there. The historic value of these dwellings (the living quarters left behind for the "luxury" of inside plumbing and water as noted in my first trip to China) led to paying families with long histories in these hutong to continue living there with government sponsorship and a willingness to have groups visit with them periodically. Some of them had become bed and breakfasts places. I could see the way of the past, in an upscale way, while remembering the words of our angry guide from my first trip.

A trip to the Great Wall was a must-see and despite it being much more difficult for me to climb the stairs, I was grateful for the amazing view and sense of the history of this 3,500 mile long wall originally begun in the fifth century B.C.. Again, a visit to The Temple of Heaven. This temple might be the best expression of mixing Chinese architectural balance and symbolism, blending the monumental with the delicate. I stood with my arms outstretched in the chilled sunlight and send out gratitude for this opportunity. We strolled through the Summer Palace grounds hearing yet more stories of those days of the Emperors. Our time in Beijing ended with a drive through the 2008 Olympics complex, which had not been there on my first trip. During the drive, we heard stories of each buildings use and details of how the "birds nest" was built.

With only nine of us, we just needed one van and the hope that traveling with such a small group would be harmonious. There were couples from Las Vegas, Connecticut, and Washington D.C.. In addition to myself, there were also two women who had originally met each other in Peru. One was from Alaska and the other from Ohio. They had been taking an international trip together each year since first meeting. Heavy snows showed up the next day in Beijing, but we were already in flight to Xian.

An evening arrival in Xian had us more focused on the hotel and some sleep than in trying to make out the streets and shapes in the dark. The following morning, we headed out to China's greatest archeological discovery: the Terra Cotta Warriors and Horses. Actually there were chariots too. The dig is still active and by the day we visited over six thousand warriors, each individually sculpted and customized to an actual person, had been unearthed. These warriors, their horses and carriages had originally been used as guards twenty two hundred years ago. They were accompanied by clay archers and infantrymen as well for realism. It is said that in 1974, a poor farmer in the area found the first of these while digging a well. It is impossible to explain how mammoth the site of all these creations is and how the dank cool earth where all this is contained and viewed creates the sense of an ancient world.

We spent most of the day with the warriors, returning to town and a special Tang dynasty dumpling banquet followed by a traveling back in time stage show. Our final day in Xian included a visit to the Wild Goose Pagoda. This seven story Buddhist landmark was built in 652, housing the sutra as brought back from India. Our last stop was a visit to meet a family whose home was in caves. In this area, many families still lived in caves, usually cooking outside communally and growing whatever crops possible. The Yao Dong caves actually stretch through six provinces of China. The extra income from the tour visits to these families helped them buy the necessities they couldn't produce themselves. Our guide talked about their everyday lives and then some of the family came out and we met them. One lady was introduced as the grandmother. I asked our guide to tell her I was a grandmother too and he did. I pulled out a picture of my granddaughter to show her and she beamed at me, inviting me with a motioning arm to follow her to see her home. I went with her to her cave. It was like a simple studio apartment and she showed me, with great pride, pictures of her granddaughter. We just nodded with approval at each other's photos. The unspoken love of the grandmothers supersedes any language. I gave her a pencil and piece of candy from my purse and then realized with embarrassment, she wanted to give me something in return from her limited resource. Finally she smiled and led me outside where she presented me with two persimmons from her garden. I had never eaten one before. I asked our guide to tell her this was a big new treasure for me and I was very appreciative. He did and this pleased her very much. It is these random interactions with everyday people that give me assurance we are all more alike than different.

A late afternoon flight took us to Guilin, which turned out to be the city that made me feel most at home. Guilin is best known for its natural landscapes. Like my home town, a river runs through the city, with paved walkways on either side of the banks. People of all types use the paths for running, exercise, hanging out, and finding their way to parks, businesses, and the river. Like home, the river atmosphere seems to promote smiles and sociability.

My earlier talks with the travel agent had made it clear this first day in Guilin's agenda would be one I wouldn't be able to handle. My guide wanted me to go, although verifying there would be a long bumpy drive and many, many stairs to climb. It wasn't until I told him about how much metal is in my back, and that my feet were already swelling, that he understood my dilemma and assisted me with a free lunch buffet access and local tour ideas. Between his suggestions and talks with staff at the front desk, I decided to walk along the water to a park at its banks called Elephant Trunk Park. What a great day I had. It really was nice to be on my own after many days of constant companions. I slept in, had a long hot shower and leisurely breakfast. The hotel was across the street from the river and I slowly wandered toward the park, stopping to join with boom box armed groups line dancing or practicing tai chi. Down the steps toward the river and after paying the seventy five yuan entrance fee, I found the amazing rock formation of the elephant trunk, lots of little pagoda style shops, a mystery garden and new people open to practice my Chinese and their English. The people watching was delightful and when I saw a group of Chinese women with a guide explaining the area, I knew these ladies were also on a tour. When they saw me, many of them started going through their bags, it turned out, looking for diction- aries. I said, "Good morning, how are you?" in Chinese and they were delighted. They in turn answered me in broken English. My Chinese and their English were on the same par but understandable and creating another people to people bond that is long remembered. Over a little bridge and by a beachy area stood the rock formation that indeed looked like an elephant from the side view with its trunk creating an open space to view the lush greenery behind it. I had to check out what a mystery garden could possibly be and it truly was a mystery to me. In an area, amidst trees and bushes were many larger than life figures made of rock, plastic, and some other medium. I couldn't tell whether these were abstract animals in a zoo, dinosaurs, alien creatures or ??, but they stood fifteen to twenty feet tall.

In high spirits I headed back to the hotel and indulged in an amazing lunch buffet followed by a nap and two brief walks toward the city center. By the time the rest of the group returned from their day trip, I was rested and ready for more action. They were ready for massages and hot showers. The two and half hour ride each way had been marked with pot holes and even the fittest of the group had leg cramps from all the stairs. They said the view and experience of the Dragon Spine Terraces out in the country were worth it all. I was glad it was a worthwhile experience for them but was just as happy for my decision. They spent the evening getting massages and much needed sleep. That was a good call because the next few days would find the end of sunny skies and provide wind and rain for us just in time for our half day trip down the Li River.

We motor coached to the landing and noted every passing moment brought colder air, whipping winds and more rain. We wondered how much of this magical river we would really be able to see. We had been told the Li is reminiscent of classical Chinese landscapes. Typically, we would be treated to fishermen on bamboo rafts, birds and water buffalo, soaring pinnacles of limestone hills and mist shrouded peaks appearing at the varied twists and turns of the river. The famed mists hanging in the air appeared sporadically and then gave way to more driving rain. However, by stepping out of the comfort of the boat's interior and out onto the pitching deck, the view was incredible. After all, a hot shower later with space to dry out clothing in our hotel rooms would remedy the cold and sogginess. This one time opportunity was worth the inconvenience.

Shanghai, Suzhou, and Tongli were the goals of our last three days in China. The rain continued as we landed in Shanghai and I was eager to see what changes might have taken place in the years since my first visit. Shanghai was to be our home base as we explored the city and took day trips to Suzhou and Tongli. My jaw dropped at the extraordinary change to the basic landscape. The Pudong area on the far side of Shanghai's Huangpu River, was mostly undeveloped in 1998. Now it was a futuristic skyline of skyscrapers, metal and glass and towers housing every type of commercial enterprise.

The cloverleafed multi-lane freeway system was terrorizing to me in comparison to Beijing's circular and cosmopolitan roadways. We visited the eighty-eighth floor of the new Jinmao tower, third tallest building in China in 2012. From its lofty platform one could see stunning views of Shanghai, we were told, since the rain and clouds allowed only a peekaboo of the vista. It was pleasing to return to the Shanghai Museum. With a different perspective this trip, it was enhancing not repetitive. The evening ended with a group dinner followed by a performance by the still famous Shanghai Acrobats. I had gotten quite used to having dinner at large round tables with lots of people and circular trays filled with six to ten choices of scrumptious food. I sensed that once home, it would be a hard transition back to my dining room table and whatever happened to be in my refrigerator.

The next morning we headed out on a motor coach headed first to Suzhou, often called "the Venice of the East." Suzhou is a 2,500 year old city, and noted for both its traditional gardens and silk production. The gardens, also designated as a UNESCO World Heritage site, are the ultimate example of scenery and serenity, a Taoist philosophy of nature contemplation. To develop such a place in urban areas was a highly cultivated art. These are not gardens filled to overflowing with bountiful flowers, bushes, trees but rather a more thoughtful and minimalist design of rocks, water, plants and architecture. Touring the gardens, even in less than ideal weather, truly was a lesson in peace, relaxation and beauty. We saw silk production from hatching silkworms through the process of creating fabric. It was in the smaller town of Tongli where we engaged gondolas, and through sheets of rain, viewed stone bridges, tile roofed houses and cobbled lanes. We ended our ride at a marketplace to browse souvenir stalls. Of course there was tasty street food for a late lunch.

The return to Shanghai found us wet, tired, happy and ready for hot showers and dinner. The next day would be the last of this trip to enjoy China.

Our itinerary showed this as a day on our own to enjoy Shanghai, noting our guide would be happy to give us suggestions. However, our wonderful guide offered us another option.

He said, "If any of you would like, I could take you from the hotel on the metro, their subway system, to the bazaars and toward the center of town. I would point out some special places at the bazaar and later you could retrace your steps and take the metro back to the hotel or catch a cab. I also have an uncle who has a friend whose cousin runs a shop with specially discounted wrist watches and hand bags."

Most of us were eager to take the metro and explore the bazaars. I wrote down all his directions for the metro and bought an all-day ticket, planning to take the metro back. It was a lovely adventure. The bazaar was no longer what seemed to be an acre of homemade appearing stalls. The bazaars had gone upscale with most in large buildings. Our guide gave us practical information, including where one could find a four star bathroom. Traveling through the country, he had rated the various bathroom stops so we could determine comfort versus need. He showed us a teahouse that would provide free tea. Of course it would be polite to listen to a little information about their wonderful teas that were also for sale. Time slipped away in checking out the art, crafts and trinkets. Sampling a vast selection of fried and steamed goodies took care of lunch and the need for dinner as well.

A couple from our group asked if I wanted to join them for an evening river cruise for the last night. I really wanted to but didn't need to eat and the busy pace of the trip was catching up with me. Wants and needs considered, I settled for a hot shower and good night sleep.

The next morning we rode to the airport on the Maglev, the world's fastest magnetic levitation train. It would travel at 287miles per hour and cover the 20 mile distance in less than eight minutes. The ride was exceptionally smooth and it wasn't until I realized the cars we were passing so quickly they were almost a blur, were all moving at sixty miles an hour.

On the flight between Shanghai and Beijing, where I could connect to my San Francisco flight, I reminisced on the past eleven days.

First, it was most fortunate that in a group of only nine people spending a great deal of time together, we got along so well. Although I was a solo traveler, there was always an invitation to join someone for a stroll or meal. Our conversations stayed away from the typical controversial topics and focused mostly on travels. Then there was the matter of scheduled stops at factories and shops to learn about their wares, processes and have "purchasing opportunities." These stops were much longer than most of us wanted and for those who had no interest in the subject or desire to buy anything, they became a source of discontent. I felt too much time was given to these side trips too, but welcomed the opportunity to learn and do some early holiday shopping for family and friends. In Beijing we stopped at a jewelry center where we could walk around the large shop and learn about the primarily jade jewelry and the history of the use of jade. Four star bathrooms were also there as well as the opportunity for a free cup of tea and a place to sit. I found the history quite interesting and their talk of "finding the jade that speaks to you" a bit cheesy. However, I did see a ring that I just kept coming back to. Although I don't wear much jewelry, I bought a jade and gold ring that did seem to beckon. It was a big gulp purchase for me, but I still wear it and am glad I didn't pass on it as too impractical.

More shop visits occurred in Xian and Guilin. Xian housed a factory of carpets, furniture and lacquerware. All of this was beyond my budget, especially considering the cost to have some of those pieces sent home. But it was akin to being toured through a truly beautiful museum of these arts. In Guilin, the opportunity was presented to visit a pearl museum and its shop. I got a brief and interesting lesson on the difference between salt water and fresh water pearls and how to tell real pearls from fakes. Fresh water pearls are considered more valuable because they take four to seven years to form and are more regular in shape. We were told real pearls feel sandy when rubbed together while fakes feel totally smooth. We saw lots of samples and were shown how the value was measured via weight, luster and color. I bought pearl earrings as gifts.

About half of the group joined me for the opportunity to hold silk worms in our hands after watching them emerge from cocoons. We then followed the process of viewing the webs of silk become threads and then woven into beautiful fabrics. Not surprisingly, many of these fabrics were for sale in the adjacent shop now in the form of shirts, blouses, and most anything else that could be made from silk.

Finally, my reminiscing brought me to consider the difference between my two China trips. Taking a subway to the bazaars and their classier location, education on pearls, jade and silk as well as acquiring a new friend who lives in a cave were big changes in this second trip. The rapid changes to China's infrastructures blew me away. On this trip, so many Chinese people I saw were wearing western brand logo clothing. Each of my trips offered different slices of this vast country. But it left me wanting more. After all, I still hadn't yet been to West Lake in Hangzhou, known as a special spiritual and peaceful place. And clearly, I had to see what had become of the Yangtze River and its people after completion of the dam.

Later, flying homeward from Beijing I noticed the sky as a soft wash of pink lavender slowly sliding into blue greens, white and green tinged clouds. Languishing below were ocean wave like clouds providing a gentle exit from a trip of much happiness and good fortune. My mind was considering what and how I would handle my next trip here as I dozed off.

A TRIP TO THE MAINLAND, HONG KONG AND TAIWAN

The beckoning Yangtze River and its transformation, finally became my destination with a change of travel timing to early spring in 2014. For this trip I wanted to go to specific cities and do specific things to make the most of my time, energy and money. I thought of how I had used a travel agency to line up a personal guide and driver when I went to India. It had worked very well so my goal was to find a reliable company that could do the same for me in China. I located one where I would have a different English speaking guide/driver in each city I planned to visit. My travels would start with Chongqing, where I could see the city after so many years and embark on a ship to travel on the

Yangtze and visit the new dam. Following would be a trip to Hangzhou, Shanghai as only a stop on the way to Hong Kong, and a brief visit in Taiwan to see my son, who had just moved there for work.

This agenda and its possibilities were very exciting to me. There were just two items that caused me trepidation. First, getting to Chongqing would involve twenty-eight and one half hours of travel, switching planes in Los Angeles and Guangzhou. I would be met at the airport, have a full day of sightseeing and then board the ship that evening. I couldn't imagine how I would pull that off with minimal sleep and the international dateline time changes. But I would somehow manage it. The other concern was a domestic flight just prior to this trip where I succumbed to a nasty stomach flu. This involved me getting violently sick on the plane, passing out and spending a night in an emergency room. The prospect of this happening again, but in a foreign country, made me shaky. I had travel insurance and logically knew one bad experience didn't mean I would have another, but emotionally that fear was hard to get rid of. Fortunately, a close, calm friend offered to take me to the airport. Her reassurances were just what I needed.

The flights to China were uneventful, arriving in Chongqing at 9:50 a.m. their time. I hoped the gentle cool temperature and rain would help me stay awake through the day. My guide was a young man, well-spoken in English, with lots of knowledge on the history of the area. By the time we got my luggage and talked about our days activities, it was time for lunch. I was already used to the random time and type of meals from the plane so it was fine with me. We stopped in an older part of town and I had the opportunity to explore it a bit, agreeing to meet him at the noodle shop at the end of the road. He parked the van and we watched an old time noodle maker create a fresh batch of noodles we could customize and have for lunch. The small shop was full of local people sitting on upside down pails and slurping down their noodles. We did the same. Next stop was the famous Chongqing zoo.

WE ALMOST HAD THE ZOO TO OURSELVES, PROBABLY because it was a work day and raining pretty hard. The only down side was the inability to stop and rest on the benches along the way because of the standing water on them. The highlights of the zoo for me were the display of pandas and the Siberian tiger. Not together, of course. First we saw the adult pandas, each in their own fenced off area. Ambling, somewhat territorial big guys who methodically scratched, located bamboo, nibbled and napped.

Next came a two and a half year old panda. He was like a typical two year old child: super busy exploring, playing and expressing outrage when he didn't get his way. Never mind being tired. I could have watched him all day. He played on logs, ran around bushes, stumbled a lot and always had an eye on his food bowl at the back of his area. Eventually he went over to it and stood there for a while looking toward what seemed to be an entrance to an interior space. Finally, he kicked the bowl and looked again. No response brought a series of progressively harder kicks. His impatience finally got the best of him and he ran to his play area where he proceeded to make wailing sounds and tear up the bushes and most everything else he came in contact with. It was quite a commotion and not long before the door in the back opened and someone appeared prepared to feed him.

The Siberian tiger was not out in an open area. There was a very tall glass wall between us since they are very powerful and the actual fenced area was close enough to the public that a determined tiger could probably have leapt for lunch. The tiger definitely saw us. He was gorgeous and his eye contact while pacing the length of the wall clearly showed he would have made quick work of us given the opportunity. The lack of sleep was catching up with me so we left the zoo and headed for a place where I could sit and have some tea or coffee. I was relieved to be just sitting with no requirement to move or be alert. So it was easy to agree to wait there while my guide left for, "a quick errand, twenty minutes at the most, enough time to drink a cup of tea," he said. Two cups of coffee later, I checked my watch and realized he had been gone forty five minutes. I was now awake. Normally I am very careful about keeping all my belongings close but now realized I had my purse and passport, but everything else was in his van. What if he was in an accident? What if he was less than reliable and not coming back? What was the name of the cruise ship and where was I supposed to catch it? I was too tired to remember any of that or contact phone numbers of the tour agency. I waited. Shortly after an hour he returned. There was no explanation about the time, but when he said he'd arranged for me to board the ship two hours before the original 8:30 p.m. boarding time, all I could think of was a soft bed waiting for me. First, dinner was required. Mostly because it was in his contract to provide dinner for me, but also since there would be no food served on board until breakfast.

I could tell from the day's drive, Chongqing had grown larger and become much more urban. My guide said he would take me to a dinner place where many young professionals

working downtown stopped for dinner on their way home. I was not prepared for what lay around the next corner or the restaurant. We made a right turn and for a moment I thought I had been transported to Times Square in New York City. In front of me where several streets converged stood towering buildings and lots of shops with a big electronic billboard shining down on everything. It had a tower clock of independence and was called the New York Square Building. The restaurant with jazz playing in the background and beautiful furnishing was a chain pizza restaurant common in the United States. This swanky version was filling up with very well-clad young men and women and the pizzas had more exotic toppings. So there I sat, completing my day in Chongqing eating pizza in Times Square. Even as exhausted as I was, there was no way to not laugh.

Eventually, a short ride brought us to the waterfront and boarding of the Century Line Cruiser. I was shown to my cabin. The joy of knowing I could finally take a shower and sleep in a bed filled me with delight. My cabin was beautiful, with a sofa, desk, lots of amenities, and several pillows.

Just before getting ready for bed, I got a knock on my cabin door and a member of the crew indicated as best he could when breakfast would be served the next morning. I assumed they sent someone who didn't really speak English only because I arrived early and the whole crew was not ready for work yet. My assumption was not correct.

The next morning I felt so good after finally being able to shower and sleep. Exploring the ship and a good breakfast were next on my agenda. Since my prior trip provided so little opportunity to speak Chinese, I didn't bother to truly refresh myself on speaking, but did bring my trusty two way dictionary. It wasn't long before I realized I was the only non-Chinese person on the ship. One member of the crew said he spoke English and would translate for me. None of the other passengers seemed to know English and were actually looking at me with shock and confusion as to why I would be on their ship. I kicked myself for not being better prepared but had brought two items I thought might make me feel more welcome. For dressy occasions I brought the beautiful red silk blouse I had purchased on my first trip. It had held up well and I knew any Chinese person who knew good old school sewing and design would recognize and appreciate it. Also, it was worn as a sign of respect for their culture and that would be noted too. I brought pictures from my first trip of Chongqing and the Yangtze River in that area. It was with me to compare the differences with time, and now I hoped would help me connect with fellow passengers. I wore the blouse and a nice skirt to the captain's welcome party and received many nods of approval. This made me feel more a part of the cruise group. The next morning the English speaking crew member was out on deck with all of us explaining in Chinese and English what we would be seeing that day. I brought out the photos and showed them to him. He became very excited and told the other passengers about them. Quite a few passengers came over to see and via translating, shared where they had been at that point of time. At least twenty passengers, it turned out, could speak a little English and many others pulled out their phones to find translation apps. Now I was just another member of the group on a river vacation. One of the delights of the cruise was seeing and being part of the partying and laughter of these vacationers. This side of life in China I hadn't seen before and this group would have fit in to any cool place I've ever been.

We did not stop at Yueyang on this trip, but I heard the temple had been moved successfully up the hill. Some of the hillsides we passed had been rock and trees, with houses and small farms. Now there were many refineries, factories and housing, I suppose, for the workers. The river now carried all sorts of commerce barges carrying multi-levels of cars and most everything else. A memorable stop occurred at Shibao where we were able to hike a bit in the area and tour the Pagoda Temple. This temple was now only available to special groups of people. The locals were not allowed in and that must have seemed strange and perhaps sad to them. As we moved toward the Three Gorges section I thought of the small fishing villages which were no longer there. This was now the entrance to the new locks at the dam.

The Three Gorges Dam is considered to be the world's largest water conservancy project. The dam is adjacent to a large park and building which houses the blueprints and models built prior to the actual start of the dam itself. Facts and figures, and books for sale with the whole story abound. Since so much information is available about the dam in books and online, I won't go into it now, although I bought a beautiful book with great photos and all the details. Our ship took its turn in line and we went through the locks on our way to Yichang where we would disembark and I would fly to Shanghai.

Shanghai, this trip, was only an airport visit with me rushing from one side of it to the other in order to catch a plane to Hangzhou. So much about the grace of green tiers of tea plants at the plantations and mystic beauty of West Lake had me in great anticipation. That was fortunate because the hotel room proved to be a frustrating situation. Across the street from my hotel was a lush park, museum and both pine and palm trees. People were playing and some doing tai chi. The room itself had a comfortable bed and reasonable bathroom but none of my adapters seem to fit the outlets for power and the noisy heating/air system usage directions were in tiny print Chinese as were directions on how to turn on adjust the television. A visit to the front desk produced a tacit reminder that I am in China and if I don't speak Chinese that's just too bad. I remind myself that I'm not moving in, just spending two nights. Nothing this petty should be allowed to spoil my vacation. If I wanted to be concerned about anything, it could be my knee, which I twisted attempting folk dances the day before. It was mildly throbbing and I noticed I was limping.

Aside from the one-to-one contact, the injured knee was another reason it was so helpful to have guides on this trip versus being on my own or part of a group. I was able to get around but needed to stop and sit often. Since it was just my tour, the day rolled out to handle our agenda and also accommodate my needs. My guide, Jack, had visited Indiana several years prior and that state was his view of the United States. He was fascinated to hear all he could about life in my part of the country and we had memorable conversations about the similarities and differences of everyday life in Hangzhou and cities in the United States. He was newly married and full of confidence, energy and good will. First stop was the famed West Lake, a UNESCO World Heritage Site. During the lake's evolution, over ten centuries, its integrity has been preserved and refined. It covers sixteen square miles and is adjacent to numerous pagodas, gardens, including several man-made islands. But, oh so much traffic getting from one side of town to the other. At least it was reasonably quiet because the masses of motorcycles were all electric. In fact, regular ones were not allowed in the city.

The park surrounding West Lake was designed with so much intention and grace it would have been easy to spend days there. We wandered, enjoyed and took a ride on the lake in one of the boats designed to look like those of ancient times. The sheer beauty, floral fragrance and calm in the midst of this busy city made just breathing and smiling a welcome and fulfilling adventure. A quick lunch was followed by a drive into the hills. This is where we ventured through the terraces of tea plants receiving a tour and education about the growing of tea and how to brew a proper pot of it.

We finished up the afternoon with a stroll through the Hefei market. This well-known market is made up of souvenir stands, amazing statues, and travelers from every conceivable place. It was great fun but my knee told me it needed a little TLC, and by then it was late in the day anyhow and the next day we would be flying off for my first visit to Hong Kong.

There was no one with a name sign waiting for me at the Hong Kong Airport. I checked my paperwork again and realized it said to take a shuttle to my hotel and there was paperwork to hand in somewhere that showed this had been prepaid. I followed the signs, fortunately in several languages, and eventually had transportation confirmed. Soon I was catching views of Hong Kong as we headed to my hotel. This was the largest and most elegant of the hotels on this trip. I checked in and found my room to be most unique. It faced the hillside and lush gardens but also had a patio containing an old style wooden soaking tub. It was huge, requiring a small ladder to get in and out. A note had been left for me at the front desk so I opened it before making any other decisions. It stated my tour for the following morning was leaving earlier than scheduled but I had no information on a time of the tour. Since I was having phone problems, I went to the front desk and asked them to call the Hong Kong contact for more information. After several attempts and being bumped to several people, it turned out they had no tour details beyond having set up my two tours while I was in Hong Kong. Further, they weren't particularly interested in checking anything out. The most helpful people at my hotel front desk, phoned my travel agent in Los Angeles at my request. She said she would check into it all and get back to me. This is the reason for working with quality people. Within an hour, I had all the information I needed for a great tour the next morning. The room was luxurious and I had just enough energy to head to their coffee shop before heading to bed. I would usually expect a coffee shop to have a basic menu and be clean and comfortable. Here, the coffee shop was more like a small luxury restaurant with table linens serving me a magnificent crab bisque and house made warm buttered dinner rolls. Sleep came easily.

The full day tour started off with hotel pickups. As we rolled off toward the island of Lantau, a head count and "where are you from" found me and a couple from Texas representing the U.S. and the rest of our group from Australia and United Kingdom. I have to admit it was nice to just hear and speak English. I hadn't realized before this trip that Hong Kong is a series of islands. Our tour took us over bridges where possible and on ferries when that was called for. Lantau consisted of very rustic houses on stilts. These belonged to generations of fishermen, most of whom could no longer fish. Though shabby on the outside, the government was assisting these folks to live in and save the village as a historical site. The interiors were filled with large screen TVs and quite an array of modern technology. Next up, we drove out in the countryside for a close-up view of The Giant Buddha and Po Lin Monastery. The Buddha is so large it can be seen from outer space. We toured the grounds and stayed for a tasty vegetarian lunch. A leisurely drive back to Hong Kong proper came with historical and geographic information. I arrived back to my hotel in time to watch the spectacular sunset with it streaks of color and shadow across the city skyline and a late dinner.

A morning half-day tour turned out to be almost a private tour. The other participants, more Australians, were only on the tour as far as our first stop, the Ocean Park water park full of goofy cartoon characters, water slides and a carnival atmosphere. After a brief look-see, the guide and I took off for Victoria Peak. It was too windy for the cable cars to be rideable, but the views were still amazing. A street of shops on still another island led to my sole purchase. It was at a classy looking store named 'The Opera Shop' and had all matter of souvenirs from the Beijing Opera. I couldn't imagine what might be in the store and it was the widest array of products imaginable. My purchase was a small mask. Although all the writing was in Chinese, the shop owner assured me each mask represented an opera character and emotion plus it was, as I noticed at closer look, also a vegetable peeler.

Back at the hotel, there was time to take a long walk around the hillside and with the hotel's assistance again, confirm the next day's flight to Taiwan and my son's ability to meet me at the airport there. A short flight, a long line through customs with new country arrival paperwork, and finally my son's smiling face.

Hugs, luggage retrieval, car to the expat section of Taipei, and most important, being with someone who really knows me. That's one of those things so easy to take for granted in everyday living where I have community. There's a lot to be said for simply appearing in a new place, meeting new people, just existing and experiencing in the moment. But equally important is the sense of being somewhere people really know not just your name, but who you are- your history and you as a person. It was dark out and since the next day was a work day for him, I was dropped off at my cozy hotel located close to where he worked. There, I was thoroughly welcomed and my attempts at greeting in return were met with smiles and corrections. The room was not large but designed so efficiently everything I might need was at hand.

Morning brought another style of breakfast buffet. My big discovery was an amazing coffee machine producing the most luscious chocolate mochas. Whatever else I ate for breakfast, it wasn't complete until I'd had my two mochas. When I returned home, I vowed to find a smaller home type machine that would do the same and I now enjoy them with regularity. Since my son was working that day, his wife met me later that morning and we took the train to downtown Taipei. This was her first venture to Asia and she was happy to share her latest finds with me. We went to the iconic Taipei 101 Building, until recently the tallest building in the world with ninety-one stories. A super express elevator whisked us to the top viewing area and the wraparound view of Taipei was spellbinding. On the way down were floors given over to all sorts of arts including jade carvings, exquisite coral jewelry and gems. Of course there were floors of fast food, souvenirs and all sorts of Taiwanese-centric objects. The extremes of these being a giant multi-floored item resembling a bee hive. It was the damper running through the atrium of the entire building and placed there as a means to temper the swaying effects of such a tall building in a setting known for typhoons and earthquakes. At the other extreme, a souvenir I purchased of what were called "damper babies", representing ecological and mindful things to do. They came in the form of cartoon characters from billboards and television. There were key chains, little action figures, and more. I purchased a green action figure, the container informed me, called "Happy Healthy." As we landed back on the main floor, I could see it was sectioned off into a collage of food, clothing and whatever else one might randomly want to buy.

We took a cab back and I was dropped off at my hotel for a rest, to be followed by dinner with my son and some of his friends from work. I'd had a somewhat sore throat for the last few days, but waking up from my nap, found my voice had been reduced to squeaky sounds and whispers. As is in so many places, little hole in the wall restaurants provide character and stellar food; this restaurant was no exception. It was great to meet and listen to the group, manage to add a little to the conversation and mostly enjoy a banquet of fish, meat, noodles, and vegetables done to perfection. Everyone was understanding of my squeaky whispers with thumbs up or other gestures that enabled me to be a part of the group.

The next day was my son's birthday. I had the day on my own to browse the neighborhood and visit him at work for a tour. This was followed by time to participate in dinner and birthday cake that evening. Over the weekend, the three of us explored a large night market with streets of food, clothing, luggage, and live venomous snakes in a topsy turvy of stalls. During the days we ambled through the flower market and a jade market. In between we indulged in all sorts of great Asian food.

Monday morning was time for a prearranged half day tour of the city set up by my travel agency. Even though I'd already enjoyed so much in Taiwan, clearly there was so much more. There were lots of stops and we moved as quickly as our guide could manage and still give us a quality experience. We visited more than what I've listed, but what caught my attention the most were the Chiang Kai-Shek Memorial Hall, surrounded by landscaped gardens, ponds and pavilions. Much history of art and rebellion is housed there. Soldiers guarded the shrine at Martyr's Shrine, dedicated to fallen heroes of China's wars. We cut through lines to skip from exhibit to exhibit at the National Palace Museum. So breathtaking, I vowed to return and take my time to go through the entire museum someday. We wrapped up the morning with a stop at a high quality handicraft and souvenir shop. There I purchased a bird carved from a stone that is noted for Taiwanese carving. It fits in the palm of my hand and seems, when I close my fingers around it, to impart a sense of connectivity.

My last evening in Taiwan was spent with my son over dinner and a visit to a shrine seen earlier. But at night its luminescence took on a whole different aura. Back to the hotel to pack and catch at least a few hours of sleep before heading home.

Once on the plane, I tried to organize my thoughts and feelings about this most diverse trip.

- First it felt like I had been on three separate back-to-back trips; one trip being the Yangtze River cruise; the second traveling through Chongqing, Hangzhou and Hong Kong; finally, a first trip to Taiwan.

- I liked the variety of guides because it added texture to my trip. Different viewpoints in each city, for example, the guide in Chongqing focused on that part of China geologically, politically but primarily on his time and money. Jack, in Hangzhou, being happy, newly married, optimistic about the future of China and the world. In Hong Kong the two tours were very professional and knowledgeable but also served as a reminder that even if you think all is prearranged and contacts are in place, sometimes you have to take the initiative to ensure you have a quality experience. Of course, my son as a guide in Taiwan was the best, and it added flavor to have a brief professional tour to fill in the basics.

- I wished I could have gone back to the Yeuyang Temple and still felt the power of the river. But I had to acknowledge it is not the same river. It is changed and tamed. Sometimes profound experiences are best left remembered as they were.

- And a big note to myself to always brush up on a foreign language I've learned and let lay for a while, even if I don't think I'll need it on "this particular visit to that country."

- This had been planned as probably my final trip to China, yet leaving it with that thought in mind, I found myself tearing up and not ready to say no more. There is nothing logical about this feeling, it's just there.

- I also found myself thinking, "What is there about travel and this trip in particular that makes me feel better in my own spirited, mental, emotional and physical skin or self?" Lots of time on the plane to ponder this question and the best I could come up with before we landed was, "Without pressure, demands, producing results (mostly placed on me by me), I am stimulated by learning, new people, new sights, information and ideas. Nothing is really asked of me except to show up and be present, and it all changes daily. That, apparently, is my happy place."

TAIWAN, 2018

After multiple attempts for a longer visit to see my son and his wife, a plane finally launched me into the air, bound across the International dateline in January of 2018 to Taiwan. The magic decider turned out to be an epiphany of time use; my family didn't need to have more than a day or two to spend with me because traveling to other parts of Taiwan and exploring Taipei on my own could work really well. Trying to adjust dates, when everyone involved had continually changing schedules and an extra handful of the unexpected, can cause even the most enthusiastic traveler into a weary "maybe this just wasn't meant to be" mumbler. Sometimes this proves to be true, but often, it's just a matter of finding a new kind of flexibility.

This would be a nine day trip, counting about nineteen hours of air and airport time each way. This was not as daunting as it sounds. I've learned to accept the non-time of long distance flying. Letting go of how I normally measure time and allowing it to pass as a series of naps, movies, random meals and beverages with zombie excursions down the aisleways is the key. Seating on the plane can be pleasant "whatever it is" for some or an important part of the flight. Because of some physical limitations I have, getting an aisle seat is really important to me so it is my priority in determining where I sit in the plane. Miraculously, on this trip, I had not only the aisle seat but the entire row. I was not the only one with such good fortune. The flight wasn't actually full, although the attendants stated it was a full flight as we boarded.

Breakfast was served a couple of hours before we landed in Taipei at 7:50 p.m. This is why it's helpful to accept all meals on the plane as appropriate in airplane time. My son was there to meet me. So great to see him. I know I could have made arrangements for a driver to meet me and take me to my hotel, but having someone you know pick you up when you finally arrive, and it's dark out, is very, very appealing and appreciated. It's also a little extra time to spend with someone you want to talk to when the total trip time is limited.

Finally settled in my hotel, I reviewed the plans for my visit. I knew I wanted to take at least one full day to see some portion of Taiwan outside of Taipei. I was hoping to tour the Palace National Museum with my son. I wanted to spend time with my daughter-in-law but wasn't sure what activities we might want to do. My plans included a trip to Taipei 101, the tallest building in Taiwan again, to return to the little restaurant that served the best squid on the planet (per my taste buds), visit my family and their kitties, and get a sense of their home in another country. A little extra time to explore in Taipei was on the list as well as any possibilities I wasn't even aware of. The excitement was such that I could barely sleep. Additionally, not helping in the quest for a good night's sleep, was the extra firm mattress in my room. China has a culture of firm mattresses as a requirement for good body alignment, and prior to a spinal surgery, that had been my comfort point as well. Now, the softer the mattress the better and it took resourcefulness to create a surface soft enough for me. A creation of pillows and a comforter helped. But the energy and creativity involved left me wide awake for hours. My alarm clock announced breakfast time only a few hours after I finally fell asleep. The energy of waking up in a different country and all its potential, had me up, in the shower and eating breakfast at the buffet in the hotel's dining space. The breakfast buffet was included in the room price, so it was assumed all guests would most likely be eating the breakfast. Therefore, breakfast was a variety of dishes from many different cultures with the hopes of meeting everyone's eating preferences. Particularly, when I travel, starting the day with a hearty breakfast and coffee sets me up for the day… days where unexpected and interesting things will occur and I may not eat another meal till much later in the day.

On the ride in from the airport, we determined my daughter-in-law would contact me mid-morning to see when I might be ready to leave the hotel. We connected and agreed she would meet me at my hotel early afternoon for a late lunch at a well-known restaurant in the basement of a large department store. Later in my trip I saw the main restaurant in the Daan area of downtown Taipei. Both are set up with precision in portions of food and timing of seating and serving. We looked at the menu and then put in our order and request for seating. An electronic clock showed the ticket number issued and time until a table would be available. This allowed for time to wander the area or wait at the entrance. It was just a few minutes after being seated that our orders appeared. Given the pace of service and turnover of customers, the food was delicious and we never felt rushed.

After eating we wandered through the aisles of both exotic and local foods before taking the escalators to check out clothing. I brought my great Chinese dictionary. This was helpful in asking about fabrics and other words that I was not prepared to use from my intro to Chinese class taken the prior fall term. A cab dropped us back at my hotel and left an opportunity for me to take a quick nap before meeting my son and a friend of his for dinner. We met his friend from work at a local casual restaurant we had visited in my first visit to Taiwan four years prior. I was hoping to order the squid from that visit. We ordered a squid dish, but it was not that special one, and a great sizzling platter of meat with a fried egg. Both the food and conversation were satisfying and created a pleasant end to my first day in Taipei.

Day two's plans included another item from my to do list. I wanted to revisit Taipei 101, the tallest building in Taipei again. I didn't need to go to the top this time for the view (which is good because the weather was overcast) but did want to see the floors of art and design that we had just walked through before as an afterthought. A person can only absorb so much at one time, so this opportunity for a leisurely look was appealing. Massive displays of coral, jade and ceramics were as internally satisfying as the great food we'd eaten the night before.

That evening we all went to a great Italian restaurant across town. I was curious about the reason for visiting an Italian restaurant in Taipei when there are so many terrific Asian restaurants. The story given explained it all. When my son had just arrived in Taipei, he met an American chef who ran an Italian restaurant in the States. This chef fell in love with a young woman who finally told him it was an ill-fated romance since she had accepted a job in Taiwan and would be leaving soon. He determined he would also go to Taiwan and find a way to open an Italian restaurant there, since that was his specialty and passion. Opening a restaurant in any foreign country is a challenge and this was no exception. He let my son know when the restaurant was ready to open and my son and his wife soon became regulars. First the visits were to be supportive, but the extraordinary quality and freshness of the food became the prime reason. They were not the only ones who thought so. As we arrived to enjoy dinner, it was noted he was about to open a second restaurant close by. Business was very good. This chef made his pasta fresh every day and meats met his eagle eye for quality, cut and freshness. Wow, was that a lengthy delicious meal! The décor and clientele made us all feel like a loosely knit family enjoying a Sunday supper.

I was still on a run of insomnia, counting on the value of lying in bed and simply resting my body with an accompanying three to four hours of sleep each night. But I was up and excited about the next day. In my prior brief trip to Taiwan there was a fast paced and informative tour that included the National Palace Museum. I was awestruck and knew on this trip I would want to spend more time in it. I told this to my son when he asked for my wish list of things to do, also adding I hoped we could see the museum together. As it turned out, he had assisted the museums docent training program at the school where he was teaching. He picked me up and we were to meet one of these docents who would give a private tour of the museum. He asked us how much time we had and used that as a guide for the pace. He was so knowledgeable, humorous and passionate about the history and art. This made the tour such a treat for us. I learned so much. For example, only the emperor was authorized to have yellow ceramic diningware. While dragons show up on many of the ceramic pieces, only the emperor's dragons have five claws on each of their limbs. Higher up officials might have four claws and the average person would have three. We walked through the many centuries' development of tools, adornment, serving pieces, design and materials. I wanted to be able to see this again and share it with friends so I bought two DVDs in the museum gift shop. This trip to Taiwan was not about buying souvenirs, but I couldn't resist the opportunity to continue enjoying the amazing art.

It seems we kept enjoying each others company, in part, because we took breaks between doing activities together. This allowed my family time to do their lives and me to have quiet time and my own time too. After a nice break following the museum, we met and headed out to dinner at a department store. This one had a full floor for a variety of fast food restaurants and a separate floor of fine dining spots. We had reservations at one of my son's favorite fine restaurants for a nicely paced ten course dinner. The ambiance, fresh clean flavors and creativity made this a lovely evening to share in conversation and yummy appreciation sounds.

After dinner we picked up my suitcases, I checked out of my hotel, and we cabbed to downtown Taipei for a new adventure. I stayed at the same hotel chain in their downtown location. This was probably one of the smallest hotel rooms I've ever stayed in. But it did have a window overlooking the center of a downtown park I was planning to explore, as well as lots of local shops and bakeries. Most importantly, it was a location where I could be picked up for a trip to Sun Moon Lake in central Taiwan. In fact, I was scheduled to be picked up at 8 a.m. the next morning. I was hoping the change in rooms would help me sleep better. No such luck. Still, I was up and ready to see more of Taiwan on time.

Our van held two English speaking guides, the driver, a couple from India and a family of six who were living in Australia but visiting relatives in Taiwan. Everyone spoke English, which made it unnecessary for me to need my Chinese notes, but I was glad to have them in case there was an opportunity to use them. We were headed to Sun Moon Lake, a three hour drive away. In the central mountains of leaf shaped Taiwan, sits Sun Moon Lake. We were told the lake was so named because east side of the lake is round like the sun while the west side is long and narrow like a crescent moon. The area is known for the sacred Formosa Sika deer. Legend says the lake was discovered by following these deer through the mountainous terrain.

We stopped on the way at a rest area. I'm used to more rustic rest areas… in a wooded area, parking places, some grassy areas and, of course, large rest rooms. This rest area had a very large rest room area, restaurants, shops, and a lovely park. Even though we had been driving for less than two hours, it was surprising to me how many in our group rushed to purchase meal-sized portions of food to eat on the bus. This made we wonder if they knew more about the "lunch" we were supposed to be getting on arrival. Apparently they did not. Our van dropped us at the top of a busy street leading to the lake. We were asked to not stop at the shops on the way down the hill to lunch because we would have time after touring the lake area. At the bottom of the street was a building we entered. On the second floor, a large round table had been reserved for us. It was right at a window overlooking the lake and soon we were being served a multicourse luncheon. Each dish was placed on a large moveable platform that I grew up calling a Lazy Susan. Everyone ate as though food had not been available for days. I was pretty hungry by then and our table was a vision of much eating, conversation and anticipation to go out on the lake. The weather was sunny with a light breeze and a boat ride sounded terrific to all of us.

Our guides led us down the pier and maneuvered us to be the first on board our assigned boat. This allowed us to select seats all together and outside where we could feel the cool water spray and view the lake and landscape around us clearly. We slowed while passing the sacred island of Lalu, or as it more recently called Guanghua Island, in the middle of the lake. The island is rumored to provide shelter to sacred deer. Eventually, our boat pulled alongside a dock to continue our adventure. We started on a pathway up the hillside which led to steep wood and stone steps. As the rest of my group bounded up the stairs I got slower and slower. The heat of the day, too much lunch, too little sleep and pain from my disability stopped me as we started the next flight. The second guide stayed with me and looked concerned. "Is this the last flight of steps?" I asked hopefully. "Oh no," he laughed. "Two flights and then, of course, the same for the next two temples we visit as we move around the lake." I had to sit down and then lie down for just a moment at the edge of the pathway. My body was just telling me it needed to stop doing everything for a moment. This totally scared the poor guide. I sat up, let him help me to my feet and told him this part of the tour would be too much for me. Even though I'd asked lots of questions to determine if I could handle the tour, I've traveled enough to know there are always things that come up you can't anticipate. My compromise was to enjoy time on the boat but at each of the other stops I would wait at the pier where I could enjoy local musicians, the lake, people watching and the shops while the group toured the hillsides. The guide promised to not leave me behind and I still enjoyed the excursion.

On the way back to the bus we were all given an hour to eat at some of the well recommended street stalls and souvenir shops. Back at the bus our group consensus was an A+ on the yummy food, a display of goodies purchased and I had some extremely luscious local tea ice cream. All this was helpful to remember for the very long ride back to town. Sunday night city travelers returning home from weekend travels choked the roads as completely as any freeway back home. The bus dropped me off around 9:30 p.m. at my hotel and the bed looked as compelling as the lake's sunshine had.

The next morning was a time planned to wander through the large park in downtown Taipei, and practice my Mandarin Chinese at the local shops and bakeries.

After breakfast at my hotel, I walked across the street and entered the green oasis of Daan Park. In the middle of downtown Taipei lies this verdant space with walking paths, a Buddha, amphitheater, athletic fields, lots of benches and a small lake. A minute island in the lake is home to a variety of birds, noted with pictures on a nearby sign. It was so relaxing and pleasurable to take my time wandering, sitting, watching and feeling the quiet. I'm sure the park is crowded on the weekends, but this Monday morning, mostly the retired and serious photographers had gathered. Fuchsia hued flowering trees and a small grove of trees, with zebra stripes in many shades of brown circling the slender trunks, caught me most particularly. Too bad I can't rewind the experience because I'd like to know the names of the trees even though the explanatory signs were not in English. I could have taken pictures of them and asked the ever helpful people at my hotel. Such things happen when there is so much to see and do.

Feeling refreshed, it was time to wander down several side streets in the area to poke around in a variety of shops and bakeries. It was surprising to me that wherever I went in the Taipei area, there were always wonderful bakeries containing a variety of not only Chinese and Taiwanese goodies but European breads and desserts. At the end of my wanderings I stopped in one such bakery and realized I had worked up an appetite. So much looked and smelled delicious I couldn't make up my mind and left. Almost back to the hotel, I realized the small chocolate bread was calling to me. I went all the way back and bought it figuring it was closer from the hotel to the bakery than going back to the bakery from my U.S. home. That was a good call, since I munched my way through that light as air chocolate goodness most of the afternoon. In a clothing shop, I bought a traditional silk sort of vest/blouse that can be worn a number of different ways. It was too beautiful to not buy. I was able to ask questions and complete the transaction with my few memorized phrases, my Mandarin dictionary and a patient shop owner. In practicing my beginners Chinese, it was curious how each person I talked to had a completely different reaction. Some corrected specific words differently each time I used them, some understood me quite well , a few simply didn't want to make the effort to understand my slow and often mispronounced sentences. Someone pointed out I should be speaking Taiwanese. Yet, I think they all were more gracious than many in my own country when dealing with tourists not fluent in English. Mid-afternoon had me packing up my things and calling a cab to take me back to the expat section of the city, to my original hotel, and time for a rest before joining my family for another amazing dinner.

At dinner, we realized the next day was my last full day in Taiwan. The time had been well used but the week had gone by too quickly. What to do for the last day? We decided I would spend the day with my daughter-in-law while my son was at work and then finish the evening with just him at dinner, where we hoped to find and devour the elusive squid of my first visit to Taipei. The morning would be spent at Yangmingshan National Park. The park was up in the hills just behind my family's apartment and very diverse in its landscape and features. I had a plan for the afternoon. On the way to my tour of Sun Moon Lake, we picked up some of our passengers at the famous Grand Hotel in Taipei. I remembered my daughter-in-law had pointed it out on the way to Taipei 101 and commented she hoped to see the inside of it someday. My tour guides mentioned it had quite a history; and also served tea that was open to the public in the afternoons. I asked my daughter-in-law if I could treat her to tea at the Grand Hotel followed by some exploring of the mysterious hotel and she was delighted.

We hired a cab the next morning and, as we moved up the winding streets, the sunny skies turned grey and a light mist moved in. We stopped at the park headquarters for the view, but already the mist was turning to a dense fog. The park is huge and their tourist safety notes include reminders of the geothermal springs' instability, and what to do if poisonous snakes or wasps appear on the trail. On arriving at the geothermal area, it was chilly, and dense fog swirled around us. Other people partially appeared as we walked toward the springs and the smell of Sulphur took over every sense. Large groaning and uprooting sounds came from the general area of the hot springs. Within the space of half an hour we had been transported to a whole different world. It was pretty startling. After our ride back down the hill, we each went our separate ways to change clothes and relax, later catching a cab to the unknown Grand Hotel.

I have to tell you the Grand Hotel is truly grand. The Grand is a large hillside structure, bright red with black trim. Walking inside provides an immediate sense of space and grandeur. But first, the Asian perspective of Anime and creative cuteness appears in the form of large glass and golden statues as tribute on bright red platforms surrounded by equally large red pillars. Once past the display and to the left we saw the Grand's version of "afternoon tea". Crowds of people surrounded a staggering array of stations serving every conceivable type of Asian food specialty and, of course, an equal variety of desserts and teas. We were first seated at a lovely formal style table overlooking an outdoor garden, and then, wandering back and forth between stations, systematically ate as much as we could possibly manage. It was tremendously satisfying. It also made exploring the facility enticing as a means to walk off the results of our food frenzy.

We didn't see any of the guest rooms but noted the historical photos showing the original site where the hotel was built in 1952. In 1978 the Grand was also the site of negotiations for the United States to break diplomatic relations with the Republic of China. A beautiful door of golden designs and coins turned out to be the entrance to a ladies room. Golden dragons spouting water graced two side entrance lobbies. Ceilings, stairways and pillars were elaborately decorated with carvings, paintings and ornate designs. What an amazing afternoon. I spent the ride home anticipating a short nap and wondering how I would be able to eat dinner with my son.

Dinner turned out to be no problem at all. We met at the restaurant that hopefully had the squid we both desired and it was approximately four hours after the massive "tea" meal. The squid arrived, little puffed circles of squid fried with red yeast and so delectable, no one would have believed I had earlier put away a massive meal. Good conversation and incredible food with someone you care about is the best kind of meal to me. As I finished packing late at night for the next morning's flight, I was filled with happiness that I had stepped past practicality and embarked on this visit to Taiwan. The following morning, my daughter-in-law went out to the airport with me to return the mobile hot spot equipment that had enabled us to communicate. As we parted ways, I headed for my flight home grateful for their hospitality and the ability to still travel the world.

Chongquing Old Market Street

*Chongqing Old Market Street Noodle Maker
(we ate lunch there)*

Temple and bridge at Shibao—on Yangtze River

Morocco and the Canary Islands

2000

"Liar!" I muttered under my breath, thinking of how the airline rep behind her counter had explained, "You could catch the ship you've missed by taking this flight on our airline. The airport is adjacent to the port. "No," still talking barely out loud, "I'm in the middle of the desert, and the only water around here might be in that small building everyone else has headed for." I was the only woman and non-Arab on the nineteen seater plane. I still had my juice box with Arabic writing on it in my hand. I dropped it as I turned and faced a man walking briskly toward me from the distant building.

Completely exhausted from work, a cruise in the Canary Islands at an insanely affordable price seemed the perfect thing to do. I'd heard the Islands were the equivalent to Europeans as the Hawaiian Islands were to Americans. In addition, a visit to Morocco was included. I signed up and started marking off the days on my calendar.

I might have realized the trip was not going to be a spa-like experience as I stood at the airline counter in my hometown being told, "You can't go on this flight." I was stunned. "Why not?" I asked, scarcely believing I was having this conversation. "Your ticket was for yesterday," was the sympathetic response. I thought I was going to throw up. I stumbled to a row of seats and tried to figure out what I was going to do. I thought I might have options because this was pre 2001 and the layers of security that came from that time were not in place. I remembered someone telling me once to not say no for people so I went back up to the counter and said, "Can I fly anyhow?" The woman looked startled but I could tell was considering and after looking at the flight information said, "There is space on today's flight so you can fly to New York. But once you get there you change airlines to get to Madrid. I don't know if the next airline will be so accommodating." "Thank you, thank you, thank you, yes, I'll take my chances," I murmured, grasping the new ticket and moving toward the gate before she could change her mind. On the plane I thought, "If they won't let me use my yesterday ticket at the next airline, I'll go someplace in the U.S., affordable and warm, like Florida," considering my suitcase full of sunny weather clothing.

Arriving in New York, I found the next airline and handed over my ticket while going through the line with my bags. I tried to look nonchalant but the airline rep wasn't having any of that. "This is yesterday's ticket, ma'am, she stated with surprise. I just looked at her, woman to woman, working gal to working gal, shrugged my shoulders and told her, "Work has been so stressful… they let me fly from Oregon to New York." My plea ended on what I hoped sounded like an optimistic note. She looked at me hard and said "Oh, I hear ya." I was on my way to Madrid. Now I relaxed. As we neared Madrid I spent time looking out the window at the sky show. It was a blazing deep erotic blue rolling into sunnyside egg yellow and at the skyline a defiant color, not red or orange or pink, all but none. Suddenly the volume of the dark earth cut it off mid-sentence. There was a smile my face as we rolled up to our gate. My flight from Madrid to Gran Canaria was just a shuttle plane ride leaving

Madrid every few hours. My travel problems were over! So when I realized my flight was late in arriving, I just went up to the airline counter to catch the next plane. But that flight was full, and the following one was cancelled. This meant I missed my ship and would have to catch it at its first island stop. No planes were headed there until the next morning.

Between airline reps and taxi drivers, I found a hotel, somewhat abandoned not too far from the airport. It overlooked the ocean and had an air about it and layout of some place definitely not like my home. It was intriguing... embodying a lot of what going on vacation is about.

The next morning at the airport, I found out the island I thought I would head for was engulfed by a sand storm and my ship didn't stop there, heading for its next port, Agadir, Morocco instead. Now I was panicking. I had to catch the boat in Agadir because the port afterward was Casablanca, a port so large I would never find my ship. I finally found a small airline that flew to Morocco and they assured me their terminal was next to the port. I felt a little iffy on this small commuter plane with conversations all in Arabic. The plane started its descent and I craned my neck to spot the port but seeing only desert. We all disembarked, the men walking briskly toward a small distant building. I just stood on the runway looking at endless desert in every direction. My ship would leave the port in Agadir soon. Maybe I would find a ride there eventually and just have a vacation in Agadir. I had read something about Agadir stating it has a seaside resort. A man appeared to be headed my way. I thought French and Arabic were both used in Morocco and I still remembered a little high school French.

"Parlez vous Francais, Anglais, monsieur?" I queried

"I speak English, Madam. Where is your husband?"

His question reminded my how important it is to know something about local customs and traditions when you travel. I knew a woman traveling alone would not be acceptable in this society so I answered, "He is working and could not come."

"Where is your oldest son?"

My response, "He could not leave his family."

"Madam, I will take care of you. Let me see your paper-work. I see you are in need of catching a ship in Agadir. I will arrange this for you. Come with me."

I followed him to the small building that was actually not that small when we got there. I don't know who he was, but he was amazing. He got me a beverage and a seat. He changed my money and contacted the port to have my ship held. I'd heard ships leave whether someone is late or not. They keep their schedule. So to be told the ship was being held for me at port was hard to believe. He hired a cab driver for me, telling me as he loaded me and my bags into the cab, "Your driver will drive like the wind across the desert for perhaps forty minutes. Don't let him stop till you are at the port and don't pay him until you get there." I thanked him demurely and we roared off into the ocean of sand. There were little outcroppings of villages, children playing, goats, adobe housing, shanties, and donkey carts. The women were mostly covered completely. As we reached the city, police were everywhere.

The ship indeed had been held for me and the captain was not in a good mood. "Finally here! Grab your bags and get on board," he snarled. But it seemed the ship would not be released until there was confirmation I had been helped on board and was settled in my cabin. When the call was completed, the captain smiled, had a member of the crew help me with my bags and soon I was in my cabin, the ship sliding out of port, and on toward Casablanca. I felt I had just finished one crazy trip and was now on trip number two... the reward trip for having survived the first trip. I was exhausted.

I was so grateful for my cozy little cabin and the opportunity to finally relax and have a leisurely cruise through tropical islands. But first, after a great night's sleep, Morocco. We stepped off the ship and drove through the large and very cosmopolitan city (the port and city so vast, it confirms my earlier thoughts about not finding my ship at the Casablanca harbor). The old city, the medina, is a maze of narrow streets we drove past, and soon we descended onto wide boulevards, palm trees and eventually the countryside. I was surprised by how green, crop laden, and river rich this area was. My original thought about visiting Marrakesh was-it probably would be highly commercialized these days but how could someone come this far without taking a look? I was so wrong. The only problem with Marrakesh was having that one afternoon instead of several days there. We drove around seeing hotels, fancy homes, and government buildings as well as hearing a good slice of the area's history.

Originally, just a point where Berbers came to trade goods, it became a town where all Middle Eastern groups coexisted peacefully... Arab, Berber, Muslim, Jew, Christian. The core of this town was now the old town, medina, filled with mystery, history and shops of every sort. This included a large open area for the daily market place. I remembered driving through a small village in China on my first trip there, exclaiming it was a smaller version of a Moroccan market place. I assumed it was a reaction to something I might have seen in a travel magazine. Now I realized that it really was like a small, toned- down version of Marrakesh.

Before entering the amazement of the marketplace and medina, we stopped for lunch at a restaurant with outdoor seating, where we were serenaded by musicians and belly dancers. The sun was fiercely hot, in a different way than I was used to experiencing. I sat with a couple from Norway and a couple from Scotland. We laughed and shared travel stories while dining on an amazing lunch of spiced carrots, eggplant, cubed potatoes, cucumber something, chicken in lemon sauce with olives, and couscous. All followed by oranges, cookies and mint tea. While not a regular tea drinker, I now enjoy mint tea and always think of Morocco. After such a lunch I might have been tempted to take a nap any place else, but Marrakesh was magic and there was no sleeping going on.

The best way to describe it is in layers. At first, the square was not too crowded. Our guide from the ship led us past the snake charmers, hooded cobras peeking out from their baskets, women who could read our fortune or create henna designs on your hand or arm. There were women in veils at our side trying to sell cheap bracelets and men in fezes selling synthetic caftans as we wove through the maze of narrow streets. As we passed a carpet shop, I asked to stop there, realizing I wanted a souvenir of Marrakesh and a Berber carpet would be just the thing. I wanted one small enough to hang on a wall but large enough to lie on the floor, perhaps as a meditation rug. I was left to my own devices by the group, but our guide said she would be back shortly to see how I was doing in bargaining for a carpet.

I entered the shop and a very handsome man asked if I was interested in purchasing a carpet. I nodded and the dance of bargaining began. It seems each culture has its own way of negotiating prices. I've participated in some that are almost a war of words being hurled at each other. Others involve ever increasing information on the value of the item, some just perfunctory. Here, was the most gracious process.

The seller started with, "I am honored by your interest in the weaving of these most beautiful carpets, my family's proud tradition. If you allow me, I will show the most exquisite variety and design now."

I, of course, replied, "I am honored for the opportunity to view these most beautiful carpets, product of your family traditions."

We moved from room to room, with evermore variety, honor, praise and a bit of seduction implied. I was growing a bit uncomfortable after receiving a gentle, unexpected kiss on the cheek and pointed to a specific carpet stating, "This is a most beautiful carpet I should like to see in the daylight now," while moving toward the sound of open spaces and other people. He quickly followed, carpet in hand. We continued the floral verbiage to price agreement just as the agent from my ship returned. She verified I was paying a proper price and we left the shop.

As we returned to the open marketplace, I saw changes rapidly taking place. The square was filling up with portable restaurants, cobras dancing out of their baskets, fruit vendors, dancers, musicians, and crowds of people appeared. I was told this would steadily intensify and continue until early morning hours. The sounds, smells and sights were all encompassing. I wanted to eat, dance, have a henna design drawn on my arm, engage with the cobras (they place them around your neck and take a picture for you, of course the cobras are old and defanged). But no henna, no cobras, not if I didn't want to miss the bus back to the ship. I'd had my fill of missing the ship so off we all went, arriving at the ship late that night.

We spent the next day at sea and I had time to explore this lovely ship and its amenities. Considering I started off looking for relaxation, the next few days were heavenly. Sleep, eat, hang out and eventually explore exotic islands were the only items on my "to do" list. On board there were always lots of activities and it was fun to dress up a bit for dinner, hit the casino, attend all sorts of live shows including a ventriloquist and Broadway musical, game night, and, of course, the midnight buffet with its mammoth ice sculptures. Some new friends talked me into playing bingo with them and I won a jackpot.

After luxury time to watch the waves and sky at leisure, it was time to visit one of the Canary Islands. A half-day tour took us up the rugged terrain on the north side of Tenerife. Staggering cliffs, jungle and then, high up into the valley we found what seemed to be the ideal place for banana plantations. The bananas seemed very small and we were told most of them were dwarf bananas intended for commercial use. On the way back to the ship we had time to wander the harbor area availing us the opportunities of shopping for souvenirs, sampling snacks and beverages, or enjoying the black sand beaches with water pounding on the rocks. Actually there was time to do it all.

A full day visit to Madeira, Portugal turned out to be a special treat. We started by exploring an expansive botanical garden. Plants I had seen at home or in neighboring states were dwarfed by their namesakes in the proper environment. Bougainvillea blossoms showered down as tree like formations while orchids could hardly contain themselves in their beds. Birds of Paradise were eagle-sized and everywhere were masses of eucalyptus and poinsettias. The mingling scents were intoxicating. As the morning progressed, it became quite warm and humid yet, for some reason, I was the only one who ran through the sprinklers spread over the well-manicured lawns. I noticed several people looked enviously at me and how cool and comfortable I appeared. After lunch we were dropped off in town and told where to meet for return to our ship. The small city tumbled down hill ending abruptly at the sea. There was no real beach, just boulders, smaller rocks and crashing waves. Some trips I like to bring back souvenirs for friends and family and the quality of the shops in Madeira created an easy way to do so. I can't say what there was about Madeira, but it seemed like a special place and I felt both relaxed and creative there.

That evening we had our last dinner on board and I shared the meal with a table of folks from Britain who had just joined us and were starting their cruise. It was fun to answer their questions about the ship and tours. I finished up with a visit to the casino and an excellent show of dancing and singing in Spanish. Back at my cabin, packing was completed and I was deep asleep shortly after midnight.

Breakfast on the ship was followed by a tour of Gran Canaria countryside. This is what my shipmates had seen while I was stalled in Madrid and none of us were able to see the island of Lanzarote so it all evened out in the end. We drove high into the hills unable to ditch the humidity and heat, but still able to enjoy the jungle and spectacular views of the island and out to sea. We stopped in the old town and visited the museum of Christopher Columbus, who sailed out of Gran Canaria. The museum had a way of presenting the old history with current times that made it exciting and entertaining. Returning to the ship, we noted our bags had already been picked up. Lunch was served and we were escorted off the ship. My cruise had come to an end.

Interestingly, my luggage was dropped off at my hotel in Gran Canaria but I had to walk to the hotel. They gave me directions and while initially I was unhappy with that arrangement, it turned out to be a great time… I had forgotten it was Mardi Gras or Carnivale as it is called in the Islands. Early versions of the celebration were going on with a parade, floats, costumes, cheering and general carnival goings on. I let myself feel a part of the celebrants, parade watching, and dancing a bit as I slowly made my way to the hotel. As the hotel came into view, I saw it was on the boardwalk, so after checking in, I kicked off my shoes, crossed over the boardwalk onto the beach and just enjoyed the sand and cool water as it splashed against my legs. Dinner was with a couple from Ohio I met on the cruise and then off to bed. I had to be up at 3:45 a.m. in order to catch a very early morning flight. So lying in bed was restful, but trying to sleep on Mardi Gras night was as much wishful thinking as it was actual sleep.

Coming back from the Islands toward the U.S. west coast is a study in moving backwards in time. When it was 9:15 in Gran Canaria, it was 4:15 in New York, and 1:15 at my final destination. Traveling home, I would have thought, would be incredibly easy in comparison to my attempts to go on vacation but the flight gods still weren't through with me. My luggage was tagged to the right city but wrong state. This is when I learned to always check the tag as it is put on my checked in bags for not only the city, but also the state. Fortunately I arrived at the airport early, because I was faced with the news I had been labelled as "cancelled" from my flight home, since technically, at the start of my trip, I hadn't been on board for the date my ticket had been issued. Again, the flight wasn't full so I got to fly home and even had my choice of seats. I couldn't be upset. I was just supremely grateful because the reservation clerk told me my flight was the only one that day that wasn't booked completely full.

So my cruise to "relax", play in the sun-no brain, no pain had its sunlit deck chair moments but also the thrilling adventure of chasing a cruise ship and the mystery of not having tickets to fly, yet always finding myself on those flights. I guess my final analysis, my take away from this adventure, was a need to acknowledge I am led and blessed and wherever I need to be, there will always be a seat for me.

India Beckons

2003

S ometimes it takes just sitting and being in the right place to hear our inner selves telling us what we need to do next. Some folks find that space while driving, some at the laundromat as their laundry goes around in the dryer. I felt I needed to go to Agra and meditate at the Taj Mahal. There was trepidation. I had never wanted to go to India before. I had heard of vast grinding poverty, so many begging and in need as well as a lack of welcome for women traveling by themselves. Still, if I was determined to go, there would be a way to do so. An early spring afternoon had me on a major airline's inaugural flight to Frankfurt, Germany on the way to Delhi, India.

A crowded plane, me wedged in between snorers and crying children, the discomfort all erased by the sunrise moving with us toward Frankfurt. There are ribbons of hot pink and purple, rolls of pale yellow sliding into soft blue, all rolling up from a dark sea, which turns out to be navy blue clouds. It was good to stop in Frankfurt. The staff where l stayed for the night tried to explain how to find a tour for the late afternoon but I realized I was too tired to take directions and used the time for a walk in the woods by the hotel. Stretching my legs along with being in nature set me up for a big bowl of soup and good night's sleep before the long flight to Delhi.

It seems all international flights arriving and departing from Delhi occur in the middle of the night. So it was just business as usual to move through the process, set foot into airport proper and note the exit ramp was lined with men holding up signs of greeting for clients or guests at a hotel. I had been told my hotel had such a service and a man with a sign would be there for me too. I saw a sign stating "Welcome Carlo Palo." Of course, they were expecting a business man and "Carol" was just a typo, and as such had secured a room on the business floor of the hotel with the perks that go with it for me. The driver was startled at my insistence I was the person he was picking up but he drove me to the hotel. The hotel manager was gracious and we struck up many interesting conversations while I was staying there.

I had recently found out my aching back was more than just a few pulled muscles. In fact I was in the process of checking with many doctors to determine what my options might be for resolving increasing pain. This had been a factor in determining how I could manage this trip. I didn't feel safe going solo and thought being part of a group tour might sap my energy and abilities on many activities I wasn't interested in. I decided to hire a guide and driver to take me specifically to the places I wanted to see and went to a well-known travel company who provides these kinds of services around the world. Surprisingly, it was much less expensive than I thought it would be. This also gave me the opportunity to talk with someone local who could share their viewpoint, lifestyle and ideas as we drove through the countryside. There were a few times I simply couldn't go further that day, no matter what great sight might be missed and that was okay. My driver was called "uncle," which seems to be internationally common for loose family, friends and connections. He and my guide, Vinny, took me to their temples and explained the dos and don'ts, and a bit about Hinduism. We stopped and ate many meals where they and the other guides and drivers ate and Vinny gave me details of what we were seeing that I think surpassed what I might have had on a standard tour.

That first drive took place in Delhi, both old and new, diplomats' row, the Muslim neighborhood, parks, shopping districts for the middle class, tombs, temples and monuments. It was a whirlwind of information and sights. As we returned to the hotel, lots of military pulled up and escorted a man in a turban and a Buddhist monk who looked like the Dalai Lama. Vinny said the man in the turban was the Prime Minister of Education and the other man was an important Buddhist leader. He said he heard the actual Dali Lama was staying at my hotel. This kind of good energy made me feel I was in the right spot at the right time. When I mentioned this to the hotel manager the next night he said, "Pity I didn't know you were interested. Yes, the Dalai Lama did stay here last night. I could have arranged a visit with him for you." I couldn't even imagine such a thing happening and told him, "Thanks for such generous thoughts, but just knowing he was here feels like a wonderful omen."

After Delhi, the plan was to go to the Taj Mahal in Agra; Ranthambore, which is a wild animal reserve; Jaipur; and some time out in the countryside. The drive to Agra took us over four hours along small towns and we shared the road with a mix of local taxis, bicycles, pedestrians, and trucks. Of course, wherever we encountered a cow in the road, the cow had right of way even if it was taking a nap.

How to even begin to explain the effect of the Taj Mahal? Approaching it through an archway, it completely took my breath away with its serene massive beauty. The original gardens were first laid out in the early 1500s and architectural features were added over the years. As the dynasty continued to prosper and grow in stature, Jahangir came to rule both peacefully and opulently. It was under his rule that the first tomb, a jewel box encased in white marble with intricate inlay work was built. By 1628 Prince Khurram became Shah Jahan (conqueror of the world) and ruled with his most beloved companion, Mumtaz Mahal. She accompanied him on many of his military expeditions. Unfortunately, being pregnant and ready to deliver her fourteenth child on one such expedition, she died in childbirth. It is believed that just prior to her death the Shah promised he would build a beautiful monument in her memory that would symbolize their eternal love for each other. Twenty-two years of intense effort were needed to complete his vision. That vision is what appeared to me as I entered the gardens and stood facing it, head on.

I slowly walked around the gardens, tomb and commemorating structure, just absorbing the pristine marble, encrusted with jewels and painted designs. Finally finding a bench that seemed the right place to sit, I relaxed and hoped, as I attempted to clear my mind and simply be, something would come to me that would make me feel I hadn't been an idiot to come all the way to India. After some time I was able to realize it was not clarity I needed, rather the gentle touch of real courage to take action and active compassion for my most vulnerable self. It was a most emotional experience.

I was suddenly very tired. The sun was making hot and sticky objects of all of us sitting under it directly and I was ready to leave. We stopped at a shop by a marble quarry before leaving Agra. I bought a small table. A wooden frame for support to hold a jewel laden marble top, they said from the same quarry as the Taj Mahal. Whether that was true or not, it is quite beautiful and when held up to the sunlight you can see the light through it. Fortunately, they had the ability to ship it to my home. When it arrived at customs several weeks later it was like stepping back into my adventure. I also learned a good lesson about human nature and its universality. As a thank you for purchasing a table, the shop owner wanted to give me a small souvenir. He led me to a shelf filled room full of statues of various sizes and in various states from crudely cut to sublimely smooth. He yelled for his assistant to bring me a small souvenir. The man, bent over and not looking up, handed me a lovely small statue.

"No you idiot!" yelled the shop owner, continuing with, "Get the one we usually give… the man is too stupid to be doing this job." As the shop owner turned in disgust I saw the assistant look up at him briefly with the quiet rage of anyone who is being demeaned. I knew as a passive way of getting back at his boss, he would give me the better statue. The owner demanded to see the statue for me and the assistant showed him the rough one. But when I got home and unwrapped the souvenir, I found both statues. What a graphic reminder: it is a human state of being, having no national boundaries, but an inward need by all of us to be treated with respect.

For a total change of pace, I was next delivered to what appeared to be a century back in time. I wanted to go on a camera safari in India and found myself at a series of little round huts adjacent to a small club house, all very colonial British, just in time for afternoon tea and time to prepare for an evening in the jungle. Because of a major drought, the roads were bone dry and deep ruts kept the jeep jumping.

Mercifully, for my back, we slowed down to minimize the noise and therefore see more animals. In the twilight, the shine of eyes, stops to view freshly made feline tracks, and an occasional sighting filled the evening. Later, I headed to the mini fridge in my bungalow, not to drink, but to pack my fairly swollen torso with the cans' icy goodness. I had another safari set for early morning and I made arrangements to go in a Jeep with just the driver for a shorter and gentler route. On the way we saw several lovely Indian women, in their gorgeous saris, walking in the same direction. I asked the driver where they were headed so early in the morning. He informed me with, "This drought is taking its toll on people and animals alike. With no water for farming, the men have gone off to the cities to earn money for food. The women were hired to dig wells in the Ranthambore Reserve for the animals and that's where they are headed. They're lucky to have these jobs and they know it." I suggested to the driver we give them a ride. He gave me a look of disbelief stating, "We shouldn't. If they get a ride today, they'll want a ride tomorrow." He turned back to the road, considering the situation done. I wanted to give them a ride. It felt like a woman to woman thing. Why should I ride and why couldn't they? So I replied "I want to give them a ride. I'm your client. Pull over." He did and translated my offer of a ride. They looked reluctant but finally got into the jeep. When we arrived at the point where they needed to be, we stopped. There seemed to be some confusion about whether they needed to pay for the ride and I had the driver explain I only wanted a photo of them in exchange for the ride. I had been expecting a photo of solidarity, perhaps a smile and look of happiness for riding instead of walking so far. But the ladies looked somewhat hostile and there were no smiles. I don't know what the driver actually said to them, but it also occurred to me after some thought, their feelings were probably, "Who is this uppity woman who does not know her place and why should we let her take our picture?"

Even though my trekking was less than the other visitors, I still had an amazing time. One highlight took place in a clearing where we met a ranger. He was overseeing some activity in the area and pointed to a deer not too far from us. "That deer is so used to seeing us around he is not startled by people. He is still somewhat wild but if you move slowly toward him you might get a picture." I didn't have to move. He came right up to me and I patted the side of his face as he looked at me (about the same height as me) as though he wanted to be my new best friend. I think, realistically, he was sensing I had salt on skin and that would have been very appealing. The ranger took a photo of this friendly deer gazing into my eyes for me and I still enjoy looking at it.

Early morning seemed to be the time for animals to be relaxed and on the move. We saw a leopard casually crossing the path not too far ahead of us. His grace belied the speed he was moving at and quickly there was only a blur of yellow black and the flip of a tail. Lots of deer, an astounding assortment of birds and so many monkeys moved in and out of the camouflaging plants and terrain. The experience was tremendously satisfying but the combination of heat and intense pain in my back had me feeling nauseous and grateful to find the end of the rutted roads and the entrance to my bungalow and the ice.

The afternoon held plenty of time to write postcards, nap and of course, ice my back. I was feeling pretty fine by dinner time and enjoyed sharing great food and conversations about our adventures and what we had seen on our jungle drives. The last safari was mostly an adventure of finding tracks all over the paths, rustling in the tall grasses and so many eyes in the brush and trees that it was hard to tell who was watching who.

Packing, icing and a bit of sleep before breakfast took up the rest of my time at this lovely space outside the realms of regular time, and soon I was back in the van with my driver and Vinny headed for Jaipur.

If the American wild west had been painted pink, well, that's what Jaipur looked like. Perhaps not the entire city, but all that I saw of it and certainly the area where Vinny insisted we must stop because of the fabrics. Standing on the veranda in front of his very pink shop was a large, smiling man, heavily mustached, barefoot, pant legs and shirt sleeves rolled up and arms akimbo. "Welcome to my shop! We have a dazzling array of fabrics and can make any item of apparel for you imaginable... enter, let me show you all we have," bellowed the shop keeper effusively, as he opened up his arms and held the swinging doors open for us. His pride and excitement were palpable. How could we refuse? His good energy was contagious. The interior was orderly and so much cooler than the streets of continuous heat and blowing dust. He moved around the shop unrolling one bolt of fabric after another as he explained what kind of garments might be made from each and extracting from me any thoughts about what I might want sewn for myself as well as anyone else I could think of. I suddenly found myself wrapped in a sari, but declined having one made. I made a feeble attempt to explain I probably wouldn't have any place to wear one, but I could see he was having trouble visualizing how I could go out in public or attend any celebration without a sari. Finally I explained, "Just a little something for me, a blouse and matching pants, the rest of my shopping will be for family and perhaps some fabrics to take home." This was acceptable. They measured me, but as for my daughter, son, son in law and a couple of close friends "about so tall about this fat or thin" were good enough and amazingly those garments fit each person quite well. "Give us one day to make up these garments. They will be ready for you the day after tomorrow" was his promise. We left, headed to another part of town for souvenir shopping and a bit of time to be immersed in the city scene. Oh, and as we rounded a corner of a bustling street we encountered two men cross-legged on the sidewalk with a cobra snake. The opportunity I thought I'd missed was here waiting for me in India. At least that's what I thought in the moment. I explained to Vinny how I wanted a photo of the snake around my neck. He thought I was kidding and then realized I wasn't. He couldn't talk me out of it. He approached the two men who paled visibly at my request, even turning down my willingness to pay for their assistance. Finally all realized I wasn't going anywhere without my cobra photo so they motioned me to come over and sit by them. They were clearly apprehensive and the snake was even more upset about the situation. It took both men to hold the snake firmly enough for the photo. The snake, clearly, was all about curling its tail around my leg and biting me anywhere possible. It was only later, looking at the photo, I truly realized the difference between an old defanged snake and a wild one barely trained to uncurl from its basket at the sound of a flute. I'm glad I got the photo, but it was sobering to realize having a strong intention isn't always in my best interests. There is more than a subtle difference between determination to accomplish and blind stubbornness.

The following morning we headed out of Jaipur for the day, heading toward the Amber Fort with its exquisite buildings, a spice market and elephant rides. The road there was an array of anything goes. We were among vans, cars, camels, bicycles and cows. Still, the only rule of the road appeared to be that the cows always had the right of way.

We started with the elephant rides. I know there is controversy about how this affects the elephants. At that time and place the elephants seemed to be treated affectionately, the one I rode was not chained up and didn't appear to be upset with me perched on a small wooden platform on his back. The rolling motion of my seating took a few minutes to get used to. We wandered slowly up a slight hill, paused to take in the view and came back. The getting on and off took me longer than the actual ride, but it was a unique experience and part of the itinerary planned for the day. When I heard we were visiting a fort, I visualized something formidable and austere. But just inside the walls was the amazing Maharajah's palace. The palace was designed to maximize any opportunity for a breeze to pass through. The intricacy and precision were impressive. Scalloped marble archways, too numerous in every direction to count, caught the air efficiently; moving it again and again to the outside even in the heat of the afternoon.

We moved to higher terrain and an outdoor spice market of spectacular size and color. Even in this somewhat remote location, mixed in with the open piles of spices was a section containing small bags of American potato chips. A turban wrapped smiling man was in charge of this massive setting of spice and clearly proud of the array. I asked, through

Vinny, if I could take his picture. He said he had no photos of himself. This would be the first time he had his picture taken. I promised to send him a copy and then we had to determine where I could send the picture since he had no address designated for mail. Shortly after I returned home I had the pictures developed and sent an enlargement to the address given to me. I hope he received it and has enjoyed it.

Our last stop, before returning to Delhi took us back to Jaipur to pick up the clothing and fabrics I had purchased. These goods were all ready and as I examined each one, the quality of workmanship was impressive and I was so pleased, already imaging how much they would be enjoyed. As I looked at the pile of material, it suddenly hit me there would be no room in my suitcase for it. A frown must have passed over my face.

"Is there a problem? Do you wish you had ordered more? We can accommodate that," came the concerned and opportunistic voice of the owner.

I told him, "I'm just realizing I have no room for any of this in my suitcase."

He laughed and replied, "This is no problem. We will make you a fabric bag with a drawstring for your purchases. We can make it to match the outfit you purchased. No charge, of course. They will make it while we chat."

And so they did, and it was sturdy enough to survive the baggage hold through two flights home.

That afternoon, as I returned from Jaipur, my aching body demanded a stop at the hotel spa for the bubbling jets of the hot tub. When I stepped in, the water was quite cool. I was concerned. I went to the attendant and mentioned how cool the water was. "Yes, it truly is," she responded with a smile and obvious pride. I looked back at the other women in the spa and they seemed to be fine with the cool water. It took me a minute to realize that, of course, they would want cool water when outside of the hotel the weather was extremely hot and humid. I stepped back in and appreciated a whole different way to enjoy a spa experience. In the spa I spoke to a young Indian woman. She asked about why I was I India and I shared my love of travel and enjoyment of her country. She seemed very surprised that I would travel at all, let alone by myself. She said somewhat wistfully, "It sounds so interesting. My husband travels on business." "Maybe you could go on a trip with him some time," I suggested. She looked at me as though I'd said something completely irrational and just shook her head. I sometimes forget that the freedom I have is not that common in so much of the world.

I had reserved my last day in India as an open day back at my first hotel in Delhi and was glad I did. I needed a day to just relax, absorb the past week, and prepare for the journey home. I started the day at the hotel pool quite early in the morning. The afternoon was left for a nap and packing as my flight would be leaving in the middle of the night. I would find that small financial "appreciations" could mean the difference between waiting in endless lines just to get into the airport versus a side door to the terminal. But that was for later. I still had the morning to hang out at the pool. I think only in India could 7am find me at a lovely pool, with lush jungle plants attempting to intrude on the pristine poolside area. To my right and above me, large numbers of jumbo pink and green parakeets conversed and flew between the trees. Half an hour passed pleasantly this way. Then a man, his wife and small child came out to enjoy the pool. I had noticed a few large monkeys hanging in the trees as though assessing the pool area. I kept my eye on them. When the man started moving the lounging chairs around for his family, the monkey chatter increased. When he walked close to the back area of the pool a sudden territorial dispute began. Several monkeys jumped down to the pool area and made aggressive moves toward the man. His wife and child quickly ran back to the hotel pool entrance. The man clearly felt a need to defend his family's right to use the pool area and was not going to back down. He moved toward them waving his arms as though ready to push or shoo these pesky monkeys away. They ran toward him and he grabbed a chair for defense. The monkeys were fearless and clearly were claiming the back area of the pool as their own. The scene ended with the man on the run back to his family. Apparently I was in safe territory, but it was no longer a restful oasis for me. On entering the hotel, I let the hotel manager know the monkeys were taking over the pool area. He just shook his head. Clearly the ownership of much that is India is in constant flux, the native plants and animals versus the human beings.

Once again, in the middle of the night we drove to the airport. My driver asked for extra money and next thing I knew, we had bypassed the long lines in front of the airport and slipped in a side door close to my check-in point. The trip accomplished its goal and additionally sent me a strong message that desires to have travel experiences as I wanted them were not going to fit well with my body's needs.

Girls in Saris, India

Deer, India

Brazil

(Brasil as it is written by those who live there)

When I first determined to embark on a major trip each year, Brazil came immediately to mind. But, at that time, it seemed there was a great deal of civil unrest, too intimidating for me on my first big trip. Now, a decade later, it seemed the perfect place to have a grand trip just prior to major surgery. My back had become a bigger issue and the surgical approach promised the greatest chance for complete recovery.

I had enough frequent flyer miles accumulated for a round trip ticket to Sao Paolo. Ten days of vacation were available and I needed to narrow down the vast array of things to do in Brazil. I also needed to decide whether to travel in the wet season, dry season or at the shoulder (in between seasons). I decide to travel on the shoulder and use Sao Paolo as an exit and entry point. I would focus on Rio de Janeiro, the Amazon River and jungle area, and Iguassu Falls. In Rio, I knew I wanted to stay at the Copacabana Beach and certainly travel to the top of Sugar Loaf Mountain. After a little research, I decided to stay in a tree top eco resort on the Black River, reported to have a cleaner, easier approach in the jungle. I would visit the majestic Iguassu Falls that divide Brazil from Argentina via Iguassu National Park on the Brazil side of the falls. I needed to arrange intra country flights and passage via air and small boat to the jungle, on to the Falls via air, and finally back to Sao Paolo. It seemed to me there were lots of components to be set up in a country where I didn't know the language and had physical limitations, so I called the company that had gotten me set up in India the prior year. I didn't want a guide and driver, but I wanted to tell them my desired itinerary and that I might need assistance on anything physically rugged. They were happy to do that and also sent me lists of what I would need for the trip in terms of visas, shots, clothing and weather. The internet today makes it much easier to scope out these things but in 2004 this approach was the easiest way for me.

Mid-April found me waiting, what seemed like endlessly, for a connecting flight from Washington DC to Sao Paolo. Of course the plane finally arrived and I was headed to Brazil sitting next to a woman who spoke Portuguese (the language of Brazil), Spanish and a little English. We managed to communicate pretty well and I got my first opportunity to use a word she taught me in Portuguese on that flight. A man helped get my suitcase back in the overhead bin and I thanked him in Portuguese. He understood me and grinned when he found out I was trying my Portuguese for the first time.

The skies were dark when we left. Every time I lifted the window shade to check, it was still dark until finally there were dark whale shaped clouds, eventually turning to a gold and pink sunrise over the Amazon basin. I was mesmerized as mist came and went over multi shades of green and dark areas of water, fields and then farms followed by mountains, the city and suddenly we were landing.

All I saw of Sao Paolo came from the window in the plane since I immediately transferred to a plane bound for Rio. Again a man with a sign met me at the airport to whisk me away to my hotel. Unfortunately, he was not familiar with the hotels along the beaches and it took a while for him to locate my hotel. He started with the swankier hotel and eventually found mine (there were many similar hotel names), smaller but clean and directly across the street from Copacabana Beach. Dinner at sunset at a small restaurant close to my hotel provided fresh fish and a view of the ocean, close enough to hear the waves rush onto the beach. I thought, "Life is good today." On Sundays the street separating my hotel from the beach is closed to motorized vehicles so families and all who wish can simply enjoy the beach and area in general. My first full day in Rio was a Sunday. The plus side was a picture postcard experience of sunbathing, people watching and splashing in the waters of this famous beach. The minus was realizing, as I got closer to the beautiful blue waters, the amount of pollutants actually in it. Still, everyone else just took it as it was, enjoying the beach and so did I. The next day I wandered back into an area of shops and bought some souvenirs in the morning and wandered on the beach until late afternoon. I had signed up to attend a dinner and folklore theater performance in the evening so I slipped in a late afternoon nap too.

I knew the folklore performance was set up specifically for tourists but that's what I was and knew I'd enjoy the music and hopefully the food. A small bus picked me up at my hotel and our bus full of assorted tourists started off at a Brazilian Meat Restaurant. There was a small token salad bar but the star was meat. Waiters kept coming by with different types of meat, slicing off as much as you wanted… delicious but overwhelming. Then we were bused to a very large music hall and seated at the main floor level close to the stage. The place was packed, including the balcony. The master of ceremonies welcomed us and told us the historical story of the musical we were about to see. But first, he wanted all of us to be a part of the welcoming and feeling welcomed process. "I'm going to call out the name of each country and when your country is announced, please stand up and let us applaud you," he bellowed with delight.

He called out the names of an amazing amount of countries and anywhere from five to fifty people stood up each time to vigorous rounds of applause. Finally he announced "The United States," and I stood up. Just me. No one applauded. The people from my bus group all quietly moved their chairs away from me. Then I sat down. I'd been traveling long enough by then to know that Americans are not always popular overseas and even less so when tensions are high between the governments. But in the comfortable comradery of the moment, it never crossed my mind to consider my citizenship a liability. Fortunately, the light went down and the show started. I determined to enjoy the show and hoped they'd still let me on the bus back to the hotel at the end of the evening. The show was lively and enjoyable and I did ride the bus back to my hotel although it was a conversationless ride for me.

A new day, a new experience is the best way to enjoy travelling while, I figured, remembering to keep a lower profile. I was up for a great day of city sightseeing and a trip to the top of Sugar Loaf Mountain. We started in the city through lush parks, the municipal theater, past the hillsides of hodgepodge housing, almost a city within the city with warnings to not visit there at night and probably not at all. Architectural features of Brazilian National Heritage, some history of the commercial areas and a tour of the bay by Sugar Loaf had us leaving the bus and preparing for the two phase trip to the top of Sugar Loaf Mountain.

Sugar Loaf Mountain, so named because it resembled the traditionally packed form sugar came in, is the best place in Rio to view the city and beyond. It has also become a well-known site for rock climbers. Cable cars took us to the first level where, part way up the mountain, we could eat at the restaurant and enjoy secluded views of the yacht club and Botafogo Bay. It was an opportunity, as well to escape from the steamy and humid cable cars. Once reaching the top, the sun, wind, views and great people watching created an exhilarating afternoon.

A quiet evening of packing and fresh fish dinner sunset viewing ended with a sense of excitement for the upcoming jungle adventure. I dimly remember wondering if jungle rigors might be more than I was bargaining for as I drifted off to sleep. Barely into my dream cycle, my morning alarm clock rang.

Reaching Ariau Amazon Towers felt like a whole separate trip. First, a flight across and northward through Brazil to Manaus. I had never heard of Manaus before, but it is the capital of the State of Amazonas and began its current history as a fort in 1669. It is accessible only by boat or air and is a main point of entry to the Brazilian Amazon. I didn't have time to explore the city but it is surprisingly diverse with not only the surrounding jungle, but also an opera house, cathedral, botanical gardens and a museum dedicated to the native population. I was met at the airport by a representative of the eco resort and boarded a motor boat with several other tourists for a two and one half hours, sometimes choppy ride literally moving through ever darkening waters from city to dense jungle. The Black River, 1,398 miles long, I learned, is the largest tributary of the Amazon and largest black water river in the world. We were all exchanging looks of "where in the world are we and will we ever get to that resort?" when the motor died down and we sidled up to a rustic wooden dock. We had been sitting in the small boat for two and one half hour so when outstretched hands reached down to help us out of the boat we all gratefully took their help. We were in the jungle.

I had picked this resort after reading it had originally been inspired by Jacques Cousteau after Dr. Francisco Ritta Bernardino met him. Dr. Bernardino's dream was to build a resort up in the tree tops which would provide visitors with a respectful and ecological learning experience in and with the jungle. In 1987 it was one of the first to be built in that area. The travel notes provided to me talked about blending into the forest canopy and they weren't kidding. The main dining and meeting hall were on the flat cleared area by the dock as was the sports bar. But the cabins, in varying degrees from Spartan to ultra-luxurious, were reached by bridges that completely blended in with their surroundings. My cabin, at first glance, seemed to be merely an intricately carved tree but then expanded into a simple but pleasantly functional air- conditioned room with bath.

We arrived just in time to find our temporary homes, freshen up and return to the dock area for dinner in the large hall. For each meal we climbed a flight of stairs and shared long tables. At that first dinner we marveled at how quickly it was getting dark and realized the agenda sent to us prior to the trip, was only a possible list of what and when. We thought we would have an early evening to catch up from traveling but we were just getting started… dinner was followed by a night ride down the river to attend a native Indian ceremony which was followed by an admonition "5 a.m. wakeup call (we had phones in our rooms, I suppose mostly for safety). We'll be going out in canoes before breakfast to watch the sunrise." It was a long day but the exhaustion was wiped away in that night time ride as the stars and their constellations bloomed clearly in the sky and the only sounds were occasional monkeys and soft unknown sounds.

I have an enlarged photo hanging over my fireplace of the shot I took as the sun came up that next morning. Our patient waiting in the dark eventually became exciting as the jungle woke up, birds first, then monkeys and who knows what as the sky slowly turned from darkness to dark grey, grey blue and eventually slashes of dusky orangey pink, yellow emerging and brightening as the daylight blue took over. It was like waiting for the big show to begin in a darkened theater. Suddenly there's the performance, and after, just like an audience, I felt like applauding. But I was happy to settle for breakfast.

I don't remember at which morning breakfast this occurred, but I will likely not forget the morning we were gathered, peacefully munching on goodies from the buffet when an extremely loud crashing sound filled the air. It was coming from the dock and we all ran over to that side of the dining hall and looked down to see a giant pale yellow Anaconda breaking through the dock. The workers grabbed machetes trying to avoid the snake, but either beat it or chop off its head to stop the carnage. It was unbelievable! They beheaded the beast and it slithered back down into the giant hole it had created. It was so bizarre, there was only one thing to do. We looked at each other wordlessly for a moment, and went back to the table to finish breakfast. No one spoke until later that day.

This jungle adventure was fulfilling on so many levels. The artwork on and in the cabins was both a tribute to our surroundings and skill of artists who created the beautiful, rustic wooden carvings and paintings on doors and panels. The wooden catwalks sometimes led us to large covered areas where we could stand or sit and enjoy the sounds of leaves rustling, creatures of all types, especially amazing birds and the ever present monkeys. Jungles can't stay green without enough rain, so there were sudden and dense showers randomly each day. The rain beating down on the thatched roofs of these refuges provided an extra dimension of interest and often, a chance to dry out. Panels of wood in these structures were carved and painted featuring large tropical birds, plants and fishes. Hammocks were strung everywhere and it was the nicest novelty to wander through treetops and randomly throw myself into a hammock to swing or just contemplate the good fortune to be there. Other catwalks took us to our clusters of housing. My cluster included five doors to five rooms or cabins, each with an elaborately painted door, which made it easy to remember which door was mine. My door had a yellow and red parrot almost hidden by large green jungle leaves on it. Inside, the simple room was made stately and seemed better furnished by use of more painted carvings of flora and fauna. Monkeys, iguanas and wild parrots were prevalent. One of the staff had a bright red trained parrot that didn't say much but was very attached to her and regularly murmured her name lovingly and a little more sternly when she wasn't paying enough attention to him. Get too close to her or the parrot and you risked getting a nasty bite from the protective bird.

Once out of the canopy of catwalks, the dock and its surrounding buildings held the means for more adventure. The dock was repaired quickly and anyone who was not present the morning of the anaconda incident would never have known about its appearance. On our last full day, we were told to prepare for a lengthy canoe ride and hike through the jungle. I was concerned it would be too much for me and told those in charge I regrettably would have to stay behind. They would have none of that and set up a shorter hike that would meet up with the main group towards the end of the activity. We all started off in canoes and commentary as we moved through more deeply into the jungle. On the river banks, our guide informed us, "The natives first, and truly anyone who now lives on the river, will build their houses on stilts both for ventilation and to accommodate the river rising in the wet season. Their children travel in canoes on the river to attend school. And now we will drop Carol off with Antonio," he finished, turning to me. The boat stopped and a surprised Antonio got off the boat and offered his hand as I stepped out too. A few words I couldn't understand were exchanged between our guide and Antonio followed by the canoe disappearing around a bend in the river. I was truly appreciative, but I felt bewildered and sorry for the boatman assigned to take me slowly through easy paths in the jungle. This was particularly so because he spoke only Portuguese. But his ingenuity and willingness to show me his jungle and what it meant to his people made this a very special part of this trip. The language barrier turned out to be no problem because Antonio showed me all sorts of jungle plants and showed me how they were used. In some cases he demonstrated their use and I then copied him to show I understood and wanted to learn about the jungle. For example, giant plant pods had multiple uses: dishes, trays and turned upside down as rain hats. We wore our rain hats for a while and then tried our hand at painting, decorating ourselves with yellow "lac" we dug out from under tree bark. We used chalk from the underside of chalk plants to write and create designs on large leaves. We found slender brown leaves with a texture almost like plastic or fiberglass that was used to weave water proof items. Another tree had a rose water scent which we dug out with our fingernails releasing more of its pleasing aroma. Antonio cut down nuts directly from a Brazil nut tree and we ate them. I noted they had a crispier and better taste than those I would find in a hometown store. I let him know with gestures and a smile how delicious they tasted and was rewarded with a proud smile. We eventually met up with the rest of the group wearing our rain hats, yellow makeup, smelling quite nice and carrying our decorated leaves. As I explained all we had done I could see on their faces that I had gotten the best hike of all.

I heard there were approximately one hundred visitors at the resort at the same time I was there, and we were grouped by the main languages we spoke to better customize and explain the experience being provided to us. This semi seclusion worked quite well as I never had the sense of being just one more person in a sea of tourists hungry for a jungle experience. Our group shared all our activities and meals and a real sense of comradery developed rapidly. It was easy, especially over meals, to discuss not only the day's events, but where we were from, why we were in the jungle and, between the lines, lots of who each of us were at our core. I remember an afternoon when we went out on the river to catch piranhas. We were warned to be careful as we reeled them on board. They were feisty little fish with disproportionally large jaws, lots of very pointy teeth and a clear desire to bite whatever dared enter their range of reach. We shared lots of nervous laughter and delight as we took turns catching the constantly darting fishes. That night we were informed one of the entrees in our dinner buffet featured the piranhas we had caught that afternoon. I now know piranha lasagna is delicious.

Each of us received a certificate with our name on it and reviewing all the activities and ecological information we had experienced. It proclaimed us environmental protectors. Certainly, we had all been changed by the beauty, diversity, strengths and fragilities of the Amazon basin and had a greater awareness of its value.

By the time we were returning to civilization, eight of us were planning to be on the same boat back up the river to Manaus and hang out at the airport until our flights were ready to leave. Our little group was also planning to take a brief excursion to see the meeting of the waters, a local phenomenon creating a confluence of the Black River joining the Amazon River. I learned the confluence would be the dark Black River joining its parent river, the pale sandy colored Amazon, meeting but not merging, running side by side for over three miles. When we first arrived at the resort, we had all been informed about possible add-ons to our scheduled plans and the meeting of the waters, on an individual basis, was a bit expensive. Our group had figured it would be an advantage financially and more fun if we all did it together. In fact, they even offered to pay my share so I could share in the unique experience when I hesitated. I was touched by their thoughtfulness but my hesitation was not financial but a result of being smug and thinking I didn't need to buy the bottled drinking water most everyone else was buying, and that I could drink water the locals were drinking. It caught up with me that last day and my real concern was a very queasy stomach and desire to stay as close to a bathroom as possible. I explained, and even though they thought I should give it a try, I was physically done with that part of my vacation. I saw them later at the airport. They shared all about the excursion. Hugs and well wishes followed as we, one by one, headed for our gates. Most were headed home. I was bound for Iguassu Falls.

After a short flight, I arrived at a small airport in the early evening and was transported to the only hotel allowed directly on the Brazil side and inside of Iguassu National Park. I was told to stay in my room until daylight. Since the hotel was in the national park, native animals, which included jaguar and pumas, would be roaming the property in the dark. My room seemed to have been an afterthought in preparation for a guest. Large cobwebs and flying bugs, some large, were sharing the space with me. I wasn't too happy about the situation, but it was only one night and I was tired enough to sleep regardless. Early morning, with only a few bug bites to show for the unwelcome company, I was up and ready for breakfast and a chance to explore the property before heading down to the falls. The somewhat spooky menacing area of the night had transformed in the sunlight to a lovely patio where a sumptuous breakfast was served. The grounds directly around the hotel had lush green lawns and beds of enjoyable tropical flowers, including wild orchids. The jungle clearly would have liked to overrun this space, but a diligent group of gardeners weren't allowing that. I was told the hotel had originally been a mission and was redesigned as a hotel in hacienda style. It was well-maintained enough to note my room experience was not a common occurrence. On the land between the manicured lawn, parking area and jungle I spotted several animals I had never seen before. They looked like a cross between raccoons and anteaters, certainly the raccoon tail, neutral body and anteater face. They were small and strangely cute and were absorbed in eating caramel corn from a bag someone had dropped. The desk clerk at the hotel told me this was their favorite food and while it made for fun viewing it was also distressing to see how people were probably putting these interesting animals' health at risk.

I wasn't sure I really needed the guide I'd hired to assist me to the falls but I was glad I'd set it up pre-travel. I didn't know how arduous a trek it would be and after the Amazon, knew it would be better to find out I didn't need the help than to struggle and miss this great opportunity. Late morning, my guide came and we started down a path toward the distant sound, more a whisper, of water. The dirt path was clearly meant for easy access and I might have handled it on my own. But then I wouldn't have gotten all the good tips on how to best enjoy the waterfall and interesting information. As we moved toward the increasing sound of roaring water, the whole sense of it filled the air. Was it also raining or was the wind just blowing the might of the spectacular falls in my direction? In a clearing through the trees I caught my first look at the massive scape, one of the widest falls in the world with a water drop of 269 feet. My guide noted the park around it held many rare or endangered species of plants and animals and that yes, it was raining but that didn't matter since to truly experience the falls I would want to be a part of them. We headed to an area that would accomplish this. I purchased a clear hooded plastic poncho and after putting it on, headed out onto a long wooden walkway over the water. The further I walked, the more the falls could be viewed and soon conversation was difficult. The sheer width and variety of Iguassu Falls was incredible and the roar was engulfing. By the time I reached the end of the walkway, I was completely surrounded by the sound, mist and waters of the falls and it was the most exhilarating and uplifting experience. I felt truly one with the waters. I don't think I will ever forget it and it might have been the best part of my Brazil trip. Certainly, trying to get past the screeners and customs at the Sao Paolo airport to get home was not.

As I started through customs and the baggage check, security came over and escorted me and my luggage to a separate room, some distance from the actual screening area. They looked at my passport and tickets several times asking me repeatedly where I had been in Brazil, my activities, my purchases and reviewed all my receipts. At some point there were people from the airline, and officials from both Brazil and the U.S. I think. I was alarmed, but mostly angry.

"I'm going to miss my flight and that means I'll miss my connecting flights too! Why are you going through my bags again? You better not break my souvenirs!" were all I could sputter at them.

"You won't miss your plane," they calmly responded and repeated the whole process again. Finally they said they were done. They said they would take me to my flight.

"My flight's due to leave in ten minutes and how will I get my luggage on the plane in time?" was my final retort.

They assured me they would take care of the luggage and I would be seated in time. We wound our way through tunnels and suddenly were beside my plane. I got on board, quite relieved, and my bags were on the carousel at the claims area when I got to my hometown airport. I couldn't make any sense of the whole situation until I realized the airport officials were probably wondering why a single woman from the United States would be traveling by herself to three separate regions in Brazil. There were probably drug rings operating in the area and I had read women were often used to move drugs in and out of countries. This made me grateful for a trip taken simply for the joy of being a part of these amazing places. Arriving home, I reflected and was grateful for all the amazing trips I had taken, hoping that my future would allow for more.

Iguassu Falls

Cruising Adventures

Recovering, whatever from, is never a quick deal as far as I know. My recovery from surgery took a lot of patience, physical therapy and time, but eventually I was back to work full time and getting the travel desire again. I needed a way to test my ability to navigate new places and how to handle aspects I had not questioned before. So travel-yes, but like before-no. Because I had been on a few cruises in the past, I considered how that might be the best way for me to still participate, taking baby steps to enjoy the amazing world we live in.

On a cruise, I would only have to unpack and pack once no matter how many places we visited. If I was too tired to take an excursion or they all seemed too difficult for me, there would be plenty of activities I could do on board ship, plus my room would always be with me on the ship if I needed to rest. Meals would be available on the ship at all hours, no cabs or steep hills to get something to eat. There would be a doctor on board. I also came to realize lots of groups of people plan cruises together and I was able to connect with one so I would actually have a few people I knew to go on excursions with and share meals. The only downsides I could come up with for travel reentry on a cruise was how much walking one really would be doing on a large cruise ship and, of course, the fear of not knowing if I could pull it off. I was going to try.

In 2008, a cruise meeting the criteria had me boarding a ship in Miami bound for lands in the Caribbean. We set sail in November, which seemed appropriate since the Thanksgiving theme of gratitude was very much what I was thinking of as Florida disappeared, replaced by sky and sea.

The few people I knew expanded to a pleasant group and the bonus was sharing the days' adventures with new friends. This cruise was just right for me, and for those in our group who could, scuba diving was a featured activity. I never felt shortchanged in adventures. I have a photo of a pirate and I walking a beach as I learned the history of that area. There is warm crunchy sand between my toes, and I am on a swing at a thatched roof café. This was my first time to swim with dolphins, although I couldn't exactly swim. But the dolphin swam around me and gave me a big kiss on my cheek. I took a ride in a small submarine with all glass walls and it felt as close to scuba diving as I could imagine. After having been through an extended period of time when healing took up all my energy and eating was too exhausting, my appetite had certainly returned. It was delightful to just show up with my friends and find a wealth of delicious options available at every meal on board ship as well as a new variety of entertainment every night. There was one day when the island we were scheduled to visit could not accommodate our ship directly into port so small boats were available to take us to the island. After checking with staff, it seemed the sea was choppy and the ride to the island would be pleasantly rolling for some but beyond my comfort ability. Rather than bemoan my loss of an excursion, I was able to focus on the shipboard spa, steam room and other amenities, usually booked up, but very available that day. Enjoy what you can.

In planning this first post-surgery cruise, I also planned a two day stay in Miami after the cruise; either to recuperate for a long flight home or to further celebrate the ability to vacation again. Those days turned out to be both. After the cruise I took a cab to a wonderful art deco hotel one block from the ocean. Every detail of the hotel and my room vibed old school art deco and beach. I was pretty thrilled. Sand and sea, tours of the other quirky hotels on the beach strip and a jaunt on foot and by bus to the art district were soul satisfying. I booked a tour of Little Havana for my second day which also took us through waterways and peeks at homes of the rich and famous. My first day in Miami started with breakfast at the hotel patio. I was relishing this since home in November would not provide such an outdoor opportunity. I followed directions, crossing the street, down a boardwalk and onto a sandy pathway lined with palm trees hearing and feeling the roar and close-up presence of the beach and ocean. That afternoon I took a bus to a close by section of Miami with coffee shops, book stores, art galleries, and artists in residence studios. The art was as fulfilling as any good meal and I actually bought a sugar bowl in a posh shop of functional art by a South American artist. It was all I could afford but still provides sugar to my guests and me every day. The bus had been easy to catch on my way there and I had assumed would be just as easy going back to the hotel. Yet I never saw a bus as I started walking back to my hotel. I was glad to have a second day to take a relaxing tour and just hang out at the pool and cabanas on the roof of the hotel.

I had not stayed at a hotel with a roof top pool before and it was quite spectacular to cool off in the pool and look past the roof at the ocean and view. There were cabanas, lounges to bask in the sun and of course a bar. While enjoying it all, my phone rang and it was my work place, apologizing for calling me while on vacation but a quick question please. I was smiling broadly as I replied, "No, you haven't really interrupted anything. Just hanging out at the roof top pool, cooling off from the sun and heat." There was a long pause at the other end. I knew it was rainy and cool back home. "Well, see you soon," came through the phone at me. And they were right. The next day I was on a plane headed home. There were lots of wonderful moments and activities on this trip but the best was learning I could still travel.

The Mediterranean Sea

2009

*T*he next cruise was more ambitious. The same group had booked space on a new ship's inaugural sail in the Mediterranean Sea. The cruise would start and end in Rome, Italy. Along the way would be a sampler of Italy, Croatia, Barcelona, Spain, Monaco, and France. This would be a great way to see many new places and determine which I would want to return to. Another great plus for me was the addition of single cabins, which meant no roommates or high single supplement charges. We'd be traveling in September, ideal, after the family rush of summer but before the unpredictable cold and rainy weather.

My cozy and snug cabin was tantalizing. I was the first person to sleep in the bed, use the shower, and write at the desk. The other side of being the first travelers on a ship was the reality of being on a first time out. How well does the kitchen function, do the door locks work, is the paint dry?

But first, we had to get to the ship. We spent our first night off the plane in a hotel in Rome. The streets in Rome have a most unique layout and methods of remembering how to return to the hotel after a brief walk, that usually work, were not usable here. A friend of mine from the cruise and I started out on that walk and realized early on we were almost already hopelessly lost and made our goal a return to the hotel right away. It's important not to lose track of the actual goal of the trip, which for us was a good night's sleep to prepare for a lengthy motor coach ride to the coast where the ship was actually moored. I later wished I had remembered that actual goal in Croatia.

The ride to Civitavecchia passed quickly and soon we were in that city and seaport, still considered part of metropolitan Rome.

Every morning we received the ship's daily guide to fun, detailing all that was available on the ship and information about that day's excursions. This first partial day on board, the guide was waiting for us and it was dizzying in its array of possible recreation, entertainment, places and times to eat as well as upcoming excursions to prepare for. Our group shared dinner together and planned for Naples.

We arrived in Naples, Italy at 7 a.m.. I felt safest going with an organized group and was glad I had done so. This third largest municipality in Italy was entrancing, with the history of Mt Vesuvius, tour of the royal palace, museums and just amazing architecture. After returning to the ship and a nap, I was ready for people watching on board, dinner, and a musical revue. No problem staying up late, since the next day was spent at sea. This meant lots of time for a leisurely breakfast, time poolside, hanging out with friends and opportunity to take my turn at silly games and trivia contests. Next up was Dubrovnik, Croatia.

Dubrovnik, in southern Croatia, is one of the most prominent tourist destinations in the Mediterranean Sea. Its most famous feature is the wall enclosing it and built in medieval times. I heard rapturous reports from some of our group who had actually walked a portion of the wall, seen amazing buildings and experienced great souvenir shopping. I had planned to be one of those people having that experience, but that's not what happened.

But before the stop in Dubrovnik, our bus joined many other tour buses going way up into the hills of Croatia to visit a captivating lakeside town. I made a mental note of where the buses dropped us off and when to be back to continue the tour. I wandered around the lake of crystal waters and lush plants. The weather was so sunny and warm with light breezes. Adjacent to the lake were shops and an outdoor market with all sorts of interesting handmade items and, of course, ices and ice creams to enjoy at the public square. Although not many natives seemed to speak English, it was a very relaxing and rewarding experience. I glanced at my watch a few times and marveled how much time I seemed to have. Eventually, I wandered back to where the buses were parked. I was startled to see no buses. I walked around a bit, thinking I was on the wrong road, but there were no buses. I looked at my watch again. Half past the hour, just like I'd been told... except the hour was an hour past when we were due to leave. (I've since bought a watch with larger numerals on its face). Wow... what to do now. First of all, don't panic, even though the ship is leaving in a few hours. Stranded in Croatia. I could do worse. But the goal was to continue my cruise. Turning around, I saw a travel agency across the street. It seemed likely someone who worked in a travel agency might speak English so I went in.

The woman behind the counter spoke English and understood my plight as I explained how I had enjoyed her lovely community too much. I was embarrassed. Considering myself an experienced traveler, I was appalled at having just lost track of the time. She was gracious and after getting the name of my cruise ship, called them. She hung up and explained to me "The ship is sending a driver for you. It will take about forty five minutes for him to get here. You can wait here in the agency if you like." I translated that in my head to "one more idiot tourist forgot to get on the bus. You have to go all the way to that lakeside town to get her." So be it. In today's drama I was playing the idiot tourist. I would live through that and wound up having the most interesting conversation with the woman at the agency. It was a rare opportunity to talk to a native, just one on one about her growing up, the Serbian war with all its ugliness, the economy, family and life in general. Maybe a good tradeoff for missing Dubrovnik.

The driver came and the ride back to the ship was uneventful. The ship sailed in the early evening and we were on our way to Venice.

Having been to Venice fifteen years prior on that first trip I took to Europe on my own, it was easy to skip the "must do and see" items already done and focus on what I thought would bring me the most pleasure. We arrived midafternoon and spent the night in port leaving at 5 p.m. the next evening. That first afternoon was spent wandering the streets and waterways, plus a tour by boat with a bit of historic sightseeing. The next day, it was easy to pace myself through the islands of Murano and Burano. Fewer photos were taken and more time simply spent enjoying the demonstrations of art, and feel of each island. Burano is most noted for its tradition of handmade lace and colorful houses. The houses are bright yet somewhat muted shades of green, yellow, tan, pink, and purple. I heard owners wishing to paint their houses must apply through the local officials and select their colors from an approved list. There were demonstrations of various kinds of lace tatting and incredible styles of every kind of lacey item imaginable. It was fascinating to watch how evenly and rapidly their fingers flew with the threads, not something I could fathom ever being able to do. I bought a lace trimmed dress for my granddaughter and some lace handkerchiefs. Murano was next. The island is actually a series of little islands connected by bridges. Again, I spent most of my time watching and enjoying a masterful demonstration of glass blowing and the deft shaping of vases, animals and bowls.

After another day at sea we landed in Sicily. We started in the curved harbor of Messina, viewing the Duomo and adjoining piazza… which is the most prominent cathedral and plaza. The main event was an eerie drive up the rugged hills to Mt. Etna, rising 10,912 feet into the air. We were left to wander through the even eerier landscape of a volcano that appeared on the verge of erupting. Yellow green gases and steam nearly blotted out the sun and lent a sulfurous odor to the air. It was like being on some foreign uninhabitable planet. The strange quiet had an effect on all of us. There were few conversations and those were more in whispers. I was grateful for the opportunity for this unique experience but relieved when we headed back to our buses and I know I wasn't the only one feeling that way. Looking back toward Mt. Etna I noticed the one incongruous feature was a wall that reminded me of a smaller version of the Great Wall of China but with the view of a volcano instead of Chinese landscape.

The next day at sea left me restless for sun, streets to explore and adventure. Barcelona was just the right place to be. I'd had the good fortune to spend some time there with a friend who lives there several years before, so I had no frantic rushing to see all the sights that this lovely city offers. The major walkway through part of the city is filled with sculpture, interesting art, shops and great international people watching which filled my afternoon. More sun and Mediterranean cities were up next and I was ready. Villages in the hills of France brought a whole new set of luxurious aromas, lush flowers and the Principality of Monaco, which is just a magic place. Via motor coach, we climbed the winding roads high into the French hills to Eze-a medieval community most easily identified by the swirling aromas of spices, perfume and jaw dropping views of the French Riviera as it sprawls along the Mediterranean Sea. From the bus we trudged up a cobblestone road that felt completely vertical and almost left me wondering if anything around the corner could be worth another step. But it was, as we came across a spice market like I hadn't seen since India. There was, of course, a whole different type of spices but just as alluring. Their textures and mental pictures of how I might use them was enjoyable and I purchased a few small samples presealed in little plastic envelopes. The fine spice encounter emboldened me to continue forward to a perfumery. I was told one of the most prestigious perfume brands in France was manufactured in Grasse, just an hour and one half by train from Eze. I had never been to a perfumery before, yet the clear quality of both individual and combinations was easy to note. I received help in finding a blend that not only appealed to my sense of what smells wonderful but additionally smells just as good on me. I used that small but affordable vial for special occasions for several years.

Next was a very full day in Monaco. We started with a bus tour of Nice, followed by a brief tour of Monte Carlo, which gave us a feel for what to tackle on our own. Most everything was walkable. My itinerary would be the palace and grounds, the adjacent open air market and of course the up the hill storybook gardens and casinos. The palace grounds were regal and it was easy to think about the Former American, Grace Kelly, and Prince Ranier living there. The open air market would have been a joy for dinner shopping and I was smitten by the variety of marzipan shaped animals and fruits. I have been making marzipan fruits from scratch for over forty years, first with my kids and our exchange student, then, most recently, my granddaughter.

I think a brief cab ride brought us close to the next part of Monaco we wanted to check out. We strolled up a hillside, and as we entered the gardens, the first thing I saw was an exquisite fountain. Then came their neighboring night clubs and casinos, which at first glance, made me feel like I was about to go on some exotic adventure. This came from probably having watched too many movies showing luxury, high rollers, winning and intrigue. In my reality, I had no fancy gown, big bankroll or secrets someone might die for. Reminding myself of this, I was able to chuckle, and walk into the front end of a casino designed for tourists like me. Afterwards, we were treated to the view of Monaco, rolling from the yacht filled harbors up through a landscape of beautiful homes and lush greenery. It was picture perfect. It was easy to see and feel why so many people are drawn to this area to visit and often with hopes to stay.

A little time on our ship brought us back to Italy and continuation of amazing geography as we approached Cinque Terre. I think the rough translation is five lands, which physically translates to five distinct villages, each tumbling down steep terraced hillsides to the sea. These villages, the whole coastline and adjacent hillsides are all considered part of the Cinque Terre National Park which is also a World Heritage Site. I wish my notes and pictures had been more detailed. I think it was just a time to thoroughly enjoy the moments and the unique experience. The result is a hodge-podge of what interested me the most with no regard for which village we were in. Usually my notes and photos remind me of the sights and sounds and I get to relive little flashes of my travels. This day was no exception. I know we didn't have time to see all five villages. We walked along coastal trails and some of the terraced hills, home to well-tended vineyards. There was minimal access to these areas by road or rail. The villages are also home to fishermen, and boats are the easiest way to gain access. Whether on a hill looking down to the sea or in a boat looking up at the villages and vineyards, I remember the views as breathtakingly beautiful. I remember one village in particular where flat land is at a premium, utilized and treasured. People parked their boats in front of their homes like we park our cars in my home town. I remember a lunch of the freshest possible seafood and leisurely strolling along the long slender warm beach. You will have to go there yourself if you feel the need to truly know more.

Our ship continued on as we headed back toward Rome on the last day of our cruise. We stopped along the way at a surprisingly beautiful cathedral with dramatically lit archways and a sense of deep peace about it. Palm trees beckoned toward its entrance and it was really a welcome point of calm after so many days of great energy and so many new experiences. I took a short tour on the way from Civitavecchia, where our ship docked. This was a bit of extra sightseeing on the way to the airport. It added a bit of history and views of The Coliseum and much of old Rome. As we started our approach to the airport, I looked back and hoped I would return one day.

Puerto Rico

2011

It was time for another Caribbean cruise, this time to islands I hadn't been to before including the luscious Puerto Rico. I was still cruising with some of the group from my first Caribbean cruise which turned out to be a great idea. In between we visited St. Thomas, Barbados, St. Lucia, St. Kitts, and St. Maarten. I was in a cabin with a balcony this time with a companionable roommate. As I watched the island slide into the background, a double rainbow appeared over the ocean, which was easy to take as a sign this trip was bound to be terrific! What initially stands out to me is the luxury of a bit of light breeze, shade on the serenity deck with its cushy seating, steamy whirling spas, perfect pools, and enough quiet to hear the ocean. Each island I visited was palm filled with enticing beaches and its own feel or sense of identity. They were all a delight to visit.

I'd had a small health issue flying on the last leg of my flight to Puerto Rico and so wasn't up to taking an excursion to St Thomas. I had to remember this was part of the bargain I'd made with myself in order to continue traveling. Enjoy what I can as my health allows, accept and make the best of the times I need to take it easy. That day, I didn't get my way and missed the island, but looking at the whole trip, it was phenomenal and one missed day didn't need to matter so much.

Barbados is in the Lesser Antilles of the West Indies. Well known for its rum, monkeys and sugar plantations, it has an eclectic mixture of British and West African influences. I took a tour where we saw all of these in the countryside, museums and garrisons.

We sailed on to St. Lucia. Wow, what a day we had, from the white sand beaches, glistening like sugar in the sun, through botanical gardens and finally a tropical rainforest. We saw the rain forest from eight person aerial trams that started from the heat of the lowlands up through forests and into the tree top canopy. Our guide emphasized the ecological concerns and efforts and was knowledgeable enough to answer all our questions. The tour felt expansive, relaxing and still exciting in the slowly changing scenery.

St. Kitts and the neighboring Island of Nevis are considered one country. On this island, we had lots of options to snorkel, and again, more beaches, lagoons and lush jungles to enjoy. It also offered an extinct volcano, Mt. Liamuiga, but too deeply entrenched in steep jungled area for us to attempt to hike.

A few of us wandered St Maarten on our own. It has the added dimension of being Dutch on one side of the island and French on the other. The Island has been divided like that since 1648 at a 60%/40% ratio but evenly divided in terms of population. The French side, known as St. Martin, is actually considered a part of France and so, a member of the European Union. The French side had a quieter feel with its historic area, galleries and shops, more reminiscent of a village in France with added beaches and boating. The Dutch side boasts the Boardwalk and Front St in Phillipsburg with their duty free shops, beaches, restaurants and a more relaxed party feel. One unique feature we found involved the small airport on the island. It was situated next to the beach so every time a plane took off it felt, to those of us at that end of the beach, as though the plane was going to run right over us. I guess the novelty wore off for those who spent more time there and, in fact, no plane actually hit anyone. We shared a relaxed and happy time just wandering the beach, the boardwalk, shops and restaurants until it was time to board our ship again and head back to San Juan.

Two nights and three days might not seem like much time, but I really got a great feel and appreciation of the island, its beauty and people. I started with a tour of San Juan's Old Town. This included the history and walk through of the old fort that guarded the bay, pastel houses and shops, the rum factory, and gracious colonial style buildings. My hotel was not in the Old Town but just one block from the beach. I spent that afternoon crossing the street and entering a lovely park. It was Sunday and whole families, dressed up in the best clothes, gathered and played. It felt like a trip back in time. Crossing through the park, a path led directly to a small beach. It wasn't as lengthy, not did it come with cabanas like the expensive hotels next to it, but it provided a place to lay down a towel and room to splash and swim in the tropical waters.

That evening I got together with some friends from the cruise for dinner. I had passed a bland gray building as I walked that afternoon. It had an advertisement posted announcing itself as a Latin Asian roof top lounge with terrace dining and jazz. We decided to give it a try. A rough looking fellow, doorman or bouncer-hard to tell, was posted at the entrance and nodded for us to go up. At the end of the first set of narrow stairs was a landing and another set of stairs. We were hungry and curious so up we went. We were well rewarded. On the upper deck, aromas of deliciousness greeted us as well as a lively crowd and most lyrical jazz. The view of the ocean was spectacular and the fresh seafood we ordered was too. We had a great evening and I found myself humming those tunes as I drifted off to sleep later. I was hoping the next day would be just as rewarding.

I was picked up at my hotel by an almost full van and we headed out for a day at El Yunque, the Caribbean National Forest of Puerto Rico. It is located twenty miles east of San Juan and I learned some of the native mythology as we drove. The indigenous Taino people called the largest mountain peak Yuke, meaning white lands because the mountain is generally wreathed in heavy white clouds. Their story of creation was handed down orally and one rendition stated the full name of the God, who dwells in this mountain as Yucahu Bagua Maorocoti. Yucahu, translates to giver or spirit of fertility, peace and goodness. Bagua is master of the sea and Maorocoti indicates immaculate conception from the mother, Atabey, who created the heavens.

The jungle, as it was when I visited in early 2011, was thick with nature trails and waterfalls throughout its twenty-eight acres. I saw so many beautiful and interesting birds and plants. But I didn't see even a small percent of the thirty five species of migratory birds; nor the two hundred forty species of native trees, vast varieties of orchids, fish or insects. It was easy to see how beloved and well taken care of all inhabitants of this bountiful place were by how well the trails were maintained, and how every so often benches and little covered stations appeared where one could sit and just slowly enjoy the environment, its sights, smells and sounds. I may have noticed more of these than many others because I was not focused on getting to the waterfalls and climbing them as some in our group were. For me, the jungle venture contained an incredible amount of stairs in the forest tower that, of course we would climb for the spectacular view. And it was spectacular. But then came steep pathways as we headed toward the waterfalls. I finally asked our guide if we would be coming back the same way after the waterfalls. "Yes, we'll be back this way. We're really close to the falls and will be back this way within the hour. Are you not coming to the falls? Are you okay with waiting here?" came the concerned response. I told him I wasn't able to walk any further and didn't mind, at all. It would be a pleasure to be at this covered station as a point of nature enjoyment. Relieved, he nodded and the group continued up the path. It was a relief to sit and just be. Little by little I relaxed, and as I did, it became easier to hear all the small sounds of leaves moving, to see and keep seeing more and more of how much was actually quietly happening right by where I was sitting. This was so pleasurable and reminded me of how much I usually miss in my busyness to get to wherever it is I am going.

Hurricanes have devastated the island and El Yunque since then. While nature always desires to restore itself, I'm afraid the flourishing home of flora and fauna may take more than the rest of my lifetime to regrow and heal completely.

Everyone had worked up a good appetite for lunch and after a short drive viewing more of the island, we pulled up to a family run grocery store and fast food stop with tables and chairs outside. It was clear our guide was friends with the couple owning the store and this was a good way for all of us to help with the local economy. I was stopped short by a stack of avocados. I do like them a lot but was totally intimidated by the size of them. The bulb part was as large as a small melon and each was at least ten inches long. They were a beautiful shade of bright green. I would have bought one but no one wanted to share one for lunch and there was no way I could eat it all nor would it keep fresh until I arrived back home. I took a photo instead.

Our driver guide was full of information about the countryside as we passed through and all things about Puerto Rico as well. He was a native citizen and passionate about his island. He was open to all our questions and had some of his own. This led to a spirited conversation on Puerto Rico politics, their territorial status, economics and more. It was one of those conversations between a small group of people that I wish we had recorded or that I would have at least taken notes on. This, of course, is one of the dilemmas of travel... to be totally in the space and moment or to step away to photo or record what is going on.

The following day left time only for one more trip to my little beach and then on to the airport. I knew I would want to return someday to see more of this most special place.

Exploring the Seine River

2018

I had one more type of cruise I wanted to experience and the opportunity came with a week on the Seine River in France. The cruise would start in Paris, travel to Normandy and return to Paris. This was a total change of cruising for me with a small ship, people in my approximate age group, and five star dining with open seating, affording the opportunity to share any meal with many fellow passengers. This would also allow mealtimes to be a time of comparing experiences of the day and learning about their travels and lives in a way that doesn't usually happen on a cruise. In addition, my cruise provided some other unexpected pleasant surprises. Usually, an interior cabin has no windows. But ours had a long window running the length of the outside wall. It was wide enough to see what was happening outside above shoulder level and actually felt light but private. We also had an occasion when the tours provided for the next day weren't offering activities that all passengers found doable. As soon as the crew heard about this, an easier tour of a city and its history was added at no additional cost. At the end of the cruise we didn't have to be up and on deck at the crack of dawn to be off the ship as quickly as possible, but rather could have breakfast, take our time, and leave at a reasonable time based on when our flights were leaving.

Again, I wanted a cabin mate and this came about in a surprising way. About two years before the cruise, I was at a get-together that an ex-husband of mine also attended. We got to talking, and he asked if I remembered a mutual friend from over thirty years prior. I actually did, and he said he'd run into her recently. He gave me her phone number in case I wanted to get in touch. I did, but promptly forgot about it. A year later, when my ex passed away, I came across that phone number and called to let her know. We chatted and decided to get together for coffee. At coffee we realized we had much in common. We both were retired, been married, raised children and loved to travel, often looking for someone to share a cabin or room with. We also found out the desire for a European cruise was mutual. Next coffee, we came prepared with cruise information and decided on the Paris cruise.

We arrived on board early afternoon and it was a day for all to arrive, get settled, hear about the upcoming day, and prepare for our first dinner on board.

The first day in Paris, we divided into three groups. A tour of the city for all; then those who wanted to visit the Louvre; those who wanted to see Notre Dame and have time to wander that area; and those who got off early on the tour, having seen the basic sights before and wanting the day to themselves. The drive into the city center took us through areas I remembered from my earlier trips and made me want to be two people at once... taking the day as it was laid out but also wandering off on my own. This meant I probably needed to return to Paris someday. I was in the group to see Notre Dame, and as it came into view, we were given a verbal list of sights to see and how to reach a book shop and some local restaurants, as well as a reminder of where and when we would be picked up by the tour bus.

It was Easter Sunday and there was quite a crowd to get inside. I spent some time reverently admiring the exquisite carvings on the doors, walls, the entire front of the church, symmetrically telling the story of everything. I didn't know then, that a few years later a fire would do terrible damage to this treasure. From there, I walked through a small park to the renowned book store, Shakespeare and Company, so I could check it out. A shop by that name had already been opened in Paris in 1919 by Sylvia Beach where many of the most renowned authors of that time spent time writing, talking and reading. An American, named George Whitman, opened this shop in 1951 and renamed it Shakespeare and Company in honor of Sylvia Beach. George said, "I created this bookstore like a man who would write a novel, building each room like a chapter, and I like people to open the door the way they open a book, a book that leads into a magic world in their imaginations."

There was already a line to the book store which wasn't even open yet, so I decided to be my version of Parisian while waiting. I went to the restaurant next door, to drink espresso, eat a crepe and people watch.

Before too long, the store opened and I was surprised to see the line was barely moving. I thought, "What could possibly be happening in there that would cause the employee at the door to only admit a few people at a time?" I'd seen that at museums and clubs but never at a bookstore. Once I got inside I found out. The shop was a series of small rooms, next to each other, up stairways, often opening into each other and all floor to ceiling with books and tables of books. If anything, once inside it felt like we had to move too quickly. I couldn't leave before purchasing a few books for myself and as gifts. It's hard to express the impact that shop has and all the details that make it special but the one that has stayed with me is the main stairway going up the second level. It is painted in reds and yellow and has an inscription on each stair, from the bottom step to the next floor. PLEASE start at the bottom of this poem as you would go up a flight of stairs and read it one step up at a time, as I did that day.

> *being*
> *of your own*
> *light*
> *the astonishing*
> *in darkness*
> *lonely or*
> *when you are*
> *I could show you*
> *I wish*

I headed back to Notre Dame, and walked around the cathedral to see more of it and do a little exploring of the area. Paris is noted for its musicians in the Metro and streets, so it wasn't surprising to see a trio playing old school jazz on the sidewalk as I rounded the corner of the cathedral. What was surprising to me was their age. They looked to be in their seventies. They were terrific and had attracted quite a crowd. I noticed a tiny bent over elderly lady in a coat and wearing a cloche-style hat. She was sort of shuffling and dancing to the music. First, I thought she was a neighborhood person and then realized she was "the girl with the band". Every band has "the girl', who's both groupie and cheerleader. When they had all been young, she'd been the one. They were still all together. I noticed that although they had the sax case open for tips, there were lots of people watching who weren't contributing so I went up and put in a couple of dollars. 'The girl' danced up to me and said, "Thank you honey" with a sweet French accent. "Thank YOU," I responded with a smile. It's these completely unexpected little jewels that come with just hanging out a bit that keep a smile on my face for days and even today, just remembering it.

I wandered through some shops, people watched, and tried a little of my high school French here and there. By the time the bus picked us up, I was ready to sit and just enjoy the scenery. My traveling partner had taken the Louvre tour and it was great to share our adventures with each other as well as at a table of equally excited fellow passengers. That dinner and every other dinner were remarkable. Each meal was a banquet of the finest order, but without the feeling of having over-eaten. Later, I thought about how they accomplished this. I think the meal was paced slowly with enough time to really taste, enjoy and absorb the appetizer, then the salad or soup course, and so on. The portions were not large but so beautifully plated it seemed natural to eat more slowly and really taste and see what was on each plate. I hoped to bring a little of that home with me for my home dining or at least for when I had company.

We left Paris that evening, sailing down the Seine and headed for the artist Monet's home and gardens. The gardens are where Monet created most of his paintings, never tiring of the play of shadow, light, sky and water. In his home, which is now a museum, artists and other friends enjoyed conversation and the fine cooking of his wife. Monet was noted for eating at great restaurants and occasionally going back to the kitchen to compliment the chef and wrangle a favorite recipe of his so his wife could duplicate it for him and their guests.

Monet was born in the mid-1800s and was mentored to paint out of doors. Monet, widowed with two children, remarried a woman with six children and they moved to Giverny. They eventually settled in a house on two acres and extensive gardens. Monet hired gardeners who not only kept up the gardens but added to them as the imaginative Monet requested. I didn't know about Monet's passion for Japanese art and gardens before this visit, but his garden makes extensive use of bamboo and quite a bit of Japanese art is displayed on the walls of his home. He died at age eighty-six and despite failing eyesight and lung cancer, continued painting until the day he died.

The thing about traveling the Seine River in early April is the unpredictability of the weather, especially in visiting gardens, considering the most lush views come in May or June. The weather was mild and not rainy. Irises, rhododendrons, and many typical spring blooms were present. It was easy to spot the precision of design and symmetry of each section of the gardens. That time of year also allowed us to take our time since the rush of tourists hadn't arrived yet.

Turning his house into a museum involved a bit of refurbishing, but is furnished as it was when he lived there. I suspect every inch of his walls might not have been so completely covered with a vibrant mix of his beloved Japanese engravings, his works and those of his artist friends. Moving from room to room, it's not hard to visualize his wife cooking on the stove in the yellow and blue kitchen, circa early 1900s, their early rising and bedtimes upstairs, and strolling out the back door to such a variety of gardens. We learned the water garden, shaded by weeping willows, had been created by diverting the nearby Epte River.

Next to the house and gardens sits a vast gift shop where it is possible to buy most every imaginable kind of souvenir. I mostly purchased packets of seeds of the flowers that grow in his gardens. It seemed like a nice sort of gift for myself and to give friends. I liked the idea of planting flowers whose kin would be flourishing in a garden in France.

We were headed for Rouen, best known as the place of Joan of Arc's last stand. It was the only stop on our cruise where the unpredictable spring weather gave us a beating; sunny and crisp for a few minutes, followed by sideways rain, and mixed with cold gusty winds. Many of us were not able to keep up with the briskly paced tour, but even so, the architecture and storied past caught my imagination with appreciation of courage and beauty. Rouen existed even in medieval times and is the capital of the Normandy Provence. It has kept its architecture of houses and places of business as close as possible to their original appearances, even though the town was severely damaged several times during the Middle Ages by fire and plague. World War II also took its toll but these refurbished or recreated buildings are not just for show but used for daily living and business today. One restaurant doing brisk business might not have been that old, but was still of major interest as the place to dine chosen by Julia Child whenever she visited the area. The town is also known as the city of a hundred spires. Not just because of the quantity of churches but more to the substance of them. Rouen's Notre Dame Cathedral has a breathtaking interior and is the burial place of Richard the Lion Heart. Standing under the stained glass and arch filled core of the church where Joan of Arc was sentenced to death gave me a sense of her devotion and determination as her vision moved her from this earth. The soaring arches, their play with light and shadow form a wordless story of earth's passion transcending into a deeper reality.

Returning to the ship was an adventure in wrong turns in the wind and rain. I was pretty thrilled to get on board, remove my soaking wet clothes for a hot shower and indulge in French baked goods and coffee for the rest of the afternoon. Next, we were scheduled for a full day at memorials and the beaches of Normandy, focusing on D-Day in World War II. Perhaps because I am first generation, my personal sense of World War II and D-Day was different from many whose family members served in the armed forces in the United States and England. But two experiences have gone a long way in shaping the views I now have and my level of appreciation and understanding. The first event happened in 2015 when friends of mine from the Midwest were visiting me. They wanted to go to the museum near me that houses planes from World War II. We explored the planes together and individually. I was looking for one of my friends and spotted her in the gift shop. As I got closer, I saw she was standing in front of a stack of books with tears running down her face. I asked what was wrong. She pointed to a picture in the opened book facing her. I looked at the painfully thin young men marching and straggling in a single file row. The caption stated, "Soldiers on the death march in Bataan." My friend pointed to one young man's face and sobbed, "That's my dad." He had survived and returned to his wife and they later had a baby girl. He never really talked about the experience. But there it was, all over his face, in this book, so many years later. His physical and emotional experience, barely out of his teens, the effects on his family, all of this gave me an insight into a bigger meaning of that war. The other experience was this current trip up the Seine River to Normandy.

Initially I was not enthused about spending a whole day paying tribute and feeling both heartless and guilty. By the end of our day in Normandy, I realized that was because I wasn't able to imagine how thoroughly and reverently we would be walked through that day in 1944. I came to understand, as we were led through the day's importance, perils, and sacrifices.

We started with pleasant ramblings through the countryside and stopped for lunch at a restaurant on a golf course, adjacent to the town housing a museum dedicated to D-Day. Even going through the museum and reflecting on the morning, there was nothing to foreshadow the emotions and breadth of what the rest of the day would present. We were told five beaches had been designated as landing points and were given code names. The Canadians would land at beach Juno. The British at Sword and Gold beaches. The Americans landed at the west-most beaches, Utah and Omaha. Other countries sent their soldiers as well.

Two separate tours had been set up for our group. One group focused more on the British and Canadian beaches. The group I was with visited Gold and Juno beaches but spent most time and focus on the American landing at Omaha beach.

Our guide stated, "There would be no way to completely avoid the Germans, dug in with heavy artillery focused on the beaches. There would be no way to avoid massive fatalities. But some would get through, they would have to, and the tide of the war would change. An airborne assault began shortly after midnight that day and by 6:30 a.m. Allied Troops started arriving. Over 160,000 soldiers landed. Records I saw noted over ten thousand deaths, sixty six hundred of them Americans."

When we arrived at Omaha Beach, we were given a map of the area and ideas on what we might want to focus on after a memorial ceremony. The ceremony took place in an outdoor architectural masterpiece. A military representative gave a short and heartfelt speech on how the day had begun, about the soldiers, the victories and losses. Next, America the Beautiful was played and we all, hand over hearts or saluting, sang along. There were no dry eyes as Taps was played. The question was asked, "How many of you are veterans… please come to the center of the area so we can salute you." I don't think most of us realized how many on our cruise were vets. We were given long stem roses to place at the base of statues honoring the soldiers. Walking through the pathways of the vast cemetery with seeming endless rows of white crosses and Star of Davids, one could only feel the enormity and loss of war. We walked down to the actual beaches and saw where tunnels and strongholds had been built to attack any who dared to land. Honoring sculptures had been placed there as well as footprints, placed where they would have been as soldiers struggled to reach sand and beyond. Heading back to the ship, I think we were all coming to terms with the day: emotional, sobering, exhausting and with a sense of gratitude for our day's immersive experience.

We sailed through the night and into the next morning, arriving at Les Andelys. The village itself is typical of those along the river but also boasts Chateau Gaillard, an impenetrable fortress built by Richard the Lionheart, also known as King Richard I. King Richard actually spent most of his life either fighting in the Crusades or living in France.

Two of the day's tours offered walks or climbs up to the castle or higher up to the cliffs. I was in the group taking the third option, which was a leisurely tour of the town, its history and time to stop by the local shops. It was a delightful time, with details of each shop, even noting the village's bakery had been burned down. During the lengthy time it took to restore the building, the baker moved on. This left the village without a baker and so they trekked to the nearest village each day for their necessary daily fresh bread. I can imagine much rejoicing when a new baker moves in.

The morning of our last full cruise day we were headed back to Paris. I woke up really early that morning. The kind of awake that tells you there is no point in lying in bed hoping you will doze off. So I quietly got up, dressed and went up on deck. It was 4:30 a.m. and no one else seemed to be up except a couple of crew members and probably the kitchen crew prepping for breakfast below. No pastries until 6 a.m., but the fancy coffee machine was always ready to brew whatever your pleasure might be, so I brewed a chocolate coffee drink and went outside. I sat on a bench on deck to be a part of the Seine and its surroundings as morning slowly came around. In the darkened stillness I finally heard a distant bird send out its waking call, then another. I could now make out the outline of trees, a light coming on in a distant house, a car engine starting. There was no dazzling pink, shocking sun glow poking up into the sky. The simple slow lightness grew and my inner peace returned at the same pace. Before long I smelled the aroma of fresh pastries being delivered to the coffee station and others wandered onto the deck with me. This little treasure of time was as valuable to me as any other activity of the trip.

Although I had plans to go on a tour that afternoon, I was overcome with the desire for a nap. It was either a nap or risk not being awake for the night tour of Paris, which I didn't want to miss. Life is a lot more satisfying with the ability to admit I can no longer rise early, sprint through the days and still carry on into the evenings too. The nap was a good call. I was able to enjoy our last delicious food and good company, then board the coaches for a tour of Paris. We finished at midnight, arriving at the Eiffel Tower as its lights came on and it became a most beautiful jewel, symbolic of all that is unique and precious about Paris.

On the long flight home, I felt so lucky to have had this special cruising experience. And being actually grateful to have experienced several kinds of cruises and noting I still have not tried them all. One of my favorite cruise moments came on one of my Caribbean cruises. It was a large ship and I happened to get a great viewing area early one day. There were no two person tables available, a larger table was and I took it. The spot allowed me to see the ocean, a pool and several activity areas. I could hear the space behind me filling up and was startled to hear "Look at that lady all by herself. She's hogging that table. It's just not right. Why is she doing that! Someone ought to… " I just blocked out the rest feeling insulted and somewhat threatened. I considered sitting there forever just to spite them. I thought of leaving in a huff and giving them a dirty look on the way out. What I did was turn toward them and said "Hi there, I have plenty of room, do you want to join me?" They looked stunned. They said, "There's lots of us." I said, "No problem, come on down." And they did. We grabbed extra chairs and chatted. The best part was that no matter where I was on the ship for the rest of the cruise, I kept running into at least one of that group and was always greeted with waves, smiles and, "There she is… hi, how you doing?" like we'd always known each other. Since then, I try to remember that experience when I'm tempted to take a cheap shot or be less than gracious.

South Africa and Dubai

November 2016

*T*aking a calculated risk by traveling by myself with a small tour group out of Canada and enduring very long flights to fulfill a major desire (more of a lust) to visit both South Africa and Dubai, were dreams I had discarded several years before as not practically attainable. Both were too rugged and too expensive. Yet the parameters of this trip seemed to meet my concerns of itinerary and costs. I made a list of questions that would have to get the right answers and gave myself over to the possibility.

First, I confirmed the dates of this trip for the listed price, I was able to take the time off from work. Also, weather would be optimal in both locations. For me, optimal is weather neither sweltering, frigid, parched, nor involving monsoons. I was able to talk to a knowledgeable agent about the itinerary, with a specific intent of finding out about excursions, accommodations and tour/trip guides. I made a point to take notes including the name of the person I talked to and the date. This particular special had the option of paying a single supplement fee or taking a chance on perhaps having a roommate. Signing up for the roommate option meant sharing a room if someone else, same sex, traveling solo, also signed up for the trip but getting a private room if no one else signs up for the feature. The agent said it was common for people to wind up with the private room so I signed up and took the chance. I also purchased travel insurance because of health issues, the distance, and the unfamiliar part of the world I was visiting. Within a few phone calls I had signed up, paid my deposit and couldn't stop grinning. A great adventure awaited me!

As the travel date got closer, the length of the flight started to weigh on me. I heard a friend talk about driving to Seattle and asked when that would happen. She was open to any time in November so I offered to pay her gas and take her to lunch if she would drop me off at the Sea-Tac airport on her way. She agreed, which made me very happy. It allowed me the comfort of a car ride and conversation versus getting up earlier, going to my local airport, checking in luggage, check points, waiting, the flight, and picking up my luggage before even getting to the process of checking in for the actual flight I had booked with the travel agency.

How pleasant to arrive at the Seattle airport relaxed and as ready as possible, since the next twenty-four hours would be comprised of either flying or waiting for a flight. The good news was all travel occurred on one airline and the only stop would be in Dubai to change planes on the way to Johannesburg, South Africa.

Again, as with so many long flights, it looked and felt like the plane has entered some parallel universe. A universe where zombies stiffly roam the aisles, randomly performing Tai Chi or isometrics. Sleep masks, snores, reading lights and lit up screens perforate the stillness as the ever smiling wait staff serves cups of water. This leads to lines at every restroom and muffled flushing sounds for the duration. At some point the wait staff hangs out in the back and we inmates take over the food prep areas, pouring our own water or juice and any snacks that may still be out. By then, even the unhappy babies have drifted off to sleep. I participated in all of this, catching up on every movie I'd missed in the past year and dozed in between. It was a welcome relief to arrive in Dubai, to deplane, and stretch my legs at the airport. I found out later, this very large airport belongs only to the airline I have been flying on. There is also an equally large airport across town for all the other airlines. As we found our seats on the next plane, I was already looking forward to spending time in Dubai. I had high expectations.

While waiting for the flight in the Seattle airport, I over-heard voices talking about this being their first trip to South Africa. I turned around and asked if they were also going to Dubai. They were and it was a good feeling to know I had fellow trip mates on the plane with me. When we all arrived in Johannesburg, we found ourselves to be a diverse group of travelers in every way. Of the nineteen of us, some were singles, some were couples. Ages ranged from late twenties to mid eighties. There were men and women and we came from Oregon, Washington, Washington D.C., Texas, Wyoming, The Philippines and Canada. The most novel trait of the group was, despite some obvious differences politically, no one was ever late, no one complained, and controversial differences we might have back in our home life, didn't come up to spoil this very special trip for us.

International flying usually has more amenities than domestic flights and, as of this writing, international airlines still treated their passengers as valued guests even in coach seats. Amenities in economy class included at no extra charge: smiles, blankets, pillows, attractive little bags containing eye masks, socks, toothbrushes and tooth paste, and plentiful food and beverages.

Over fifteen hours on the first flight and now the final eight hours on the second flight came to an end. We had arrived in Johannesburg, or we were told, Joburg as it is known to its natives. Finally, it was time for lots of walking and searching for the lines of entry process into the country, luggage pick up and the spot just outside of the terminal where all of us finally met up under direction of the local tour guide.

Our guide was phenomenal. He was ninth generation Dutch and both passionate and knowledgeable about South Africa's cultures, history, weather, flora and fauna and politics. He had been a guide and game park ranger for many years. He was patient, helpful to all with so much information I couldn't both take notes and catch everything he had to say at the same time. So this trip had a minimal level of notes to draw from, but much better was the information and firsthand experience.

I come from a cool rainy climate expecting dryness and some heat. Not having been to Africa before (except for Morocco), visions of the exotic or at least the unknown sprang to mind. So it was very surprising to find grey, cool rain-filled skies and the need for a jacket to provide warmth as well as to keep me dry. Our guide told us this was most welcome weather because there had been so much heat and lack of rain that animals were dying and plants withering. We spent the night at a large complex consisting of many hotels, restaurants and a casino. We were told most people visiting Johannesburg stayed in complexes like this and our tour of the area would explain why. This led to a free evening to catch up on sleep in real beds, and wander through the shops, restaurants and casino attached to our hotel. A recommendation for the best in local food got my attention and I headed there after stowing my bags in the room, which seemed to be all mine. I followed directions to a specific doorway and several turns right and left and suddenly found myself in a space so familiar to me. I thought, for a moment, I had found an otherworldly wormhole to Las Vegas. There was the marble statue and domed blue and white cloud-painted sky as in Caesars Palace. There were lots of tourists, shops and restaurants. For a moment, perhaps too tired to be wandering around, I groused to myself about traveling such a distance as this for rain and Las Vegas, but couldn't help but see the humor in it. Then, just past the statue, I spotted the recommended restaurant. It was lovely and featured African meats cooked to perfection. There was quite an array of vegetable based dishes as well, but as a meat eater I was ready for one of their specials. This was perhaps the most tasteful and tender meat I have ever eaten. It was the best meal I ate on the entire trip. I believe it was Kudu. That turned out to be a major ethical problem for me later in the trip when we were on safari. At one point I asked about the beautiful and graceful antelopes just ahead of us, which turned out to be Kudus. But on this first day in Africa, I just enjoyed my meal and people watching. A good night of sleep had me ready to explore the next morning.

That first day laid out the blueprint of how our days in South Africa would run. Up and ready for a large breakfast buffet at 7 a.m. I particularly enjoyed having two mocha coffees each morning, not only a taste luxury but guaranteed to keep me lively for the day. Then around 8 a.m. the day would be spent in sections of riding the bus, with discussion on the way, and getting out for experiences.

Our tour started with some basic facts about the area. Joburg is on a plateau approximately 6,000 feet above sea level with a population of six million people. It is a huge commercial center but rough and tumble. We were told there was a time when it was also a cultural center, but much had been shifted to Cape Town. When I was there, our guide pointed out no one was walking around the streets in a casual way. This was Joburg, designated as a place where you get there, do your business and get out. Since I returned from this trip I've read there is a revival of the arts now and hope the extreme grittiness and crime are edged out soon to make this a city to enjoy again.

By now, after so much traveling, it was November twelfth and we were all coming to terms with being in a foreign country just days after an American presidential election. The results were a surprise to many people, not just in the U.S. but also in South Africa. Fortunately, our focus was on discovering this beautiful country but I was asked many times what I thought of the elections. It was interesting to hear the thoughts of what the future might bring from people so far from my home and how our politics were affecting their country. Our guide was well versed in the current politics and history of South Africa and as he talked, I could see how Germany and The Netherlands focused on extracting as many valuable resources as possible for their homelands: greed, diamonds, treatment of local people as workhorses or nuisances to be gotten rid of – the unfortunate stance of most countries in the name of colonization or dominance as they pillage others.

It's not possible to talk about the history of South Africa without reviewing the diabolical system of apartheid. In a particularly slow and steady way, the ruling of the native people was taken over, and in the name of preserving their heritage, they were moved from their lands to "townships" which separated families, and then were given a hideous choice of getting an education or retaining the right to learn in their native language. We saw areas of slums, sheets of corrugated metal, meager belongings in small sheds. These were still in use but only in some areas. We also saw beautiful houses, lawns, schools, all in that same township area called Soweto, the shortened version of Southwest Township. We visited the apartheid museum. In order to really experience it, each person was given a random entrance ticket. Those receiving a ticket marked white, went through an entrance that exposed them to the white class of living ever better, cities becoming more cosmopolitan and other countries pesky questions kept at bay simply stating, "Of course there are always some disgruntled citizens, but it is really no problem." I was one of those who received a ticket marked non-whites. My experience in the museum marked how insidiously changes were made until the uprising in Soweto by students. There was much bloodshed and many students died. There is an amazing architectural monument and mural with this tribute written below "To honor the youth who gave their lives in the struggle for freedom and democracy." Photos were taken of this massacre and smuggled out of South Africa to other countries. No longer could the oppression be hidden from the world. Still, it was years before Apartheid was truly dismantled. Most everyone has heard of Nelson Mandela, whose leadership, imprisonment and later his forgiveness led to healing the country. I took a picture of a large sign in Soweto created in an Andy Warhol inspired style of Mandela's likeness and the words "Comrade, Leader, Prisoner, Negotiator, Statesman."

While we walked around the tribute to the students, we noticed many students now on the streets. School must just have gotten out. When I travel, I often bring small items to give as little gifts to our guides, people I may meet and certainly children. So I hoped there would be several students in Soweto using pencils decorated as coming from my home town. I like that feeling of connection.

This trip, like many travels covering extensive miles and places to visit in a limited time, offered more of a buffet than in depth experience of any one place. You just take it all in and make notes of your experiences and those locations you hope to come to see again in more detail.

Our fourth day of adventure had us on the road headed for Kruger National Park for safari. The long ride was made interesting by the shift in climate and terrain. At first, we experienced changes in elevation. As we moved higher, we encountered ranches and rolling hills. Heading back down provided views of pine and then eucalyptus trees. As we neared Krueger, the land became warm and flat, housing citrus groves, avocados and mangos. Our guide spent a great deal of the time talking about these changes, their effect on plants, animals, and cultures as well as the history of the area. We stopped for lunch at a wildlife reserve. The large complex had shops, animal viewing areas and a large restaurant. At lunch, as we watched the ostriches, elands, and other animals, our guide gave us the lowdown on what the reserve was all about. Their reserve was more like what we know in the U.S. as a cattle ranch. Poaching of these wild animals is a big problem in South Africa. Animals are killed to the point of extinction for either a specific body part or for food. By providing a safe and comfortable home for these animals, they are allowed to have a quality life experience. When they are humanely killed, it is thought of as a better death than in the wild where getting old or injured or whatever would slow them down is a death sentence. In the wild, life belongs to the swiftest and strongest.

Late in the afternoon, we approached our hotel, which was situated just outside the gates of Kruger. By then, we were at a much higher elevation. As we entered the hotel to check in, clear warnings were issued to us. Because of the proximity to Krueger, wild animals roamed the grounds at night. We were requested to not leave the raised walkways after dark. Baboons were prevalent and appeared to have a sense of ownership of the area. We were told to beware of even sitting in the hotel casual areas since baboons might want whatever we were eating, and to never leave our room windows or doors open or unlocked as baboons might enter the rooms and play with or take most anything. Any doubts about being in the jungles of Africa were dispelled as we carefully took our luggage to the rooms and returned to the main building for dinner. My walk seemed to take a long time measured by the rustling in trees and monkey shrills all around. A buffet supper was followed by the members of the hotel staff dancing and playing instruments of their native heritage. They lived in the surrounding area. Many spent the day at work to earn money for school and to assist their families. After spending their work days in the comfort of the hotel, most went home to where none of the amenities like indoor plumbing and electricity were available to them.

I was happy to return to the safety and warmth of my room and snuggle in for a good sleep. I was deep asleep when my alarm clock went off at 4:30 a.m., just time to wash up, have breakfast, grab a spot in the jeep and head for the gates of Kruger, which opened at six a.m.

Our feelings of excitement and anticipation bounced off of each other as the gates opened and the transportation for our safari appeared. It was a giant sort of jeep with seating for ten people in rows that were tiered into four levels. The sides and front area were open and the top was made of canvas. Our group was divided into two such jeeps, and as we took to the rutted dirt roads, both were presented with the same set of rules and cautions from our guides. "Keep your hands and arms in the jeep. No, I don't have a gun and we should be just fine. Don't raise your voices. We'll make two stops during the day to stretch your legs and for lunch." The roads we roamed were deeply rutted, but the thick seat padding made the eight hour safari comfortable enough to focus solely on the search for animals.

The talk is always about seeing the big five: rhinos, lions, leopards, elephants, and the extremely dangerous Cape buffaloes. But the jungle is full of all kinds of animals and birds, so being quiet and observant brought an amazing array close up. We saw all the big five except the leopards. But we saw what they had been up to the night before and were told we probably were in the vicinity of leopards by the water holes, who blended in so well and sat so silently, we never knew they were there. Unlike the lions, leopards watched and waited, and when they went after their prey did not just eat what they wanted then leave the rest. Upon killing, the leopard drags the body up into a tree and leaves it hanging until that night. No sharing with any other animals is done and at night they return to the tree and work on eating as much as they want through the night and perhaps for many nights thereafter. Our guide pointed out a tree where a large, partially eaten carcass was hanging.

We had many elephant sightings, some families crossing directly in front of our vehicle, taking their time and allowing our quiet oohs and aahs over the babies tagging along side their mothers. We also saw crocodiles, warthogs, giraffes, elands, nuelas (a type of antelope), kudus, wilde-beasts, zebras, baboons and so many beautiful birds.

While the guides don't carry guns, they all have walkie talkies. These are used between jeeps to warn of problems or alert to some special animal sightings. This was how we hap-pened on our moment of potential danger and excitement. Our guide got a call about something going on in a wadi, a low-lying area by water with lots of reeds. The reeds were moving strangely… something was going on. We arrived and parked next to the jeep that had notified us. We could see the reeds moving too, and as the reed movement got closer, there suddenly appeared a small wildebeest, wide eyed and clearly running toward us as though its life depended on it. It certainly did, we saw, as a lioness emerged in close chase. Both were headed directly toward our truck and I was already visualizing the two animals in our jeep. But at the last minute the wildebeest swerved and left the reedy area for low lying brush. The lioness, of course, followed. We don't know if the lioness got her lunch or the wildebeest somehow escaped. Our guide reminded us these animals don't know what old age is. Survival of the fittest demanded speed, strength and luck.

Both of our stops took place in parks set up for tourists to use the facilities, enjoy the scenery and purchase food and beverages. It felt good to stretch our legs and feel free to move around without concern. Later that day, and much exhausted, we returned to the lodge and I took a long nap. Some of the group opted to take an extra trip back to the jungle that night to look for the leopard and its prey. No fancy jeeps for this trip so this was not something my body would have done well with. I contented myself with their stories the next day about having found the leopard and how scary the jungle really was at night.

The next morning we left Kruger and headed south for the wine lands and eventually Cape Town. This required a drive back to Johannesburg, a flight to Cape Town and a drive to the town of Stellenbosch. We didn't actually go into the town, but rather made camp at the beautiful Spier Estate Vineyard and Winery. Less like a hotel and more like apartments or condos, were the housing arrangements at Spier. Groupings of these were clustered around swimming pools and formed a pattern narrowing down to pathways leading to the main building which is a conference center, restaurant, hotel proper and lovingly assembled art gallery of local and generally African art. Our full day offered us a morning tour of the vineyards which included tastings and an afternoon with opportunities to go into the town of Stellenbosch. The town is known for its Cape Dutch architecture, art galleries and shops. Because I know of my physical limitations, I always try to remind myself that listening to my body allows for the best quality of trip for me. My body was telling me it needed to slow down. I was determined to spend the day at the Spier Estate. Fortunately, the estate is massive and spread over its acreage were a craft market with local artists both working on their crafts and selling their wares, restaurants, cooking demonstrations, picnics, a waste treatment plant, wine tasting, gardens and sculptures, a spa, trails, and days could be spent just enjoying all of that. I slept in, had a long hot shower and lingering breakfast. The rest of the day was spent on the grounds and later at one of the swimming pools. I also stopped at the craft market and talked to the artists, buying most of my holiday presents there. The following morning we were on our way to Cape Town, a brief coach ride away.

Cape Town is vast and incredibly varied. Just when you think you've seen it, there is more and it is nothing like what you have already seen. In truth, it seems more of an area than a city; which makes it an excellent reminder of how the uncontrollable weather governs what you will be doing no matter where you are. We were scheduled to drive high into the hills toward Table Mountain and then proceed to the top in gondola-style cable cars. These can run only if it is not windy and on our scheduled day it was windy and cloudy so no trip to the top. The same held true for visiting Robben Island where Nelson Mandela had been held in exile and imprisonment but the waters were too choppy for the boats to make the trip on the day we were scheduled. No matter how much you might want to take part in these activities, if it's not possible, better to adjust and find out what can be seen rather than getting upset and spoiling part of the vacation. Our motor coach was able to drive us up some steep and narrow roads where we had options to climb to landmarks or photograph the jaw-dropping view of Cape Town laid out below at our feet. Missing the Robben Island tour meant more time exploring the many other facets of the area. We spent time on a walking tour hearing the history of the buildings and area. Ornate colonial styles were still being used by the government and many blocks in that core area provided lush parks. A whole block was dedicated to growing fresh produce for the city's citizens.

A visit to Kirstenbosch Botanical Garden was overwhelming. We had three hours to explore this vast and varied greenspace. Including the treetop walk, it would have been easy to spend three days there. After viewing a map of what was in the gardens and where, I opted to view what interested me the most. I wandered through lavish gardens full of stone sculptures, ducks and other birds. Some of the plants were familiar to me while others were new, not surprising since there are more than seven thousand plant species growing there. A special highlight was the expansive area of South Africa's national flower, the pink and prickly King Protea with blooms the size of grapefruits.

One evening we dined at a supper club with stage show. Authentic Cape food was featured and the musical revue highlighted the culture and history of the area. It's hard to go wrong with great food and a good show. The next morning we boarded a motor coach headed for the peninsula tour. As we drove south, communities of the wealthy and their magnificent houses went by as well as harbor towns. We stopped in one for lunch with time to wander through shops. Breathtaking views appeared and before we knew it we were at the Cape of Good Hope, close enough to the South Pole to require bundling up a bit. At Boulder Beach we stopped to enjoy the penguin colony. These are the little penguins, maybe up to my knees. This was their molting season so as they waddled in busy circles, little poofs of feathers went up in every direction. It was pretty hard to not just enjoy watching them but you wanted to be careful where you stepped too.

Our last day featured a trip to the vast harbor shopping area where boats could be viewed and a massive series of souvenir browsing and restaurants flourished. I bought a native beaded necklace and after arriving home wished I had purchased more of them because of their beauty and uniqueness. The final evening in Cape Town was set for relaxing, walking around and packing for Dubai. I walked up to a little strip mall and enjoyed the shops and conversations with some of their owners. At the entrance to the mall was a very large sign bearing a message I'd never seen at a mall anywhere. I don't know who to attribute it to but it read "7 Steps to Happiness: Think less-Feel more; Frown less-Smile more; Talk less-listen more; Judge less-Accept more; Watch less- Do more; Complain less-Appreciate more; Fear less- Love more. Enjoy your experiences at Piazza St. John." What a great recommendation for interacting with oneself and others. I'm sure it made me a more pleasant customer at their mall. Eventually I headed to my hotel to pack and think back on my great experiences in South Africa before falling asleep. In the morning we would be headed to the airport and new adventures in Dubai.

Magical and ever changing Dubai loomed closer and clearer as our plane started its descent. Our guide met us at the airport. He was a professor who had recently started guiding tours. His lack of experience as a guide was minimized by his knowledge of his homeland and pride. This whirlwind visit was more action and less note taking so the accuracy of my sharing here is based more on what I remember. One could be assured even visiting a few months in the future would render the current cityscape as inaccurate. Seemingly great and creative architects were offered opportunities to build their wildest imagined designs and so they appeared with jaw dropping speed, like plants popping up in the spring. Giant silver disks sitting on an edge revealed, at closer examination, rows of windows and the explanation that this was an office building. The slice of moon on its side and what looked like American football goalposts with cross bar all made of window were office buildings too. Curves, and nose bleed altitudes measured new hotels and it seemed every plot of sand either had been taken over by such buildings, or was in process of holding some building of commerce or residence. Also, everywhere was the pervasive sand, patient and ready to reclaim it all in time.

We stopped at our hotel long enough to drop off our bags and have a bite to eat. Although we had flown through the night and were longing to stretch our legs in an actual bed, this wasn't to be. We only had two full days in The United Arab Emirates and there was so much to do and see. This first day we drove through Dubai while our guide gave us a history lesson of the area including the past, present and plans for building the future of Dubai. While the city was in a building frenzy, there was still much of the ancient architecture, museums and forts. Man-made lakes deep as any natural lake were abundant and we stopped on the sandy beach of one of these lakes. It didn't take long for most of us to kick off our shoes and enjoy. Next we took a water taxi (a cross between an Italian water taxi and gondola) across the waters to the souks. The souks are the ancient marketplaces sectioned off by the type of goods they make and sell. We had time to check out spices and gold. The gold souk was mind boggling in array but fortunately for me, not something I wanted to spend my souvenir dollars on. Spices were a different story. I like to cook and have friends who do too. The aroma of familiar and new spices was captivating and I finally settled on saffron from Iran. The owners treated every person entering as a long lost friend, offering tea and treats and a running commentary of the various uses and delights of each spice. If we hadn't been given a time limit, I don't know when I would have left the souks. Later that afternoon we drove back to our hotel with time to relax, eat or explore. The next day's tour would be to Abu Dhabi.

But that day wasn't over yet so after a brief rest, exploration of the area beckoned, especially since we were close to one of the two largest shopping centers in Dubai. One of the building goals in Dubai seems to be breaking records of size and abundance of shopping and activities. This particular mall had indoor skiing. There was manufactured snow, a ski lift, the whole experience, as well as an interesting way of displaying shops.

My roommate and I could see the top of the mall from our hotel but needed directions to actually get there. I hadn't mentioned a roommate before because I didn't have one. I had a room by myself for all of the tour except the last two nights. The reason? Three singles, two women and one man, signed up for the tour. One had a first name that could be used by anyone. Someone at the tour office mistook her "Ms." as Mr. and assigned her to the man's room. This was not acceptable to either of them. Given the time zone differences, it took them until the last two nights of our tour to determine that this women and I should actually be rooming together and we did so to continue to have the better rate. By then, we had all gotten to know each other so it wasn't a big deal. As we approached the mall I thought I was paying good attention to the entrance we used and the road we came in from since the mall was huge with lots of streets approaching it. The first floor was like any American mall in terms of types of stores and the crowd. One exception I noticed is that I was the only one really watching people and being protective of my purse. Everyone else acted as though they were in their own home. I'm guessing it was more a matter of discreet security rather than an incredible level of random honesty. The second floor was a mix of shops I knew and some I had never heard of, those being at the high end of fashion and pricing. We only dared take a peek on the third floor. No one was up there except sheiks, their wives and attendants. Shops we never heard of and no pricing were the norm and the array of goods and their quality were exquisite.

Lots of walking and suddenly realizing it was getting dark drove us to a quick bite at the food court and outside to return to our hotel. But when we got outside none of the streets looked familiar. We picked one and walked quite a while with nothing resembling our hotel or anything landmark we had seen before. I realized waking from a nap and just "going for a walk to the mall" without thought was a bad idea. Between us we had no hotel card with address or phone number. We had no phone. Eventually we saw a young woman leave a shop and head to her car. In desperation, we called out to her and asked if she could give us directions to our hotel. She didn't know where it was but said "Hop in and we'll find it together." I absolutely don't recommend getting into cars with strangers in new cities or new countries, but we did. Seems she was French and came for a visit to see a friend who had moved to Dubai. She was so captivated by the job opportunities, friendliness and diversity of the people that on returning to France quit her job. She was twenty-two and told her parents she was moving to Dubai. They were shocked, but she came to Dubai and started a new life. No regrets for her. Eventually we found our hotel.

We slept well and were ready for breakfast and a new adventure for our final day in Dubai. We were given directions the previous day as to what to wear in order to enter the major and magnificent Sheikh Zayed Mosque in Abu Dhabi. Abu Dhabi is the largest of the seven emirates that make up the country. My view, based on this trip, confirmed Abu Dhabi as a wealthy and sophisticated city of gardens, with tree lined boulevards, high rises and the famous mosque. When our guide felt assured we were all appropriately covered, he escorted us into the mosque. It was a most interesting morning. We learned a great deal about the religion, religious observations and customs in the mosque. We witnessed the breathtaking grandeur of marble, reflecting pools, pillars with jeweled inlay work, sculptured carpeting, and soaring ceilings. On our coach ride back to Dubai we stopped at a fort. A large restaurant was waiting for those hungry for lunch. Most of our group went to lunch and reported later the meal was superb. I opted to stop in the shops and museum. Artisans were creating metal work and other crafts that were then for sale. It was fascinating to observe and have a sense of the area in less urban times. I bought a hand-detailed, small lidded brass pitcher which seemed like some sort of magic might be held within.

The afternoon was set aside for the rest of the group to prepare for a wild night of jeeps over the sand dunes ending with a traditional sunset dinner in Bedu tents, with entertainment following. With the spinal issues I have, the bouncing and hammering jeep ride would have had me ready for traction not dinner, so I came up with a plan B for myself. One reason I generally feel my travels are successful is that I acknowledge my limitations and the consequences. " I'll take all the adventure I can handle... but not more than that." So far, this has worked just fine for me.

My plan was to taxi over to the other large mall, which not only had an actual underwater shark cage experience, but also housed the tallest building in the world. I wanted to go to the top. When I talked to our guide about this, he said, "So sorry, but it's not likely. People and groups buy their tickets in advance and even then most will not reach the actual top of the building. But many are not prepared for the extremely long line to take the elevator so someone may be willing to sell you their ticket. Still, there is good reason to go. The shops are so interesting and we also have the dancing waters. You know, like the one in Las Vegas, only ours is much bigger and better. It is followed by a light show so stay until dark and find your way to the lake. The lake is part of the tower and mall complex." I was not to be daunted.

I caught a taxi around 4 p.m., enjoyed the drive and view of more amazing buildings. Soon I arrived at Burj Khalifa Dubai and the mall. I walked past the giant aquarium shark cage area at the mall, seeing but still finding it hard to believe. Then I headed downstairs and saw the endless snaking line quite clearly waiting to go to the top of the building. Walking slowly past many people and trying to make eye contact didn't produce anyone remotely interested in chatting or giving up their space. I was already thinking about how I would spend my time until the dancing waters show when I spotted a sign that said "Tickets" tucked into a distant corner of this large space. In walking to that area, I could tell someone was standing behind the counter. I was already feeling a little self-conscious about my appearance. I was wearing the loose and casual outfit planned for the next early morning transfer to the airport and flight home. Realizing I had nothing to lose by going up to the counter, I approached the expressionless woman there and told her I wanted to go the top of the building. She asked, "When?" and I replied, "Now." She just asked for my credit card and wanted to know if I also wanted to see the largest James Bond collection of memorabilia in the world, currently on display in their basement for an additional modest fee. I said, "Sure." I had no idea what the cost would be but I really wanted to go so I handed my card to her, signed the receipt and put my copy in my purse without even looking at it. I didn't want potential dollar shock to spoil my last evening in Dubai and determined I wouldn't look at it until I got home.

I barely had time to put my card away when a gentleman in a sharp suit asked me to follow him. We moved past the ever growing line, and while I thought he was taking me to the front of the line for some wonderful reason, that was not the case. He led me to a room, apologizing for a bit of a wait until the express elevator was ready. I was stunned by the amazing room. It was filled with white leather couches and lots of plants. People were sipping drinks and munching on fruits. A gentleman offered me tea and stuffed dates, encouraging me to relax with them for a moment until the elevator was ready for us. Clearly, the ticket window I went to was for VIP tickets... who knows what else was in store. We were soon led to the express elevator which took us to the 148th floor (which I think is the top floor for visitors) so quickly I was amazed my ears didn't pop. Instead, it was just like taking a deep breath. We were escorted immediately to another room where we could again have tea, dates, and ask any questions we might have before exploring the unique top floor. The area was circular with floor to ceiling windows. It just happened to be sunset and the hazy pinks, and yellows became an amazing backdrop to desert sand, mountainous structures, and the man-made lakes and rivers. After taking it all in from every window and angle, I realized there was more to see. I followed some people to a short line into a room that had no windows. On the curved wall the history of the area played out with lighting and music. The first person in line had one of their hands in a box. Very curious. When it was my turn it came to me that my hand in the box was controlling the lighting and music. What a unique experience. An additional room held a gift shop. Many items were at a moderate price but of excellent quality and of course I purchased a souvenir.

Realizing the dancing waters would start soon, I got on the elevator and when it stopped, let them know I was headed to the James Bond exhibit. Again, I was led to a different entrance and went down to what I thought would be a medium sized room with some mementos of the Bond years. I was wrong. This was a massive exhibit that could easily have held my attention for a full day. A wall of televisions broadcast all the movies in the series. Memorabilia from typewriters to full scenes from the show were on display. Automobiles, a casino, costume; it was mind boggling. Eventually I just had to stop myself and return to the main level to find the dancing waters.

My guide had been right. A cloud of mist as the night turned black, announced the beginning of the program. The creativity and sophistication of the lighting and water movements produced oohs and aahs from everyone, including me. In looking around, I saw we were outside of both the Burj Khalifa Dubai and the mall. Suddenly lights from the actual Burj appeared, changing colors and patterns over the entire side of the building. It was totally unexpected and better than anything similar I had ever seen. What a terrific afternoon and evening!

Back at the hotel I packed and tried to calm down from the day's excitement. The morning would come way too soon. But when the alarm rang, I was ready to head to the airport. The variety of experiences in South Africa and Dubai filled me and I felt totally satisfied. The jungle; winelands; Cape Town, with its bounty of mountains, shops and penguins; coupled with the true magic of the UAE, the magnificent mosque and shape shifting clever Dubai had me feeling very rich in experiences.

Australia

2018

Australia had been on my list of "one day I need to go to" places so when I spotted an almost too good to be true trip, I signed up. The catch was probably the longest flight I'd ever been on combined with only five days at my destination. I would have to make good use of those five days in Sydney. Following my own advice about not waiting for everything to be perfect, I went because it would achieve my goal. An acquaintance, who had heard me talking about the trip to South Africa and Dubai shortly after I returned, approached me stating she would like to go on such an adventure with me someday. I said sure, and just let it go. When she approached me again, I suggested we meet for coffee to see if our ideas on traveling would be compatible. She had the money and free time to just sign up when that adventure might take place. I told her it might not be for quite a while, but within a couple of months, I called her about Australia. She was ready to go. The cost of airfare and hotel was so reasonable we were able to choose the tours we wanted without worrying about their cost. We had something planned for each precious day. Meals were not included, except when part of a tour, but we were both light eaters so that worked well for us.

The airline was the best all-around one I've ever been on, when you consider my flying is almost always in the economy class section. That was fortunate because of the length of the flight. After flying in that timeless place through multi-meals, computer gaming, and a bit of napping, we arrived in Sydney and realized we would be downtown by 10 a.m., while our hotel check-in wasn't until 3 p.m.. It wasn't just that we were tired and couldn't imagine what we would do for five hours, but we were supposed to be at the Sydney Opera House at 3 p.m. for our first tour.

The hotel staff was great throughout our visit. We explained our plight and hoped we looked as exhausted and anxious as we felt. The woman who greeted us at the reception desk said, "Go have some breakfast and we'll get your room ready as quickly as we can, maybe an hour." We were relieved and asked where the closest place for breakfast and, most importantly, coffee would be. It turns out, as in some other countries I've been to, large shopping centers have excellent restaurants on their basement level as well as large grocery stores. There was one two blocks from the hotel. We had a great selection of breakfast options and lingered over coffee, hoping our room would be waiting for us. It wasn't but we still got our room with enough time to wash up and catch a cab to the Opera House.

The Opera House tour lasted only one hour, but was so well done we felt refreshed and exhilarated when we left. The tour was multimedia, and since we were there during Vivid Week (a big music and arts festival), we could hear some of the rehearsals, which was one more benefit. I am paraphrasing a bit, but our guide started with "In the 1950s, city officials wanted to have a classier presence, something that would put Sydney on the map on a worldwide basis. They decided to build an opera house on the harbor and put out requests for designs to architects around the world. There were many solid attractive plans submitted, but

Danish architect Jorn Utzon submitted a most lyrical drawing with ideas of what it should be like and do, and thoughts on how it could be built. The vision he had, captured the officials and he was awarded the contract in 1957. There were massive cost overrides and parliamentary contention about whether it was worth the money. That caused the government to alternately authorize payments to continue one year and then the next year take the funds away. The iconic opera house was not completed until 1973 and half way through, the process became too daunting for Utzon, who returned to Denmark and never saw the completion. Still, this creative and amazing building does stand in tribute to him and his vision. In 1973 Queen Elizabeth II said this about the Sydney Opera House, "The human spirit must sometimes take wings or sails, and create something that is not just utilitarian or commonplace."

Energized, we wandered along the harbor really feeling we were in Australia. It turned out to be an adrenaline rush and in the cab back to the hotel, we couldn't determine whether we were more tired or hungry. We went to one of the restaurants in the shopping center basement and ate pho, the warm broth, noodles and meat, filling us with a good meal and readiness for bed.

Our hotel room was more than we had envisioned. It was simple but had two beds, a chair, desk, sofa and TV as well as a small kitchen with refrigerator, coffeemaker and microwave, and assorted dishes and silverware. We noticed in going through our itinerary, all our tours would start in the early mornings so we stopped in the grocery store and bought coffee and fixings for a breakfast each morning. To bed early gave us a good opportunity to catch up on our sleep and enjoy our morning tour of Sydney and the surrounding area.

A shuttle picked us up at the hotel and stopped at several other hotels until the van was full. I think there were ten of us. We were given the history and highlights of many businesses, the shopping district, stopped at beautiful and incredibly blustery Bondi Beach, suburbs and coastal cliffs. As we returned to the downtown area, our guide suggested, "We will drop you at your hotels but I'm going to tell what kind of shops and interesting sights are along the way and if you want to stop and get out for any of those, just let us know." When he talked about first rate shops for their famous coffee and other authentic kinds of souvenirs, we got off, an easy call since we were only four blocks from our hotel... or so we thought. It never occurred to either of us that there might be a unique way of numbering the buildings, so when we were in the three hundreds block we assumed the next block would be the four hundreds. But when our block ended at building number 371, the next block started off at 375. We walked for so many blocks, each of us too stubborn to say, "Let's catch a cab now," and assuming if we did, it would only take us for one block. Eventually, we reached the hotel, barely moving. After a nap, hunger set in and we wandered out to find dinner. We discovered we were in the Chinese and Thai restaurant section of the city and got recommendations from the hotel's front desk. Fortunately, we both loved Chinese food. We went down two blocks and up a flight of stairs to a mostly empty restaurant, but it was only 4:30 p.m. By the time we left, the line waiting was partway down the stairs. On the way to the restaurant, we saw a long line of people in front of a small shop window. It was so crowded we determined to stop there on the way back to our hotel to find out what was so compelling. The line was gone and the simple sign said "emperor puffs" with quantities and pricing. We bought a few and found out why so many people lined up to buy them (probably on their way home from work). These mini puffs were warm and custard filled. They melted in our mouths and the whole sensation of crunch and warm custard was addictive. I'm almost drooling, writing about them now.

We had already learned the early winter weather in Sydney would provide sun, rain, calm and wind, so next morning we brought our jackets and umbrellas with us in our cab to the harbor area and a scheduled morning tea cruise. We were looking for a specific dock and simply couldn't find it. Our frustration mounted, along with wind and sideways slicing rain until we calmed down and let go of what we were expecting to see and what was really there. There was no pier with its name in large letters filled with lots of excited tourists waiting for a yacht to show up. Our pier was rustic and not well marked. No one was standing with their umbrellas turning inside out except us. We kept searching the waters for our boat but eventually all that showed up was a small craft. A man jumped off and enthusiastically claimed, "You must be here for the morning tea cruise, come on board ladies." He greeted us by name and there was no doubt we would be out on the choppy waters in this small boat. Clutching the railing, we made our way to the seating area, which was two metal folding chairs that even with us sitting on them, were prone to sliding from one side of the boat to the other.

The captain sat a few steps up and in front of us and turned to wave at us as we were introduced. It was really interesting to hear about Sydney and see its sights from the water after having spent time on land with that perspective. Before long, he told us he would go below to prepare a light breakfast and tea made from all Australian products. He was gone a while and eventually the captain noticed. He turned around, now not looking at the busy harbor waters in front of him but facing us and declared, "I see breakfast is being prepared, so I'll fill in as the guide." He informed us of the harbors history and sights to be seen, occasionally turning his head to look forward. I kept wishing he would only be the captain and look where we were headed. There was a lot of traffic in the harbor and I visualized running into some massive ship and who knows what would come of that. Finally a tray with breakfast appeared and it was worth the wait. We were finishing up breakfast and the rain and winds stopped. "A break in the weather," spoke our beaming tour guide. "Good time for a photo shoot on deck, follow me." The boat was still rocking pretty heavily and I felt I would have disappeared into water if not for my death grip on the railing. My friend and I were somewhat exhausted from all the drama, yet when the guide told us to smile and the camera clicked, the photo showed us smiling as though we had just stepped on board and into a casual sunlit morning.

By the time we returned to the pier, the sun was fully beaming and offering an invitation to spend the afternoon out of doors. Our guide and captain told us there were lots of restaurants and a weekly farmers market with additional booths of all sorts of local goods nearby. We enjoyed the afternoon there and that evening walked a little further from our hotel for another delicious dinner. We turned in early because the next morning we'd be heading out for a full day in The Blue Mountains.

Once again, a van appeared at 7 a.m. and after a few hotel stops we were on our way. Our guide kept up a stream of incredibly interesting information about everything we drove past. Observations about the cost of living in Sydney, how people managed to afford it and the intricate commutes via car and train by those who worked in the city yet lived in the rural communities we were passing through. The feel and history of each town was made known to us as well. We arrived for a break at Euroka Clearing, deep in a national park and were introduced to the park ranger, who filled us in on what we might see. There was a large variety of birds but the big draw was the kangaroos. We were told to move slowly and keep our distance. When asked how far away we should stay, the ranger grinned and informed us, "Don't worry about that. The kangaroos will let you know." We spread out, noting the areas for plants and other creatures, while searching for the kangaroos. I found two, hunched over in a grassy area and slowly moved closer to observe and get pictures. One hopped away and the other suddenly stood up on its haunches. It slowly turned its head moving its ears as though they were radar. Apparently they were. He rose to a full height, surprisingly tall, and just stared at me and stared at me and stared at me. Nothing else was needed to let me know my observation time was over.

Back on the road we were close to the mountains and they were an amazing shade of blue. Our guide asked, "Does anyone know why the mountains are blue?" No one knew, so she explained "Eucalyptus trees cover the mountains. When conditions are just right, as they are today, the sunshine releases oil from their leaves and the crispy mountain air creates a sort of crystallization of the blue oil rising in the air. Aah, science creating beauty.

We stopped on our way to lunch at a pavilion and saw a live, short, but extremely informational show. Native dancers also played ancient musical instruments and chanted, giving us their history and introduction to their arts.

Lunch was up a mountainside in an elegant restaurant with breathtaking views. I ate the best and most authentic Caesar salad I've ever had. I also had my first pavlova, which is common in Australia but totally new to me. Wow... this one was made with a base of cream anglaise with a cloud of toasted meringue filled with whipped cream sitting on it. Fresh berries were nestled in its center. I attempted to make one when I got home... not too bad, but lots more practice needed.

Our next stop was much too short a visit to Mt. Tomah Botanic Gardens. It would have been easy to wander the vast gardens and enjoy spectacular views from this mountain perch into the valley. I could easily have stayed a full day but we only had forty-five minutes.

We settled back into the van, quieter and feeling full of great experiences, but to me, the best was yet to come. As we headed for town on a two lane highway, one of the group asked, "Is that an emu behind the barbed wire fence, coming out of the woods?" Our guide told us, "Yes, there are wild emus back in that area and they do sometimes head towards the fence. Do you want us to pull over and watch it?" As we all nodded we would, she continued, "Sometimes they will be curious and come really close to the fence. Remember, they are wild animals, but if you offer them a slice of apple, they seem very partial to apples, from the palm of your hand, they might eat it. Does anyone have an apple and do you want to get out of the van to see?" Someone had a couple of apples and we all got out. I had a unique opportunity to put a slice of apple in my hand several times for the emu to eat. Several times were needed because the emu was so quick, it was hard for anyone to click the button on the camera fast enough to get a photo. The emu came up to me, about my height, and looked me in the eye, cocking its head to evaluate me I think. It looked down at the apple and back at me again. I didn't so much feel the emu take the apple, as suddenly feel the absence of the apple in my hand.

Back at the hotel, we thought about how we wanted to spend our last day in Sydney. The weather forecast, which proved to be accurate, told us there would be cooler weather and rain so we slept in, had a proper restaurant breakfast and enjoyed exploring the city. After our Blue Mountain day, I had approached our hotel reception desk and asked about a building all our guides had pointed out. It was a tall building with what looked like a revolving restaurant at the top. She told us it was a luxury department store and there was, indeed, a revolving restaurant at the top.

I responded, "It must be expensive and I'm guessing requires reservations months in advance. In fact we probably wouldn't go because we need to be up early in the morning and would want to eat dinner before they most likely start serving."

She smiled, explaining, "It's not so expensive and dinner is served late at night but service also starts at 5:30 p.m. Do you want me to make a reservation for you two for tomorrow night?"

We did. So after a day of exploring the city and packing, we headed out for dinner.

It was indeed a luxury shopping center. The restaurant was beautifully furnished and the rain we'd experienced earlier seemed to be over. Our wait person informed us we would have two hours to enjoy the view and meal and we smiled at each other knowing we wouldn't need that much time. Yet, the meal was most enjoyable and the slowly moving twinkling jewels of the city mesmerized us. When I eventually checked my watch, we had been there more than two hours. It was a great way to end the trip and I wanted a photo to show what a treat the evening was from the food and atmosphere to the view. I knew from experience there was no way our view would appear the same through my phone camera, nor would the whole sense of luxury. I took a picture of the ladies room. Green glass sinks, creative lighting, larger and fancier than most hotel rooms. When I show that picture to people as a way to explain how amazing it all was, they always say, "Oh, that is amazing!"

A Little Nostalgia Traveling
and the Bad Luck Trips

n some of the trips I've shared with you, there have been unfortunate turns or surprising adventures, but I've experienced some truly bad luck trips as well. I think the law of averages states no matter how well you plan, how upbeat you are, or how well everything seems to go for you, some travels will just be a series of everything going wrong. It's a reality anyone who opts to travel needs to accept as possible.

Here is a good example. I like to watch some of the game shows on television and, several years ago, I was offered the opportunity to audition for one in New York. I was on a nonstop flight scheduled to last around five hours. By the time we'd been in the air for two hours, I was sweating, feeling dizzy and my stomach was very unhappy with me. I barely made it to the bathroom, concerned I might have the stomach flu. The next thing I knew, I was sitting with my back against the door on the floor facing the toilet. Airline bathrooms are incredibly small. Realizing I had passed out, it was also apparent I did indeed have the stomach flu.

You read in the papers or see on TV where some petite person lifts up a car because their child is trapped underneath. Situations where adrenaline kicks in seem to allow people to go beyond any reasonable expectation. That is what must have happened to me. Somehow, I was able to catch the attention of a flight attendant by opening the door a crack and had her get my extra pair of jeans out of the small bag I'd brought on board. In that tiny bathroom, I cleaned myself up, rinsed out my soiled jeans, put on the fresh jeans, cleaned up the area and used up all the paper towels and soap. Because I was exhausted and dehydrated, probably looking every bit of it, the attendant brought me some water and somehow got a row of seats for me, so I could lie down.

That wasn't quite enough. When the plane landed, I was unable to get up and wound up in an ambulance headed for a hospital instead of a cab to the hotel and my seat at the Broadway show I had a ticket for.

That particular hospital was probably more entertaining than any show might have been. The emergency area was packed and many of us were on gurneys all over the place waiting for a bed and curtained-off area to become available. Also present were police officers and family members of those others waiting their turn. The whole mix of people seemed to be all chummily chatting with each other. A young man, in conversation with what seemed to be a family member, turned to me and asked, "What are you in for?"

It turned out I needed an IV and when it was completed they suggested I stay for one more, but I really wanted to go to my hotel and declined. I asked someone where I could get the number for a cab company and they just laughed. I approached a policeman and told him what I was trying to do. He chuckled as well and told me, "Aw, the regular cab companies don't come out here. We just have the independents. Yup, those dark cars that look like, well, dark cars. I'll go out with you and make sure you get one that will really take you where you want to go. They'll listen to me because I give the say so as to who can work the hospital." I thanked him and got into one of those cars, surprisingly enjoying the view and conversation. Finally we crossed a bridge taking us into Manhattan and my hotel. A hot shower, a clean large warm bed and I believed I'd be fine when I woke up. The problem was, I should have stayed for at least one more IV. I had a note from the hospital on what I needed to get back on my feet, but every time I tried to make it out of the hotel, I passed out in the lobby. The first two times people looked concerned but just walked around me. The third attempt, someone got the Assistant Manager. He got someone to help me get back to my room, and saw to it someone else went out and got what I needed. By then, I could tell I wouldn't be able to catch the flight home and rescheduled for the day after.

I was weak, but feeling better and was determined to go to the audition. I thought, "If I can make it through the lobby, I'll ask them to call me a cab. If I don't get sick or pass out in the cab, I'll go to the audition. If I make it into the audition, well that's victory." Surprisingly, I made it into the audition and the first section, weeding out most everyone, was a written test. They even gave us pencils with the show's name on them. I thought I'd done really well, but it was not good enough. I was not called up to go further in the process. I made it back to the hotel and after resting the following day, took an afternoon flight out.

This flight had one stop and our initial flight was running so late, I was afraid I wouldn't make my connecting flight. I was feeling better and that was fortunate. I was desperate to get home and as I was making my way to the gate I heard my name over the loudspeakers "Carol Palo, your flight is ready to leave, please report to gate, whatever the number was, now." I completely lost it. I was running as fast as I could yelling, "Don't leave without me!" at the top of my lungs. The cabin door was about to close and I had only time to sit down, put on the seat belt and we were airborne. At last, a few hours in the air, a ginger ale and biscuit, thoughts of an uneventful drive home, all within my grasp.

When we got to my airport, it was easy to see some serious rain was going on. As I pulled out of the parking garage, clearly it was more than that. The water was so deep in spots I thought it might come into my car. For a moment I considered staying at a hotel near the airport, but the desire to be home was strong. Along with not too many others on the road, we all very slowly made our way out of the airport and onto the freeways. The night and rain, in conjunction with streetlights and traffic lights, turned the roads into dark abstract puddles of art. I was grateful I knew my way home from the airport so well that I needed little in the way of visual cues. Finally pulling into my garage, I walked into my living room, dropped to my knees and literally kissed the carpet. It was the best feeling in the world to be home, plus I had one expensive pencil as a souvenir.

SOMETIMES GOOD THINGS COME FROM UNFORTUNATE situations. Many years before, when my kids were about eleven and fourteen, I was in an auto accident and there was a financial settlement. I thought "What could I do with this money that might at least somewhat make up for the pain and difficulties?" I took my kids on a trip to Washington D.C. to see the workings of government on the way to the Bahamas. My son and daughter were excited and hoping to see the Congress in action. My son hoped to wrangle his way to take the metro to see a hockey game on his own and it all worked out. As we approached the airport to the Bahamas it suddenly hit me that we were going to a foreign country. Even though this was prior to the securities enacted after 9-11, I struggled to figure out how I had forgotten to even check to see if my kids had any ID on them. My son happened to have his high school picture ID. My daughter could only come up with an expired library card. I wasn't sure what we would do if we were turned away. When it was our turn at customs, I showed my ID and they nodded. My son showed his ID and they nodded. My daughter showed her expired library card and they looked at it and then at me and they laughed themselves silly as they motioned for her to join us.

Next came the good news, bad news phase of the trip. The hotel was clearly overbooked and an angry vocal mob filled the lobby. It was made up of not only people like me, trying to check in, but people who had tried to check in and been sent to other hotels... hotels that were rat traps in the worst parts of the downtown area. They were back and they were the angriest. We calmly waited our turn. When the harried clerk at reception got to us I simply stated, "What an awful time you must be having, and it isn't even your fault. I know you are doing the best you can. Is there some way you can help me and my two kids get a room that is safe if mine is not yet available here?" I was hoping a little empathy and calm voice might help our cause and it did. He sent us to a very ritzy resort with swimming pools, a casino and rooms fit for royalty. We were awed and enjoyed every minute there. We almost forgot this wasn't our true vacation headquarters until the call came three days later that our room was ready for the remainder of our vacation. The room in our original hotel would have been fine if we had checked into it as planned, but after such opulence, it was a sad comparison. We were glad to spend only two nights there. Still, the three of us agreed it was a truly diverse and interesting trip that was a lot of fun. Looking back, I mostly think of a gentler time when a library card and high school ID were good enough for a family traveling together.

THE AUTO ACCIDENT THAT LED TO THE BAHAMAS TRIP also led me to a way of viewing life and my self differently. This was a time before wearing seat belts was mandatory. Cars came with them and it was recommended but that was all. I hadn't bothered with the seat belt and the reaction of hitting the car ahead of me while being hit from behind raised me out of my seat and I hit the top of my head pretty hard on the top of the car. I thought I was alright and just wanted to get home. I had a headache the next morning but went to work. My boss came into my office and saw me with papers spread all over my desk. He asked me what I was doing. He told me later, "When I asked what you were doing you said you were trying to make sense out of them." He knew I had been in a car accident the day before and insisted I get to the doctor immediately. It turns out I had, in my language, bruised my brain. The doctor informed me, "It's the kind of concussion where your memory and ability to retain anything have been damaged. You need to just sit and do as little as possible. Usually this resolves itself and may take five or six weeks. There's nothing else to do." I went home wondering what he really meant and hoping I was one of the "usually resolves itself" people.

I remember the slow and horrifying realization that I couldn't follow a paragraph in a book or retain what I had just seen on TV prior to the commercial. More importantly,

I realized my view of what makes me valuable was being quick-witted and smart enough to pursue the new career path I was on. What if I couldn't do my job, carry on a good conversation, or be quick to catch on to things? Would I still really be me? That led to thoughts of what makes me who I am and what is really important? Over the next few weeks, as there seemed to be no signs of improvement, cleverness, career, and being first mattered less and less on the scale of who I am. What was it for me, that I feared losing the most? By week five I knew whatever I would be facing, that's where I would start doing what I could. That part of life would be okay. All that really mattered was that I was loved by the people I care about. It was that simple. None of the attributes I thought were so important had much to do with that. By the end of week six one of my kids noted I looked like I was reading the whole front page of the newspaper, and I was. Rapidly the abilities I'd had prior to the accident returned and there was a sigh of relief and gratitude. It was a gift to learn the value of what is really important, to me at least. But I was happy to be able to pursue the life I hoped to have for me and my children.

I thought back on those values many years later when I faced the possibility of an extreme surgery, the one I've mentioned in some of my travel tales. The last actual trip I took was a domestic trip to visit close friends in Palm Springs. It was painful and humbling but I couldn't pass up one more opportunity to travel, just in case it would really be the last trip. What a difference and stark reminder of helplessness under the wrath of pain and disability. A friend drove me to the airport and I needed a wheelchair to get to the gate. It was a fairly short, nonstop flight and a dear friend was waiting for me. She also had a wheelchair for me and we were soon at her home. It was wonderful to see her and her husband, as well as the change in scenery. But the floors throughout their house were tile. The hard surface made every step an exercise in pain. The bed was too hard for my fragile body and pain pills at night barely offered some sleep. This was just a long weekend trip but there was no doubt I had come to the end of my ability to travel.

I was still working, but focusing more on how to hand over my projects and ensure things would run smoothly when I went out for surgery. I hoped that if I planned it all well and conveyed my optimism, I would still have my job when I was able to return. Aside from going to work, my world became smaller and smaller. Pain and exhaustion made going out with friends or even having conversations less and less appealing. As spring sunshine brought flowers and birds back to my yard, I spent more time sitting out there. This is when it occurred to me that just as I had explored so much of the world 'out there', there might be some exploring to do 'in here.' The 'in here' was that same place I had been when I was recovering from the brain bruising of my auto accident. I started reading more about inner landscapes that were connections to nature, the universe, god or a higher power and better understanding of who and what I am. It seemed as intriguing as travels to different countries had been. I had also taken some bad turns in my teens and eventually found my way back by finding a higher power that would help me solve my problems. All this opened me up to new ways of dealing with the frightening prospect of major and invasive surgeries that might leave me blind, partially paralyzed and perhaps not much brighter than a vegetable. Acceptance? How could that happen?

It came to me in the form of visualizations. I've often thought, "What if I'd buried myself in watching TV, eating everything in sight or in an isolation of despair and bitterness." Fortunately, sitting in the sunlight in my own backyard brought the best solution. One afternoon, just sitting without any particular thoughts I sort of traveled, in my mind, to this:

I am in a small wooden boat, sitting at the back on a wooden seat. My hands are in my lap because there is nothing else for me to do. The boat is on still water, surrounded by tall reeds. It is quiet. It is so quiet, I could hear a fly's wings if there was a fly. The air has no movement. The boatman at the front of the boat has his back to me and a tall pole in his hands. He slowly, deliberately presses the pole downward, moving us out into this vast body of water. I am calm, knowing that we are not going out to sea. Not today. The boat will land. It will not land exactly where we started from. It may be close or far away. It does not matter. When the boat lands, my friends will be there to greet me. I will get out of the boat and go on with my life, wherever that is.

A strong feeling of calm and acceptance swept through me. I still use this visualization when faced with difficult situations.

Over time, I've added meditation. I do best with a guided meditation since my brain wants to stay in high thinking gear. Being guided, even in breathing, makes the calming effect easier for me to attain. In addition to regular exercise I now do Tai Chi, which is good for overall body movement and again has the calming effect I seem to be in need of.

When I think about inner landscapes or inner travel, it is much like traveling away from my home. I go to be refreshed, for adventure, a new perspective, growth as a person, play, and to share these experiences with fellow travelers and my friends. So much of that is about connections. Connections with the places I see and feel, the people I meet and travel with, with myself as I am in contact with things that delight, amaze and startle me. The journey of traveling inward has all that. It has led to discovering a strong need to express myself, my feelings and ideas to others, as well as connecting with the greater presence in the universe.

I HAVE TALKED TO OTHER PEOPLE ABOUT HOW AND WHY they were motivated to seek the inward journey to find their greater self and that connection with powers greater than themselves. So now I am happy to step away from the writing and share the experiences of six guest authors who offer a variety of experiences that I think you will find interesting. Enjoy.

Inner Landscapes

Mandalas in Nature

by Bondi Nyary

My childhood home in Massachusetts was surrounded by woods. Nature is where I have always
felt grounded, connected to the universe, and to my
higher power. It is a safe place for me. I've pursued my love
of plants and art personally, academically, and professionally. When a friend mentioned she was going to a flower
market in order to create a mandala for a wedding, my
curiosity was roused.

I knew of mandalas but hadn't thought of them in terms
of flowers. I wanted to find out more about them. "Mandala"
means circle. They are spiritual, symbolic, and graphic
geometric symbols and are representative of the universe.

In making a mandala, everything I love comes together,
including my sense of design, my love of all things natural,
my love of nature and being in nature.

Occasionally I collect items ahead of time, but usually
I work with what I find on the day I create one. They have
consisted of leaves, ferns, stones, cones, flowers, seaweed,
and small branches. More often than not they are sym-
metrical, but my artist's eye takes liberties within any given
piece. As a painter, it is always a dilemma as to what to
do with finished works. To leave my mandalas in the wild
for others to come across or not, soon to be consumed by
weather, is a gift to me.

Being in nature and creating a mandala takes me back
to the sense of a large part of who I am. The child playing in

streams, catching polliwogs, and feeling the earth beneath her feet is alive and well. These expressions of loving nature, design and connectivity, give me a strong sense of knowing that I am exactly where I need to be.

The Inward Journey

by Rev. Clara Alexander

erhaps I have always been on a spiritual journey. From my childhood attending the Methodist Church in Arkansas where I loved singing the hymns and vacation bible school activities. Everyone was sure that "Jesus loves me, this I know." That church was full of my relatives and neighbors, which is another way of saying it was filled with love and goodwill. We moved to another state for my mother's health and there I learned about prejudice. In 6th grade I suggested we ask Joyce to play with us and was told, "We don't play with her because she's Mexican." I am grateful that my parents had taught me that we were as good as anybody and also no better than anyone else. I watched my parents and other relatives treat everyone with respect.

As an adult I moved to California where I had various interesting experiences. There were many opportunities to study theosophy, alternative healing modalities, auras, human potential, Edgar Cayce, and the dawning of the Age of Aquarius! I learned to channel healing energy for my friends. I have always had a strong intuition, being able to visualize something and then find it or walking into the room and sensing the energy when what was being said by the people in the room versus their energy not matching their words.

Fast forward to my phone ringing in Beaverton, Oregon. A friend was calling to ask for a reference so that she could apply to a New Thought ministry school. The more she said about the program the more interested I become even though being a minister was never on my list of things to be. After a talk with the founding minister I decided to apply because filling out their in-depth application would cause me to think about my life. I didn't care if I was accepted. At the time I was working full time, had a husband who wasn't working, and a daughter in middle school. The minister called to tell me I was accepted. What to do?

After attending the first meeting, I loved the curriculum and appreciated the value of learning to be able to articulate my beliefs, plus new healing modalities. With occasional financial help from friends and family, three years later I graduated. Four of us studied for another year to become ordained ministers. I never wanted the business of a church and have not started one. As a minister I have officiated weddings, funerals, baby blessings, house blessings, memorial services, and celebrations of life ceremonies. New Thought is love based and inclusive. It is an incredible experience to be with people at such momentous times in their lives. I've often said that I get paid to party as I become one of the family and get to share in their joy at wedding rehearsal dinners and receptions. Years later some of my wedding couples still send Christmas cards.

I find that I am a minister wherever I am, with the person in front of me. This was especially clear when I was working my corporate job on September 11, 2001. Co-workers came to me and asked to meet in prayer. It is an honor to be with people during times of stress and great joy. I get to be the calm presence reminding people to breathe, relax, and trust in their highest good.

My Yoga Journey

by Eva Hallbeck

My yoga journey started many years ago when my mother was taking yoga classes in Iceland. At that time I was a professional dancer and in very good shape, so when I took yoga classes with her I did not think about it too much. It was just another way of moving and it did not take my interest. The poses were very easy for me to do so there was nothing new or exciting. With time I retired from dancing and did not even think of yoga unless my mother told me about experiences for her yoga class. Her experience of calmness and wellbeing after class made me think a bit more about this yoga thing.

I have lived in the U.S. for many years and found plenty of classes that I could go to in my city. So off I went to classes, and every time I took class I felt really good in my body. Remember, I had retired from dance so I was not as active as I had been before. Now I started to understand what my mother was talking about-the wellbeing and calmness after class. I was really surprised about the calmness I felt after class; even though the asanas (poses) were very demanding I still felt calmness, strange to me. Now, I wanted this feeling all the time. And I wanted to know more about what this yoga was. I understood it wasn't just exercise, it was something more and that I needed to find out and understand. This was all new and came to me as a surprise.

My mother TOLD me, in a loving way, I needed to find a yoga teacher training program in my city. After a few months of searching I met with a director of a yoga program and I knew then, after talking to her, that this was something I had to do and this was the place. An interesting feeling, I had never felt so sure about something before. Interesting how one thing leads to another. It all started many years ago but I was not open to it. Apparently I was now. My yoga journey had started way before I even had a clue.

A new world opened up to me after the program started. We were reading about yoga, philosophy, meditation and how we can live yoga and not just do yoga. The yoga lifestyle was starting to take shape in my life and I really wasn't doing it on purpose. It just somehow sneaked into my life. A part of the yoga philosophy is the eight limbs of yoga. It's a guide to help us live more mindfully and be more in tune with our self. I like to picture these eight limbs as a tree with eight arms and each arm is important to support the body of the tree. The body of the tree is ME and the arms are there to nurture and feed ME. These are the eight limbs:

Yamas: social discipline

Niyamas: personal discipline

Asana: physical activity

Pranayama: breath work

Pratyahara: one pointed mind

Dharana: concentration

Dhyana: meditation

Samadhi: enlightenment

All these eight limbs are interconnected and when they work together, ME is feeling at ease, calm and mentally nurtured.

"I Surrender"

by *Rochelle F. Leisner*
Shamanic Practitioner, Reiki Master, Spiritual Seeker

I've always been a seeker. At the age of twelve I looked up to the sky with my arms reaching and pointing high above me and said out loud, "G-d, I'm not sure why you put me in this place." I never felt like I fit with my family and I certainly didn't have warm fuzzy feelings about myself on the inside. So, I began this search for something more, not knowing or understanding what the search or the more was. My thoughts continued, "Is there something greater than myself that can save me? Can G-d get me out of this pain? What does he want from me? What is my purpose and why did he put me here?"

I got sick a lot. I had a Bat Mitzvah, went to religious school and participated in a Jewish youth group. I drank and did some drugs. I remember being wheeled into a concerning operation. The combination of drugs, alcohol and little sleep put me in this situation. I reached my arms up, again, for the second time, on the gurney waiting for the doors to open to a room I had never been in before. I was twenty-three years old and it had been eleven years since I first petitioned who I believed to be G-d. I looked up to the ceiling and said, "I'll be better, please let me come out of this." I awoke to be told my heart had stopped on the table. I had reached out to G-d twice in my life and that was it.

A few years later it was time to join a twelve-step program. I started to search for a connection with a higher power. I had a relationship, but my yearning wasn't fulfilled. Then, my grandfather died and as I began to mourn him, I returned to the synagogue for Friday night services earnestly for a year. I started going to the beach to watch and hear the waves. In my grief I searched for an answer to my longing question. How do I get a stronger spiritual connection to my higher power? I began to find some peace in the prayers as I dissected every word, yet I still didn't wholly feel the experience I craved in my soul.

I married and had a child. I went through all the right religious motions using the correct prayer language and Jewish behavior as my child grew up. I had physical issues that created great challenges and as a result, I was unable to find the spiritual connection that I needed.

It was time to go to therapy to sort a few things out. I was fifty years old and it had been thirty-eight years since I had first reached up and questioned my relationship with G-d. I was still not fulfilled in my soul. The psychotherapist was also a shaman. I knew nothing about shamanism. I was intrigued yet totally wigged out.

First, the shaman journeys by entering an altered state. This is accomplished by listening to a specific rhythm of the drum beat which creates a deeply relaxed theta brainwave pattern. She then uses a rattle and her hands to extract energetic intrusions. A soul retrieval was performed to recover lost soul parts that leave due to trauma and are returned to the client to create wholeness. My shaman described my life to me, from in utero through my teenage years. She shared with me things about me and my childhood that gave me a new perspective on my upbringing. I had questioned my memories and my life's purpose up to this point.

I was completely sold on the power of shamanism and I began to journey to the healing spirits on my own. My purpose was becoming clearer and my spirituality was enhanced. I learned how to let go of my ego and journey with my spirit animals. My friends noticed the changes in me and started asking for healings. Soon I was receiving requests from others who heard about the powerful results of shamanism and soul retrieval. I became a shamanic practitioner.

During a whale watch in Maui I journeyed to the whales. My most beloved spirit and guide, my whale, came to me and told me her name. Since then, I have journeyed to her many times a week and she answers deep questions and has shown me how to change my behaviors. I have learned to honor, love and trust this spiritual soul.

Then came an introduction to an entire circle of healing spirits. I was shown how to interact in the spirit world with my dolphin, penguin, porcupine, deer, eagle, bear, seal, and elephant. My deer showed me a higher version of myself that brought peace to my inner being when I visited her. I bonded with my whale in the spirit world above and my mothering bear in the world below. There is also an eagle that flies with my heart and soars with my soul. Two birds fly above me as representations of my grandparents, who were so beloved to me, and live in the world with these spirits. An owl came when I needed wisdom. When I first met my snake, I was honestly repulsed. Once she showed and taught me how I could heal through her extractions, I fell in love with the healing benefits of shamanism. She took out the emotional and spiritual garbage I put in. She continued to heal my clients with ease and precision, happily and willingly extracting all the negativity with love and compassion. My snake is something I could never have imagined. My beautiful seal takes me on journeys to heal others. She leads me to their soul parts and brings healing in the spirit world that benefits the client in everyday reality.

I began to find that my inner longing was quelled. I felt and still do feel so spiritually connected to my whale that I cry in gratitude and love when we are together in journey. I found a peace and acceptance in her that I had only dreamt about and didn't know could exist. We swam together in the grace and beauty of the waves. I trusted her totally and completely like I never had before. I shared every piece of myself and she greeted me with grace, love, and acceptance in each experience. She showed me how to believe in the reflection I saw in the mirror, something I had longed for since childhood. I began to feel more whole and at peace with myself, my purpose and my higher power.

Then something devastating happened in my family. I was lost. I remember feeling that I was spiraling down. I couldn't journey. I was just emotionally surviving and greatly missing something. It was that complete inner longing in my soul for a power greater than myself. While I had found my higher power, the feeling in my soul was not quenched. I was thirsty for more and I wanted and needed it right then. Was this G-d, or an energy? Could I find it again in shamanic journey? I spoke to G-d, "Darn it Lord. I believe in you. I know you or a something is there. I really need to find more of you." I was eager for more inner peace. The pain in my heart was so unbearable. I really felt like the only choice left was to go to G-d. I needed and wanted relief. I couldn't get through this pain on my own. All my life led up to this moment. I finally surrendered to my higher power.

I went back to Friday night services often. I began to let myself feel the words in the prayers. I soaked them in as if being bathed by a blanket of spiritual light that was cleansing every cell of my being. I allowed the words to flow through me and become a part of me. I prayed and spoke to G-d as if every word was gold and I was but a humble servant in glorious receipt of that experience. I quietly felt each tear as it silently dripped down my cheek. At almost every service, the emotional experience spiraled around my soul. It entered my heart like a lightning bolt of grace that had taken a ride through my nervous system. I kept going back, and every week I felt more.

I began to say prayers more regularly and found they fed me. The Serenity Prayer, the Lord's Prayer, the Jewish prayers of Modeh Ani and the Shema... I said each prayer over and over, going from one to the next. I allowed and expected every word to fall from my lips to my heart, swirling through my nervous system cleaning each cell one by one. When I couldn't feel the words of a prayer, I began from the top saying them again.

Today I am grateful to utilize and incorporate all my hard earned spiritual work. I use shamanic tools to connect with my spirit guides in an intimate and personal way that brings great peace. The complete love and acceptance continue to generate tears of joy and serenity. The restorative value this work provides me and others is so valuable, and I believe, to the health of this planet. The ability to get answers and curative benefit through this ancient spiritual practice is a gift I am thankful for receiving.

I look forward to my time at Friday night services. I love being Jewish. The tradition allows me to be flexible in how I choose to practice. I take the prayers home with me, sometimes singing them in the shower or as I get ready for my day. I feel the presence of the words. The intention behind the love of G-d and reverence I have for this power, I feel. When it's difficult to feel while reciting prayers, I start again.

My favorite recipe for a day is to spend it on a sunny afternoon in front of the ocean. I pray and sing to G-d for hours looking for the presence of spirit in each up and down of the current as waves rush up and back. The visions of a fluffy lavender presence that is softly caressing my cheek appear. I believe in G-d. I see her. I feel her. She's in the wind and the waves. She's in the colors of the sky and beauty of the rainbow. Just look up. Maybe even reach your hands high above your head as if your life depends on it. I know mine did.

Sandra Chisholm's Connection
to The Inner Landscape

When I turned fifty-five, I realized I would be retiring in the next ten years and would need to begin forming some new peer groups. My life had been centered around my three children, work, and school. As a single parent I had little time to explore many outside interests.

About this time, a man from the Trinity Iconography Institute exhibited a number of icons at my church. Each icon is a traditional reconstruction of a holy image. They were beautiful and called to me. I signed up for ongoing classes to learn how to paint icons, and so far, for the past twenty years have been pursuing this art form. When working on a holy image, I find a deep feeling of serenity and calmness. I have been blessed by gifting them to others. The icons are anywhere from one inch to the size of a church wall or ceiling. A tattoo parlor once requested a sample of St Michael for a person in the military. Some icons are used on Christmas ornaments and others are dedicated at a baptism or marriage.

The other icon writers I met have become cherished friends. I will often make a post card sized copy off competed icons as gifts for friend. I am often surprised, when visiting some, to find these cards displayed. My painting teacher was one of the most unique, talented and amusing individuals I have ever known. She is ill and I miss her very much.

This year I met another teacher who is a thanatologist. She plays the harp for end of life care. I am at the age of seventy-seven now. I am playing a gothic style harp that stands almost five feet tall. I find the experience to be one offering serenity and calmness, but in a different way from painting icons. Painting icons is a solitary activity but playing the harp is an endeavor playing with and for others who are present. My teacher is again unique, talented and amusing. There are so many clichés about "the teacher appearing when the student is ready," and I don't know why I have stereotyped the teacher as a middle aged man in clerical garb or academic robes when my two most influential and favorite teachers have been jolly older women with paint brushes and harp strings.

Taking My Temperature

by Carol R. Palo

I'm interrupting this section of guest authors to share a perspective and practice of my own inner travel adventures. Part of the exploration of my inner landscape, just as in travels to Italy or India, is openness to new discoveries. Finding a good guide, observing the details of what I am seeing, feeling, and experiencing become avenues to the most fulfilling adventures. This best happens when I let go of resistance and become open to try the unfamiliar. For me, contemplation of meditation and prayer brought up resistance, until I realized the practical aspects and results could make giving them a try worthwhile.

I'd heard that meditation is listening and prayer is talking, implying the combination as conversations. Over a period of time, that becomes a relationship. I overcomplicated this scenario with concerns over what kind of relationship did this have to be and with who or what very specifically. What my experience now tells me is not to worry about the specifics, just bring the willingness.

I created a prayer or my side of a conversation. I prepared to send it out to whatever spoke to me... for anyone with the same concerns, the other side of this conversation could be with a religious God, nature, the universe, a personal spiritual concept of God, or ones innermost self. The important thing is to create a space of silence after speaking to get a response. That response can be actual words that come to you, a feeling, a thought, or a strong emotion. Sometimes there is nothing and that turns out to be a response too.

Below is the prayer or my side of the conversation I have been using for quite a few years. I vary it occasionally so it will stay fresh and keep me from just reciting the words from memory without conscious thought. Because it's simpler than saying, "My prayer or my side of the conversation" continually, I will refer to it as my prayer. Alongside of this prayer are explanations and examples of how I personalize the prayer. Please personalize it to meet your specific needs or goals, because this is just me offering something I have found helpful. I hope you will have an open mind and read it through whether you determine it would be helpful to you or not.

Dear God,

> (or to nature, to my inner core, to the universe, etc.)

Thank you for letting me be me here today,

> (I list things that I had nothing to do with attaining-they are luck or grace… such as being born in a country where women have so many rights, can vote, have at least some equality. Also to have been born in a country where we can speak our minds and have more freedoms than many others. I have more and you would use your own.)

Thank you for:

> (here I add items specific to me like sanity, the ability to be a good friend, to be optimistic by temperament. I often add things I'm working on to improve, like patience. Think of your own.)

Please help me to maintain, and grow in those areas

Thank you for the awareness of your presence
> (I list the ways I have awareness, like through nature, meditation, Tai Chi.)

And knowing from my own experience,

you always have my back and really all of me,

which is the best place to be.

Thank you for the quality of life I have today,

the quality people in it, and the more quality person

I have become yet am still growing into and that that's okay.
> (I think of the best of what is available to me today, some experiences, some specific people and my growth as a person of value on this planet)

Please help those who are suffering in any way to find relief and guidance through you.

I ask for your goodness and light to do its work for me and all those concerned.

I ask to be open and clear to catch your intuitive thought or intention for me,

and when I have it, to take the right action today.

Please help me to be a positive presence and bring my patience: on the road and with myself
> (I think about the day ahead, about people and situations for the day)

Please help me to not cut off people in conversation or on the road but if I do, help me to make amends and stop doing it.

Thanks for my family

Please, extra-large portions of your grace, your guidance, your blessings, your mercy, your joy, your safety, and good health-both physical and mental for my (list family members).

Please help us to be good to ourselves, each other, and close as a family.

Your grace and guidance for this very extended family too.
(all life on our planet)

Please help me to be a good _____
(listing my roles as mother, etc.)

Help me to be a good friend to them all including myself.

I ask for the strength to endure, to last, to be

the power to heal, and the wisdom to learn

How will I do that? Please help me to bring my honesty, open mindedness and willingness into the day.

Please help me to use the gifts and talents you've given me well

And be of service today
(ending with silence or amen or whatever you like).

As I go through this process, I pause, which is my listening. Sometimes I am filled with a deep feeling of joy or sadness or wonder. In the most practical way, sometimes, as I pause after asking for honesty, open mindedness and willingness, I feel a pushback against being honest, or a resentful attitude about willingness or fatigue at the idea of being open minded. There are days it is extremely difficult to even go through the prayer or conversation. Often I see my lack of patience at the very time I am asking for patience. It is not uncommon for my thoughts of almost anything else to keep intruding on the conversation. It then takes real self-discipline to simply go forward. These are all ways I can gauge how I am entering the day. Good to know if I am catching the grace and joys. Just as good to be aware when my thoughts are scattered, I am starting off with no patience, or need to look out for a lack of those characteristics that could trip me up. These are ways I take my mental and emotional temperature. It enables me to make those adjustments and catch myself as the day goes along. So as I go through this conversation, what emerges is a gauge of my temperament that day-Prickly? Fearful? Hopeful? Whatever becomes evident helps me get a sense of what I need to bring to that day for the best outcome.

Life Journeys

published in 2018 and available at Blurb.com

BY JERRY ANNAND

"I started writing poetry in the midst of depression as a way to externalize my painful feelings. As my mood lifted, I discovered writing poetry was a way of recording the spiritual journey that I had been on - the journey that has become my metaphor for life."

The sixth guest author has given me permission to share the following poems and introduction from his book. His haunting and lyrical poetry explores the internal paths and starts an exploration into the journey of aging. We start with his opening statement and move to three of his poems on the following pages.

In The Beginning

In the beginning was the
Great Creative Force.

It moved in currents swift and strong
that carved the passage of my course
and made the paths I moved along.

It entered in and animated me
On the moment of my birth,
kept me a living, moving being
and gave my life its worth.

It is a healing, cleansing flow
that brings refreshing rest.
it soothes my anxious feelings
and calms my fearful breast.

I lie upon its surface.
I feel its gentle push.
It moves me to my purpose
Without a sense of rush.

Carol R. Palo

Homeward Bound

God, when I am sitting rushed of mind
and know my face is deeply lined
with frowns that stress and worry add
or the heavy heart that's deeply sad.

Give me peace and restoration
lest I fall into frustration
and forget about my spiritual quest
to be in touch with a quiet rest.

Even in the midst of strife
or straining to direct my life
I would still desire the feeling
that my life's experiencing healing.

Not for me the proud hard head who
takes his beating but sees it through.
I would ride with life in accord
like a vessel safely guided toward
a harbor safe and sound

And a beacon – homeward bound.

The Journey Is My Home

My life has been a journey – one that I call home.
With time and space aplenty for the changes yet to come.
All the places that I've visited
have made me who I am.
Each was part and parcel
of becoming my own man.

All these places I have traveled to now form the walls
   of home.
And all the time that I have passed has made this life
   my own.
All my thoughts and my ideas,
the feeling that I've had,
are part of who I am and was,
when happy, scared or sad.

And all that I am thinking now and everything I've done
is part of who I was back then and who I have become.
They have brought me to this place
that I now call my home,
and let me know my life's not done;
there is so much to come.

For all my past heads up to now, and nothing's gone
   forever.
And all that I have been somehow blends my whole
   life together.

JERRY'S POEMS POINT OUT THAT TRAVELS OR JOURNEYS can be out there, in here and can also be journeys of time.

Moving into the next section, I wanted to share the movement through life in a number of ways. I've written my thoughts on societal and personal decades, and there will be a guest author sharing her perspective on aging and the reality of her fiftieth high school reunion. Finally, there is a unique survey completed by seventy-three people aged two to ninety-five, and a difficult journey that came later in life.

The Journey of Aging

Decades: Societal and Personal

Breaking time down and labeling segments of it is a popular way to deal with its movement. The labeling provides a minimal amount of stress or thought and, I think, it provides comfort in a sense of everything appearing to be in its place.

I'm not talking about the natural rhythm of noting day from night, or the changes in seasons. These all feed part of survival instincts needed for living on our planet. My reference point starts with large chunks of history such as "the Dark Ages," "The Renaissance" and branches out dependent on which group of people is assigning the designation. Is the viewpoint religious? Then "The Spanish Inquisition" or the "Reformation" comes to mind. Politically, as in "The Gilded Age of Laissez-Faire," or cultural via "Gothic or Impressionist periods?"

From a societal perspective, I'm focusing on the most recent one hundred years in The United States. That's the 1920's labeled "the roaring twenties and Prohibition era," the thirties known for "the Great Depression" the "united in war" forties, and the fifties which keep changing in description over time via honesty, nostalgia, repression and room for more contributing voices.

The most recent twenty years have been greatly impacted by technology. With the potential to see and hear what's happening beyond one's own neighborhood and acquaintances, we are brought to be both closer and yet further apart.

All this can't help but influence how we view our own personal decades of life. To be honest, I didn't think in terms of my decades until I turned thirty-five. I don't know why, but that year was more significant to me than turning thirty. Mid-thirties, I realized, was the point my expectation had been set for being settled in life and really knowing who I was; yet my life was all up in the air. I really started to feel the pull of time. I remember looking in the mirror, looking for wrinkles and signs of aging. I gave myself a pep talk about how silly it was to think that one day, one birthday would suddenly age me… and then, there it was right at my left temple… a gray hair. It was a getting serious about life, a half decade for me. I determined my forties would be about being a good mother and developing a career. It's true, what you focus on is what you see, and those things were the overriding theme of my forties.

As you can tell from this book, while career and other areas of my life were going on, the focus of my fifties was the promise, to myself, of a traveling adventure every year. My sixties, I'll label as the transformative decade. Dealing with a serious medical issue, the ensuing surgeries, and the slow slogging through to attain as good a version of life as possible, brought me losses and bonuses. This was the time of finding the inner travels, of my own resilience and the upset of best laid plans.

I hit my seventies calling it the "put up or shut up" decade. There was a movie I saw several years ago in which a young man didn't realize his whole life was really a filmed TV series. Friends, trying to help him accept reality, pointed out that the sky at the end of the ocean's horizon was really a wall. He argued and walked out into the water to prove his point. He wound up bumping his head against a wall painted blue with puffy clouds. This is how I view my seventies. When I was younger, it was easy to say, "I'll do that someday." And there was validity to saying this because there seemed to be plenty of time to accomplish almost anything. Now I feel the sense of finiteness. Not to say people don't or can't accomplish great things or enjoy life in their eighties and beyond, but I've seen so many people start their eighties in great shape only to be a shadow of that person by their nineties, or not around at all. So for me, it's been an interesting process of catching myself saying things like, "Oh I'll do that someday," and determining whether to do them now or let them go. I accepted a whole new short second career when I was seventy-one. It brought me fresh perspectives, new friends, new information about the world around me, and money for more travels. I wanted to share the experiences, ideas and people you are finding in this book and I have pushed myself to work on it regularly, vowing to have it published and available before I turn seventy-eight. It has taken time to come to terms with the lack of 'an infinite variety of pursuits out there at a broad horizon.' I'm accepting the discipline of making the most of choices, using the values of time, ability, and pleasure. Additionally, as a writer, I have things to say and a need to know others will have an opportunity to hear or read of those things. So, I also think of my seventies as the legacy decade. To me, that means sharing myself and whatever I have to offer that may be of assistance to another human being.

I don't know what my eighties or nineties will be noted for. I'm letting it be okay to focus on the richness of what can be balanced in each today of this decade.

The 50th High School Reunion

By Carol Brown Bintner

I have attended five of my high school reunions. During those reunions, the cliques that were so prevalent when attending school were still recognizable over the years. This year my classmates and I celebrated our fiftieth. Where does time go? Perhaps it was 'different' because we hadn't had a reunion since our twenty-fifth. Sadly, the twenty fifth didn't go well. Attendees complained about the food, the service, the music, and the place. Committee members were not pleased, after all of their efforts, so they announced later they weren't going to provide them anymore.

Fast forward to 2017: A group of Class of 1969 classmates decided we should have another reunion. They met regularly and worked diligently to create our fiftieth reunion. Flyers went out to what once was a very large graduation class. We all received the pertinent information and we were asked if we knew the whereabouts of twenty-six people who were off the map. My anxiety for the September 2019 event grew steadily.

The big weekend arrived and I was ready! It was a three events weekend. The first night was casual and about ninety classmates attended. I had moved out of state forty-four years prior to this reunion and that made me feel like a bit of an 'outsider'. It didn't take long for me to realize that I was looking at people who looked just like me. We had white or graying hair and few of us were as slender as we had been during our school days.

There were some people who were still fighting the aging contest (most of them were women) but the 'sea of white hair' definitely won that contest.

Once I started speaking to people (some of whom I had no recollection of), I realized we're all part of a big group who spent three important years together. My comfort zone rose dramatically. The evening went well. Gone were the 'cliques' that were at previous reunions. We were just one big group of Baby Boomers.

By the time the event was over, I was filled with fresh memories of good people. The aging process made us equal.

The second event was a tour of our high school. I joined a large group at the starting spot and immediately saw things and people that brought back a rush of high school memories. The school has been updated several times over the years. New buildings and larger parking lots are now part of the campus. I was most impressed by the services that are available to today's students. They go by the 'No Child Left Behind' approach to learning. Kids who need options can get them. The school's dropout rate is very low. The school is also quite proud of its security system to protect students and faculty. It was an impressive tour. Like its students, our high school has gotten better with age.

Saturday night was the BIG celebration. It was held at a lakeside country club. There were close to two hundred people in attendance. I saw a change in the crowd that night. We had grown 'closer' by the final event. People were relaxed and there were many smiling faces. Laughter was everywhere. I felt very lucky to have been able to make this special weekend. Age was no longer a factor. The Class of 1969 had bonded once again, only more so this time around.

There was only one subject that dredged up the reality of our futures: two poster boards of pictures of departed classmates. There were over fifty (and perhaps more we didn't know about). It's time to let go of the white hair, wrinkles and weight issues. 'Today' is the time to enjoy every moment of life.

Survey on Aging

Survey Introduction

The purpose of this survey is to show patterns or directions based on age, and how that may affect life changes. It was conducted, based on my curiosity about how peoples' view of life changes through the various stages of life and the effect of what I would call dimensional relationships with ourselves over time. Because I didn't want this to be a survey of simply graphs and charts, I decided to look at some definitions of 'survey' to broaden my view of this venture. My American Heritage Dictionary defines survey as a means of examining, looking over or scrutinizing in a comprehensive manner. It goes on to say surveying is the measurement of dimensional relationships on the earth's surface. I read an article recently that made me look at the possibility a survey can also to be a conversation done via a set of questions and the responses to it. These set the stage for determining what kind of survey to do and how to present it. I'll share the material with you, and a subjective scale for evaluating along with the trends I see. You, the readers, also have the opportunity to determine the changes and relationships.

The measurement of these relationships is provided via seven questions asked of seventy-three participants, ages two through ninety-five years of age. An additional question offers them the opportunity to add any other comments relating to age. For those age fifty into their sixties, there is an additional section. It enriches the information on, what I feel, turns out to be a pivotal time, mid-fifties to mid-sixties, for many people. It is explained with the data from that age group.

Here are the seven questions. If you like, complete them yourself and see how you compare to your age group.

1. What is your age?
2. What do you like best about being your age?
3. What don't you like about being your age?
4. What is your best memory from the past?
5. What are you looking forward to?
6. What are your fears of the future?
7. What do you like best about being you here today?
8. Any other comments on aging?

Breakdown of Participants by Age Groups

THE PRESCHOOLERS

You might wonder how the youngest participants were able to complete the surveys since they aren't able to read or write yet. I had the good fortune to know a preschool teacher who brought my predicament to her school. They allowed her to meet with a class of nine children aged two to four as a part of a learning section on aging during their snack time. She presented the questions directly, only clarifying if needed. The teacher wrote their answers to each question on a white board and compiled them using as an answer what the majority of children said for each of the questions. The teacher told me they didn't want to answer the first question, which is 'What is your age' unless she answered it first. She asked them to guess and got answers ranging from six to fifty-six. Strangely, when their guesses were added together and divided by nine, they were very close to her actual age.

1. Their ages averaged out to three years old
2. They best thing about being their age was making snakes and tigers. This made sense when considering it was likely based on the class's current project of being creative with playdough.

3. They didn't want to answer question three about what they didn't like about being their age. I am guessing it's because either they couldn't imagine being any other age right now or simply accepted and enjoy being who they are in the moment.

4. Question four asked what their best memory from the past was. I was told the answer was almost unanimous and it brought tears to my eyes. They said their best memories were playing in their playroom with mom and dad.

5. Looking forward to the future had them at home with friends coming over to play

6. Fears of the future held visions of bears and lions

7. Easy to guess what they like best about being themselves here today... play dough!

STUDENTS PRIOR TO HIGH SCHOOL

There were only three participants in this age group, so I summarized their responses.

- One seven year old responded with pleasure about growing taller, learning more, and viewing the future with hope, excitement and happiness.

- Two thirteen year olds responded with a mix of good news, bad news. Happy to have more responsibilities, but concerned about how much of that comes with approaching adulthood. The same situation came from looking toward high school and living on their own. Still, there was much optimism and appreciation for modern technology and the value of their friends and families.

HIGH SCHOOL STUDENTS

This group included two students from public high schools and ten students from a private high school. The private high school teacher also added a question. Question eight was 'what do you think will be your best decade?'

1. The ages ranged from fifteen to seventeen

2. What they liked about being their age-two trends emerged:
   - Gratitude for being old enough to be taken seriously and have more responsibility without the burden of paying bills and actual adulthood.
   - The joy of school, friends and learning

3. What they didn't like:
   - Too many restrictions set by parents and pressure to succeed from family, school and themselves

4. The best memory from the past brought out:
   - Family trips from camping to world travel
   - Time hanging out with friends
   - The addition of a family pet
   - Times of learning new technology
   - Anything that felt empowering

5. Looking forward to the future brought a consensus:
   - Big steps into independence
   - Finding more about their passions and interests
   - For many both excitement and trepidation about college, careers and starting their own families.

6. These students dug deeply and honestly into what, brought up fears in the future:

   - One student pragmatically declared they had no fear since fear is a product of not preparing appropriately.
   - Several responses voiced fears of a time they would have to deal with the death and loss of loved ones.
   - Some were not so concerned about death itself but of running out of time, not having enough to fit in all that they want to experience.
   - More immediately, they had fears about getting on the right career path, suddenly being without family support or trapped in a life that is meaningless to them.
   - There was fear of failure and the unknown.

7. Being me here today brought gratitude for feeling safe, having friends and family, for freedom of education, speech and self-expression.

8. Added comments:

   - This is the age where many people are trying to find themselves
   - It's hard to be seventeen because in many ways I am already autonomous but I still need permission to go out for coffee with friends

---

THE TEACHER'S EXTRA QUESTION ABOUT WHICH DECADE her students thought would be their best was answered by nine students.

   - Five students thought it would be their twenties because this would be when they could really dive into who they really are and what they want to do, which would lead to being successful.

- One student cited their thirties as a time when they will have life figured out and everything will be stable.

- Their fifties was one response because it would bring the combination of money, freedom while still having much of their physical abilities.

- The decade already complete at age ten was noted as the happiest and most carefree I will ever be.

- The final student couldn't decide citing they would love to say their twenties because of the learning and education but realistically it would probably be their sixties when they can retire and travel the world. (I hope this student will read my book and start traveling before their sixties.)

THE TWENTY THROUGH FORTY YEAR OLDS

This group all had good intentions about completing the surveys but clearly, that is the age group juggling early grownupness, school, ambitions versus realities, more intense dating marriage and children, travel, bumping into thirty and the awareness and strangeness of gaining some maturity and different kinds of realization. Then comes the zig zagging down the slushy slopes into the no-mans land of the forties with its accumulating and discarding, accompanied by side dishes of reckoning, reacting to the perspective of being in the middle of where they've been and where they are headed. This is a long way of saying I got very few responses from this age group. Seven people between twenty and forty responded. Here are highlights from each of them:

- A twenty-one year old was recognizing life's choices and how that is a double- edged sword. This age was considered an advantage for its options, while the stigma of still being treated like a child sometimes was a definite liability. There was optimism for discovery and thriving and fear only of death. They had a definite feeling of being young and active while also feeling older and wiser with each year.

- "All ages are valuable and have a purpose", was pointed out by the twenty-seven year old. The intervening years from twenty-one provided more reflecting and maturity with more looking back on their childhood with an eye to starting a family. The fear was not death, but being disappointed with their life. A pleasure was considered growing a little each day.

- Three mid-thirties people responded. All were deep into their careers, families in process and dealing with stress. They all agreed the best part of being their ages was more maturity, with a better sense of direction and having the best of both worlds. This was determined as appreciation for the knowledge and wisdom that had become more available, and professional success without the worries they saw as coming later. These worries they foresaw as a continuing thread of having to slow down and worry about saving money. Added to this were stress, aches and pains, and for one, already realizing they were not materially where they thought they would be by now. Some were already starting to deal with their own health issues or those of parents and children. Their best memories were of family and friends they had known in more carefree times. The best 'being me here today' responses were: being a mom; living in a beautiful country with a wonderful partner and great job; learning life skills that enable me to live happy, joyous and free regardless of whether life around me is a mess or not.

- Two people in their forties provided comments not so different from those in their thirties. But they had developed a deeper appreciation of being a parent and the sense of who they are and what they have to be grateful for, including having a creative mind, not needing acceptance from others so much to be happy, and knowledge or self and the world around them. One of them added "I can now relate to my father when he was raising me. Mentally, I still see myself as a kid, but I find that the older I get, the more I think about my dad and how he must have felt when he was my current age. This insight makes me feel closer to him somehow."

THE FIFTIES AND SIXTIES

Before moving on with the fifty and sixty year olds, I want to tell you about a survey I thought of several years before even thinking of writing this book. In 2003 I decided to write a book about people in their sixties or approaching their sixtieth birthday. I designed a questionnaire and thought I would ask sixty people, calling the book *Sixty by Sixty*. I had just started compiling surveys, when I read a well-known writer had come out with a book similar in content and with nearly the same title I had planned to use. I do sometimes think creative ideas are just floating in the cosmos waiting for someone to grab them. This seems to be the case in the *Sixty by Sixty* project with someone grabbing it first and bringing it to print. I gave up on the book but saved the surveys.

I found those surveys packed away and, although the questions are quite different, it will still be interesting to compare questions asked in 2003 with the survey completed sixteen years later. So, as a subset of the aging survey results for those ages, both surveys and their results will be included. The survey of 2003 involved a separate group of participants with the exception of one person who completed the earlier one then and was available to complete the current one too.

First we'll continue with our current survey of 2019 and its seven questions.

The fifties are an interesting space. The half century mark can be a big gulp. There is amazement to have somehow slipped into this decade that leads to senior discounts at restaurants while also being asked for ID because we don't look old enough sometimes. I remember going to a movie theater in my late fifties and saw the sign noting senior discounts. I asked the teenager behind the counter how old you have to be to get the discount.

She looked at me in the way only someone that age can, which is you're clearly over thirty so you're old, and replied, "Do you want to be a senior today?"

I said, "Sure", as she punched out the senior ticket and slid it over the counter to me.

Eight people in their fifties responded, with two in their early to mid-fifties and six their later fifties.

Those in their earlier fifties responded:

1. Ages fifty-four and fifty-five

2. What they liked about their age was their self-accep-
   tance, calmness, stability and the ability to travel

3. What both didn't like were the aches and pains and
   general awareness of the aging process.

4. Their best memories involved family vacations for one,
   and for the other, moving cross country for a fresh start.

5. The future looked welcoming to both of them, containing personal growth and new experiences.

6. Their fears involved potential illness for family or self and
   financial insecurity. In a broader view one talked about
   'powerful and evil political forces creating damage'.

7. What was best for each in being themselves, here
   today was their connections with people, the ability to
   be present in this moment, and one said "having my
   insides match my outsides."

THE PARTICIPANTS IN THE UPPER FIFTIES

1. Ages fifty-six through fifty-nine

2. They were pleasantly surprised to be in better physical
   shape than expected. There was appreciation for their
   independence and clarity in who they are and their
   work lives.

3. The unwelcome issues of their ages included some
   memory decline, feeling sixty breathing heavily down
   their neck with new aches and pains.

4. Their best past memories brought up the joys of the
   many roles they've been able to have, such as being an

actor, a doting father, the pleasure of throwing great parties and cycling in the annual Cycling Oregon. There was a childhood memory of a baseball game where he made a brilliant catch in the outfield.

5. Future tripping brought a list of things that are difficult to do when you work full-time: More family time, simply having fun, helping to make the world a kinder and gentler place, and traveling.

6. Fears ranged from none to our planet's livability, with a variety of health concerns, losses of people and things in between.

7. Being themselves on this day had comments on appreciation for the health they have, friends, the kindness and hope in the lives, and still enjoying and being able to play.

8. Most in this group answered the optional question for any comments:

   • "I want to create, do things I have not done."

   • "I am far more worried about illness than I am about age. I wonder if the bulk of our culture's concerns about age would be different if we cared for sick people with more compassion."

   • Age is irrelevant-it's how you live that matters."

   • I'd rather take my age now than the younger me. I'll take wisdom over speed."

   • One fifty nine year old mentioned the following— I like being fifty-nine and feel like I've been given a second change at living. It's a gift to see myself as a part of this universe. I like to remind myself to not get too caught up in society's ideals of physical appearances, that I'm okay just as I am. I enjoy thinking back on childhood Christmases with my family, especially my dad. These days I so enjoy watching the journey of my children and connections with other people. I don't want to be like some older people I know who just sit and do nothing except wait for time to pass. I no longer fear death. What I fear is wishing I was dead.

COMPARING THE SURVEYS OF 2003 AND 2019 ALONG WITH PARTICIPANTS IN THEIR SIXTIES

Earlier in the survey I mentioned a survey project in 2003. The following questions of that survey add an extra dimension to those in their late fifties and sixties since this age group is often considered the gateway to the later journey of aging. I don't know if the sixteen year difference in time and history will make a big difference in the thinking of people about themselves and their lives, but following the actual questions, I've added some information on what was going on in the world in 2003 that can be compared to the pre-pandemic life of 2019.

Here are the questions:

1. When I was _____, I thought of being sixty years old as_____.

2. The nicest thing I've discovered about being sixty is _____.

3. The hardest thing to come to terms with is_____ _____.

4. What makes me laugh the hardest is_____

  _____.

5. What would I say to some younger_____

  _____.

6. What would I say to someone older_____

  _____.

7. What I miss the most is_____

  _____.

8. What I look forward to the most is_____

  _____.

9. What's really important today is_____

  _____.

10.The one sentence that comes to mind as I reflect on
   being sixty is_____

  _____.

Again, you are invited to answer these questions too.

AN OVERVIEW OF 2003, INCLUDES GEORGE BUSH AS president of the U.S with Dick Cheney as VP. Sky marshals were introduced at U.S. airports and Homeland Security began operations. Saddam Hussein was removed from power. Four million people worldwide marched against the Iraq war and that was part of the largest protest in history, part of approximated ten to fifteen million people as part of a peace march against world conflicts. The space shuttle Columbia disintegrated, leaving all seven astronauts dead. A major outbreak of severe weather spawned more tornados than any other week in U.S. history with almost four hundred covering nineteen states. The U.S. Supreme court upheld affirmative action in university admissions and the Oakland Raiders were bested by Tampa in super bowl XXXVII.

In entertainment, Wheel of Fortune celebrated its 4000th episode since 1982, The Young and the restless soap opera celebrated its thirtieth anniversary, a new singer named Beyonce, a singer just going solo from the group she had been in, looked promising, and the Golden Globes honored Michael Jackson and the movie Cold Mountain. Some of the new television shows starting that year were The Chappelle Show, Anderson Cooper, NCIS, Arrested Development and Extreme Makeover-Home Edition. There were also losses to entertainment including Bob Hope, both Johnny Cash and June Carter Cash, and Katherine Hepburn.

The Boston Globe published an article dated December 23, 2003 with the following points of interest in politics, health and science.

- They noted the tragedy of the Columbia shuttle
- An outbreak of the SARS virus and the possibility of mandatory quarantines.
- Concerns were voiced regarding the Bush administration and the possibility they were playing politics with science by appointing pro industry experts or suppression of other experts, or changing reports on missile defense, and the environment.
- Good news for improving health endorsed both tea and red wine. Use of meditation was proven to work in the brain to reduce stress.
- Global warming reached a new level of seriousness.

- A confluence of biology and physics followed a single molecule through a living biological system; and drugs looked promising in stopping the necessary blood vessels in cancerous tumors from growing.

It's interesting, knowing I lived through 2003 as an adult, and to remember hearing about most of these events but only as punctuation to the rhythms of my everyday life. I don't recall at all, the most interesting item (to me today) in that Boston Globe points of interest: The Wilkinson Microwave Anisotropy Probe (WMAP). I didn't know what anisotropy was and looked it up. It is the property of being directionally dependent, as in a piece of wood that on the one hand splits easily along the grain but with more difficulty against the grain. It was in this manner the satellite made a map of the cosmic microwave background, a hum of radiation left over from the universe's earliest days. Scientists were able to calculate the most accurate age of the universe at 13.7 billion years. Calculations also confirmed a most embarrassing fact. Why most of the universe is missing from scientific discussion. Four percent is made up of ordinary matter. Twenty-three percent is dark matter. The rest, physicists have not detected... at least not prior to the end of 2003.

How to perceive news headlines from sixteen years ago with what is going on in 2019 is highly subjective. It seems to me not much has really changed except 2003 was the beginning of many trends that have mushroomed in present times. I am thinking of security, surveillance, the use of data, the long cycle of war in the Middle East and the chronic jostling between the isms like capitalism, cronyism, fiscal conservatism, liberalism, environmentalism. In the everydayness of our lives, progress is made in the sciences, new entertainment is made available to us as the lives of heroes and entertainers pass away. In 2019 the world is smaller in that we are much closer to each other in time, available space and communication, but not necessarily in caring ways. It seems to me today that times are much more stressful. But in 2003 I didn't know what 2019 would be like. That causes me to think 2019 feels more raw because I am looking back at 2003 when I didn't know the heightened weight of the world that I feel today. Perhaps, thinking of the people who completed the surveys, these things are reflected in their responses.

We will look at the questions that both surveys have in common and then move on to the specific questions of each survey. These will be the 2003 responders and the 2019 sixties group. You can look back a few pages to review the late fifties answers.

THE 2003 SURVEY HAD TEN RESPONDERS AND TEN QUES-tions. Before going further, this earlier survey had a unique responder. This person, from Germany, sent in not only a completed survey but a poem she had written in both German and English on aging. I was able to locate her recently and have her permission to share her poem with you now. I am considering her a guest author and so, share her name with you to give her credit.

"Autumn of Life" by Maren Zenk
The sun did not hide behind the clouds
For
Weeks
Clear summer days
But nights are rather cold

The beech ledge looses its green
Soon the leaves will be brown
Hard
Dry
Without life
The mountain-ash rises to the sky
Leafless
The berries are lost on the ground
But birds will carry the seeds to the four winds

Only the asters are radiant
As if they did not know
That everything is over
Soon there will be winter

THE 2019 SURVEY HAD EIGHT RESPONDERS IN THEIR SIXties, the seven questions plus the optional eighth for comments. Four questions in both surveys asked essentially the same questions.

The first question in common is, What do you like best about being your age or have happily discovered about your age?

- From 2003 came more contentment, waking up in the morning, no one asks them to help move furniture any more, giving and asking for advice, and being healthy and comfortable.
- The 2019 group noted feeling both active and confident, having more freedom and retirement, calmer and more appreciative of what and who they have in their lives.

What are the worst or hardest things about being your age or having to come to terms with?

- In 2003 the answers were loneliness, the loss of friends, the amount of maintenance required for daily health and living, wrinkles, less energy and worries about becoming dependent on others.

- From all but one of the 2019 responders came the process of growing older, more aches and pains, losing strength and flexibility. That one separate answer was, "I never had it so good, so I can accept my age and lifestyle at this time."

What do you look forward to in the future?

- Only one person from 2003 said they didn't want to retire but rather stay strong and keep working.

- The rest of both those from 2003 and 2019 listed travel, more time with family and friends, grandchildren or watching the next generation sprout up to take their leading role. They mentioned the luxury of time to just be, relax and try new things.

What do you like best or feel is most important about being your age or being you here today?

- 2003 had a focus on good health, theirs as well as family members', to stay in the present while learning from their own history. They were more comfortable with less stress, being a better and more helpful and giving person. There was traveling to appreciate the beauty of their country.

- 2019 included more confidence in themselves, and the idea of possibilities has become a positive. One person responded, "Having more choices, plus just being alive."

The rest of the survey questions are dissimilar for no particular reason beyond a focus on one age group versus a large variety of ages, and what seemed like good questions to me at the time that would promote the most insightful responses.

First, the remaining questions and responses from the 2003 group:

When I was_____, I thought sixty would be

_____?

- Two people didn't answer the question
- One thought as a ten year old being sixty meant you were a grandparent
- Another thought, as a teenager, sixty meant you would walk with a cane and had lots of pain.
- Six responders thought in their twenties that sixty was the end of time, impossible and could not imagine themselves at such a place probably devoid of fun and at the end of life.

What makes you laugh the hardest?

- Thinking about the absurdities of the human mind and condition

- Watching my grandchildren
- Idealism
- Conversations with my hearing-impaired spouse
- Usually laughing at myself

What would I say to someone younger than me?

- Carpe Diem, life can be a banquet; live, really live. Slow down and enjoy your life.
- Make good memories
- Set standards in life, be nice and always do the best you can. Strive for what is best for you and your family.
- Don't put off issues that may impact the rest of your life.

What would I say to someone older than me?

- Again, carpe diem
- Congratulations. I applaud you. It's not easy being older
- Asking to know what I'll need the most as I age further
- Tell me about your experiences. I'd rather listen than talk.

What do I miss the most?

- They all mentioned power, energy, loved ones no longer here, better health, young children running around the house, and knees that work without pain.

What is one sentence that comes to mind while reflecting on being sixty?

- Thank God I made it this far.
- It's not forty or fifty but it's not eighty!
- Life: what a trip.
- I think I'm not one of those old people and then I look in the mirror and guess what, I am.

There were two questions in the 2019 survey that were dissimilar from the earlier survey as well as the optional space for age related comments.

What is your best memory from the past?

- Giving birth to another human being
- "I remember at age seven or eight standing at the top of the green overlooking the valley, sky, earth, and trees. It was all so large, powerful, and beautiful. I was part of it and felt comfort from it."
- Family gatherings, so full of people and laughter. I am about three years old in Florida at Grandma's house. I'm outside in the driveway. I am playing in the 'moon rain' steam rising from the heat and sun shining. There are rainbows everywhere in the sparkling mist… so refreshing and fun."

What are your fears, if any, for the future?

- Many answers related to potential losses such as physical and mental health, loved ones, running out of money.
- One person responded they take it one day at a time. They felt society was scaring people on a daily basis and they were choosing to not tune in to that, pointing out, "If a bomb was dropped I wouldn't know what hit me anyhow. There's too much I can't control so I just try to make my life comfortable."

The optional question asks for any age related comments.

- Having the option to be young of heart and being as active as possible.
- It feels like the completion of a vast eternal cycle.
- There is no time to waste, so lighten up on yourself.
- Speaking the truth in a way too difficult to when young.

One person, in their early seventies, completed the 2019 survey and when we spoke, remembered they had also completed the earlier one in 2003. I found that survey and let them read it. It was a pleasant surprise to them to see their biggest fears had not materialized and their hope and optimism were still intact.

THE SEVENTIES, EIGHTIES AND NINETIES

To better highlight these age groups, one representative survey from each decade has been selected to read, in each case, close to its entirety. I think this gives a more detailed picture and shows the fullness of these individuals moving through their later years.

1. My age
   - 72

2. The things I like best about being my age
   - "They are a mixed bag. On the one hand I sometimes 'milk' being a little old lady so clerks, etc. will go out of their way to help me. On the other, I am easily offended when treated like a child or as if I was incompetent. This piggybacks onto another emotional conflict with aging. It seems to me at times younger people in our society prefer that seniors not be heard or seen, and believe we are just draining their resources and taking up room. I can fight that perception and sometimes I do. I can also use it to give myself permission to use the 'invisibility' cloak of age and dress for me and for no one else. I'm comfortable with my skills, knowledge and expertise I've accumulated throughout my professional career. That doesn't mean I don't like ongoing learning; it's just that now I give myself permission to learn whatever suits my fancy."

3. Things I don't like about being my age
   - "The aging process is a pain (pun intended). I miss some of the things my younger self got to do, like traveling and gardening which are not really options anymore. And I really don't like being ignored or discounted because of my age."

4. Best memories from my past

- "I have so many good memories that picking a best is hard. I love remembering my wedding day and how happy my husband and I were to be joining our lives together. I love remembering how we felt when we relocated across the country; everything was new and exciting again and the future was full of possibilities. And once there, starting our own business, watching it grow and flourish."

5. What I look forward to in the future

- "I look forward to continuing good health so I can be there for my husband and not a drain on him or anyone else. Also, what I pray for is a restoration of sanity in this country's voters and elected officials that I hope will help address the very serious issues that threaten future generations' abilities to live on a healthy, harmonious planet."

6. My fears for the future

- "I fear I'll develop some deteriorating illness (Alzheimer's runs in my father's family) that will make me lose myself and really be a drain on those who love me. I also fear that we've passed the tipping point on climate change. Just an aside, I have a perverse admiration for how the planet seems to fight back: all weather patterns are worsening, for instance. We seem to forget that we need the planet to survive; it doesn't need us."

7. About being me here today and additional thoughts

- "My general statement on aging is a 'brave new world' for sure. It never occurred to me that I would be old someday. One of my generation's mottos was 'never trust anyone over thirty' mostly because we never thought we'd live that long. I still find myself at times berating 'old people drivers' as though I'm not one of them! I pray for acceptance, gratitude and peace as the journey progresses."

THE FOLLOWING OCTOGENARIAN WRITES:

1. 82 years old
2. What do I like best about being my age?
    - "I like the lack of responsibility."
3. What do I like least?
    - "I don't like having no goals."
4. What is my best memory from the past?
    - "My best memory is motorcycling along the head-waters of the Missouri."
5. What am I looking forward to in the future?
    - "Having nothing to do"
6. What do I fear in the future?
    - "Not having anything to do is also my biggest fear."
7. With the extra comment: What do I like best about being me here today?
    - "I like having all of my acquaintances the best. Also, I miss my motorcycle."

I've included two surveys from the ninety year old group. First, one just turned ninety and then the other who is ninety-five.

1. 90
2. What I like best about being ninety is
   - "I like that I can still live independently. I still drive, am able to go shopping, do water aerobics, and can manage my own affairs."
3. What I like the least is
   - "I don't like more aches, pain, and sagging skin."
4. My best memory from the past is
   - "It is when my spouse and I retired. We sold our home and traveled full time in a motorhome for fifteen years. It was wonderful... lots of beautiful country to see and beautiful people to meet."
5. What I hope for the future is
   - "I hope to become a great-great-grandparent!"
6. What I fear in the future is
   - "I am afraid, looking ahead, at what current politics is doing to our country."
7. What I like best about being me here today and extra comments
   - "I am happy I have a nice place to live and lots of really good friends. But while I am doing well, things have been really bad for my family. Lots of health problems and deaths. Guess that's because of having lived this long."

From our oldest participant:

1. 95

2. What I like best about being my age

   - "I like my happy memories and experiences, meeting all nature of humans and creatures on earth. Life has been great, really!"

3. What I like least about my age

   - "What I don't like varies-infirmities and quirks that raise their ugly heads in my body. Also seeing friends, family members and world-wide great people leave the scene. I wish often I had done more for the downtrodden people and creatures!"

4. My best memory is

   - "It was attending a very liberal church college and found my first real love and super family."

5. My hopes for the future

   - "I am looking forward to some last experiences and contacts among family and friends, seeing grandchildren and great-grandchildren become great citizens of our country. I also enjoy my own children being superior parents and both enriching their lives and helping others."

6. My fears for the future

   - "I fear I haven't done enough to enrich all my living contacts in life to recognize the goodness in most humans."

7. What I like best about being me here today and extra comments

- I don't have to apologize for having lived and used this planet and its wonderful life and developed properly its resources. I consider our planet like a ship filled with resources which we use and also recycle. Many times I've felt 'cheated' in not being a persistent achiever, less inspired than I should have been. But then, when I am put to it in life's problems as presented above, I take an inventory and it isn't all that bad. Thank goodness for little favors in my life as well as giving little favors in return. That is gratifying."

SURVEY RESULTS

Hopefully, you enjoyed the variety of viewpoints and comparing your answers with the survey participants' responses. If you are interested in how such subjective material can be quantified, my very subjective criteria and rating system came up with some surprising results.

The criteria I used to interpret the responses involved two measurements: 1.positivity 2. clarity and insightfulness. Each of these was interpreted with a five point rating range with one for the least amount of criteria met to five for the best. First an overall reading of each of the nine age groups provided a sense of their ability to keep a positive balance in their responses along with the clarity and insightfulness to express where they stood in life's journey. One column of ratings held the positivity of each group and a second column just their ability to answer with clarity and insightfulness. The ratings of the two columns in each group were added together creating a list in order of the age group with the most points ending with the age group having the least points. I wonder if your assessment is similar to mine.

GROUP	POSITIVE	CLARITY & INSIGHTFULNESS	TOTAL
fifties	4	4	8
high school	4	3.7	7.7
sixies	3.65	4	7.65
twenty-forties	3.6	4	7.6
nineties	3.9	3.6	7.5
seven-thirteens	3.5	3.5	7
preschool	4.1	2.6	6.7
seventies	3	3.3	6.3
eighties	2.8	2.8	5.6

I see the chart results as a heads-up to fifty year olds to enjoy a second wind of great opportunities rather than bemoan fifty years gone by. To the seventy and eighty year olds, the challenge is to buck the trends and focus on enjoying all you can. For all of us, reflections and questionnaires can be enlightening but it is the action we put into each day that is our real gift to ourselves and others.

Bridge to Unwanted Journey

In 2003 my lovely mother turned ninety-six years old. She didn't want to take the survey in 2003 but was willing to give her reflections. I'm quoting as she spoke her stream of thoughts:

> I can't believe it! My head still works, still like to read and I have wonderful and exciting dreams at night. Looking back, in many ways I still feel sixty, which was a wonderful time. I could do what-everything. I still can, just can't do as much. On life's difficulties, well, as time goes on there is a distance you can live with; you are grown up and the little things don't matter so much anymore. Feelings are of your current age whether that is sixty, seventy or ninety-six. As you get older, you are more above what people say who don't know. It's like talking to one of the astronauts who walked on the moon. You know better, what they say and what you see is not the same as that experience. So at ninety six I am at a more isolated space. I can call that being alone, lonely or just having privacy-that attitude is up to me. The difference between ninety and sixty isn't just years. It is filled up with resentments and satisfactions. Help and good experiences early, help you to be more optimistic later. And expectations need adjustability.

My mom lived to be one hundred and two year olds, but as her journey of aging took the devastating twist it did, it became the kind of journey or traveling no one wants to take. At ninety-six, she still had times of peace, clarity and happiness that she could share. But it was clear, more and more often, that dementia was gaining a stronghold on her daily living and thoughts. My dad passed away when she was eighty. Looking back, it is easier to see how being on her own, after my dad passed away, allowed a slipping of conversational skills and activities that kept her life busy and full. Back then it seemed like a temporary reaction to her loss. I talked to her on the phone every evening and spent much of every Saturday with her to shop and visit. She had friends, a senior center with interesting activities she attended, and was generally in good spirits. Clearly she missed her husband. Without being maudlin, simply honest, she occasionally told me she would wake up in the morning somewhat disappointed she had woken up.

"What is the purpose of this?" she would ask herself or God. Then she would always decide since she had woken up she should make good use of the day, and did her best to do so.

It was a few years later, when she was about eighty-five, before I realized she was taking a turn away from common sense behavior. She forgot to eat and lost weight. An aide came twice a week to help her with medications and she sent one after another away, sure they were stealing from her. She lived across the street from a large mall and would walk over and then be unable to walk back. She started telling me about the nice people who would stop and offer her a ride home, which she always accepted. The senior center started calling me because my mom had forgotten to get on her bus to get home and needed a ride. I started leaving work early to pick her up, and stopped by in the evenings. She told me she was worried about getting Alzheimer's, because she had problems finding whatever she was looking for.

I told her, "If you forget where you left your keys and finally find them, that's not Alzheimer's. If you find your keys and don't know what to do with them, then you have a problem."

That gave her great peace of mind. I was not sure about what was going on but I began to doubt she would be safe living on her own before too long. I knew she wouldn't want to think about moving to a retirement community but I wanted to find some way to introduce her to that future possibility. In addition, she was living on just her Social Security. I could help some but not enough to cover the steep costs of most of those communities. I checked with local officials to determine if she qualified for their assistance. She did and they gave me a list of those places that would accept the government assistance programs. I checked a few of them out on my own and found one I thought she would like.

One afternoon I told my mom, "I've been thinking that even though you're doing well now, you are getting older and there is a possibility that you might have a stroke, heart attack or something else that makes it impossible for you to live on your own. I know you would count on me to make sure you would be comfortable and safe. But I don't know what you would really want. Would you come with me to look at a retirement community and let me know if it is what you would want someday or what is lacking?"

On that basis, she agreed and a few weeks later we toured a facility. She was impressed and told me that someday she could see herself living there or in a place like it. Before we left, I quietly put her name on the list. I had learned that without that, they might not have a room for her when she needed one. The worst that could happen would be her name came up, we wouldn't ready and it would go back to the bottom of the list. This all happened a few months before my first trip to China where I had the strange experience on the Yangtze River in which I came home knowing my mom was in trouble and I would need to take action. So it wasn't surprising to me when my mom misdiagnosed herself and took medication that brought her to the hospital. She then went to a rehabilitation facility. Her doctor and I both agreed she had passed the point of living alone anymore. I called the retirement center and someone had just moved out. The studio apartment hadn't even been made officially available yet. I explained the situation and they said she could have the room but they would need the completed paperwork and have her moved in within the week or they would be tasked to give the room to the name that actually came up just before my mom's name by officially posting it. It was clear I would need to get this apartment for my mom, with my sole purpose as doing whatever I could to speed up the normally three week process, and find help to get her packed up and moved in. The retirement center needed paperwork completed showing the government approval of payment and that in turn required information from her doctor, financial information that I would complete and, of course, my mom moved into in her new apartment. I completed my information and called the doctor's office. It seemed the forms would take a few days just getting from their business office to the doctors assistant, then as the doctor had time he would sign, and then mail back to me. I asked my boss, because I was working, for an extended lunch hour and as courteously as I could be, hand carried the form to the business office and waited for their portion, walked it the doctor's assistant and waited at the counter for her to take it in to the doctor, and finally took it with me and brought it the governmental office and the person directly working on her case. Two days later I picked up the completed form from them and hand carried it to the office of the retirement center. That left me a couple of days to find friends with room in their vehicles to help me move her things in. There wasn't room in this smaller residence for all her belongings and I let her know it was all still in her old apartment so I could bring her whatever we had forgotten. I was worried about how to tell my mom about this drastic change of events but apparently, this whole scenario had really scared her and she told me she was relieved I had taken this step. She was still frightened of the change and skeptical that it would work out for her. It was more a matter of "this is what it has come to, my life, what else can I do but go and try to accept it" she said, not with words but with her whole demeanor.

We moved her furniture and clothing on a Saturday and I moved her in the following day. Part of my respon-sibilities at work was designing space for office furniture. This was a most helpful skill in designing my mom's studio apartment to comfortably accommodate her bed and other furnishings that would make her feel at home. She slowly moved around the room to survey each piece of furniture, visualizing how she would watch television, how her bed was positioned, the size of the small refrigerator. She noted she would be able to walk into the shower and that would be easier. She was trying hard to make the best of this turn of events. I knew it would be a struggle to sit at tables with strangers for meals, and make new friends. She tried all the activities she was able to do, and looked for kindred spirits. This caused a notable spike in her social skills and awareness. I hoped this was a permanent change but had to accept it was actually a pause of wellbeing and enjoyment before the relentless progression of memory loss.

I could see it was important to her that she wouldn't be the only one at holidays or facility barbeques who had no family present. Since I'm an only child, it meant staying tuned to their calendar and making sure to be in attendance as much as possible. Her new normal became more comfortable as she found a routine that worked for her.

She fell and broke her hip in her early nineties. I knew she meant to live every day she had coming to her, and also didn't want to be kept alive artificially. She needed blood transfusions and her age, coupled with the hard effects of anesthesia, made the situation as to how to proceed difficult. Thank goodness that hospital had an ethicist available who helped guide me to determine that my mom would want to do all possible if there was a chance she would be back to her normal self. As it turned out, the surgery was successful but she was resistant to doing any physical therapy at the hospital, rehab facility, or back at her apartment. We all told her she might never walk again but she was sure she would be able to walk whenever she felt ready. Seven or eight months later she tried to walk repeatedly but her muscles had atrophied beyond a point of regaining their strength and she was in a wheelchair for the rest of her life.

It might sound awful, but the wheelchair probably saved her life later on. A few years later she tended to wander, and on one occasion, was found by some ladies out shopping at the foot of the hill the retirement center sat on. She had wheeled herself out the back door and must have taken a roller coaster type of ride down the hill before the shoppers spotted her and correctly assumed she must have come from the retirement center. They brought her back and she was neither unhappy nor pleased with her return.

But before that happened, her life fell into a somewhat pleasant rhythm. There were trips to the library and stores with the community bus, visits from me and some of her friends and acquaintances made at meal times, but with a slow spiral in her ability to perceive reality.

I recall one visit when she seemed upset and I asked her, "Is something bothering you?"

Her response was, "Yes, I don't know why my husband doesn't come visit me. Doesn't he miss me?"

I remember sucking in my breath, it caught me so by surprise. "He can't, Mom," I replied.

Her "Why not?" produced my, "Mom, he passed away many years ago".

I thought she might cry or be angry that I should say such a thing. Instead she was quiet for a moment and then, with a look of relief on her face said, "Thank you, I'd forgotten." We had that same conversation many times after that.

She forgot how to use the remote control for her TV. Sometimes she randomly pushed buttons, and got whatever and whenever was on when this happened. She seemed to have a bent for late night shows with conspiracy theories and all sorts of strange things. I could tell from the conversations we would have at my next visits. Her ability to separate out these shows, from her everyday life and her dreams created some lively conversations. I tried putting tape over some of the buttons so she could only use the on/off and a couple of safe stations but eventually we couldn't find the remote. Sometimes she would be aware of all this and express bewilderment as to how and why this was happening to her.

Because she had done a lot of office filing when she had been working, I explained to her, "Imagine that everyone, including you, gets a brand new file cabinet when they are born. It stands vertically and has several drawers. Each drawer has file folders all neat and crisp. The folders are for events that happen, ideas, and all the things that make up our time on papers to be filed in chronological order. Naturally, the first ten or twelve years show the drawers as orderly and make accessing any idea, or memory easy to reach. Imagine also, after many years, how full the folders become. Sometimes information winds up in the wrong folders because they are too full or not put back in order. Sometimes it is so hard to file that a paper or whole file gets slipped behind the drawer and winds up at the bottom of the cabinet or just gets caught somewhere. It is easy to see how difficult it is to go back and find anything that is in the cabinet. The cabinet is like our minds. At some point, as we get older, we have accumulated so much information, experience, and memories, it becomes extremely difficult to access them if even possible at all. Please be gentle with yourself. It's not your fault you have an overflowing file cabinet." I don't know how scientifically accurate my description was but it seemed to bring my mom comfort.

Earlier in this book, I mentioned an extreme surgery I went through. While arduous, it also brought tools for living that I still use today. By the time my surgery was imminent, I had recorded a video for my children to play for my mom. Her memory had deteriorated to a point where she had real trouble recalling the more current events or conversations in her life. In the video I reassured her all was well, I was just unable to see her this week, and I would be by soon. This was meant to provide relief to both my mom and my children so they wouldn't have to keep repeating an untrue story about what was going on with me.

My mom had gotten in the habit of taking my hand on my visits to her and saying, "You're my angel. I don't know what I would do without you."

How could any of us tell her I would be unable to visit for a very long time if at all.

My mom had the gift of being gracious and it created a sense that she was clearer than she actually was. If you had visited her, regardless of who you were, she would have greeted you with, "Thank you for stopping in. You look great. I like your bracelet, (or socks, or some item you were wearing). How have you been?" Then she would have listened to you, nod and smile and you would have left feeling you had a very personal get-together with this terrific and certainly clear person. In reality, she might have had no idea who you were or remember later that day you had even been there. On many of my visits she told me about a prior coworker who visited her and had found a part-time job for her, doing translation work. My mom spoke three languages and enjoyed getting out and having a little extra money. She never had that company's business card handy and assured me the staff at the retirement home always called her a cab. It was only many months later, when I was in conversation with the staff manager, we talked about her good fortune with a part-time job.

I thanked them for calling the cabs for her and they said "No, she told us you arranged the cabs." We just looked at each other. They tracked her more closely for the next few months and we realized there was no part time job except in her creative imagination.

It wasn't until after I was back on my feet from that surgery and able to be a more normal version of myself, almost a year later, the staff asked me to come in for a serious discussion. During that year she started barricading herself in her room, spit on other residents as though they were enemies and clearly was having times when she thought she was in an earlier part of her life. Sometimes in our conversations I got the impression she wasn't sure who I was and I occasionally heard her call the staff that assisted her "my angel" too. Then there was the first Thanksgiving after my surgery. My daughter picked her up and brought her to my house for the traditional dinner. At the table I saw her staring at a framed photo and I was pleased to tell her I had found this photo of her with my dad when they were younger. I asked if she liked it. "That's not me and I don't know who that man is" she proclaimed.

Later that evening, I got a call from one of her caregivers who raked me over the coals with "What a terrible daughter you are! What is going on with you? Your poor mom is crying because no one came to see her on Thanksgiving and she is so lonely!"

"What!?" I responded." She was just here three hours ago with my son, daughter, son-in-law, and granddaughter. We had a great time and delicious meal. Just look in her refrigerator and you'll see a plate full of Thanksgiving food for her to enjoy tonight or tomorrow."

I could tell from the pause, she was looking.

"Oh," was the reply. "I'm sorry for what I said."

She seemed so truly upset. We were both quiet on the

phone for a moment, I think, realizing how she had certainly and completely lost her afternoon. I think we hung up at the same time.

In that serious meeting it became clear the staff believed my mom had more needs than they could provide in assisted living. They insisted that she be evaluated at a mental facility and had already set up an appointment. They wanted me talk my mom into going voluntarily. She was already very paranoid and I thought the best would be tell her she needed to go for testing to keep her funding to stay where she was living and I would take her there. She would need to stay overnight. She thought about it for a few minutes, then said she would go and stay for the night if I promised her that, no matter what, I would pick her up and bring her back to her apartment. I didn't really know what would happen at the end of testing, but if I promised my mom I would bring her home, I would have to do it. I promised.

The day of testing came and I knew my mom was very concerned and trusted me completely, not because I am so intuitive, but because she reminded me of my promise several times along the way. It was strange to drop her off with her small suitcase and hesitant posture. It felt like dropping off a child for the first time ever at summer camp. I walked her in and got her settled in the sparse room assigned for her visit. I couldn't leave until a pleasant and reassuring woman came in and greeted my mom. She was there to show her around and let her know about what the next day and a half would be like. I felt less like I was abandoning her and with a hug, left.

The next day, around lunch time, I returned. Before I could see my mom, I had to talk to the doctor in charge of her testing.

He said, "Your mother is quite charming and seemed to get along with everyone here. That made it even more astounding to find how unable she was to do the most simple things. She could not tell me what a drawing of a clock was or what the hands on it did. She had no words to put for vegetables, fruits, parks, trees. Calendars, names, relationships with people or interest she might have drew perplexed looks from her."

I knew she had slipped a great deal but I was shocked. I asked, "Is it dementia or Alzheimer's?"

He replied, "It's so profound, it doesn't matter."

What could I say. I gathered my composure and told him I would get her and take her home.

"What?" he exclaimed. "No. We are preparing to check her in. She'll be staying here, of course."

Every nerve in my body went on high alert. "You will not check her in." I declared, getting to my feet. I could tell I had my 'mom face' on. The look that says nobody better mess with me and what I'm saying. "I promised my mom I would pick her up today and bring her home. That's what I'm going to do right now!"

The doctor softened and said, "You know she needs more care than what she has available where she is."

"Yes, but I need to fulfill my promise and then find a good memory care facility for her. I do want her to get the care she needs but I can't leave her here."

He nodded as I left his office to find my mom. She was in the room where I'd originally left her. She was sitting on the bed with her bag packed, waiting for me.

My, "Let's go," was met by her sigh of relief. I could tell she believed I was coming for her, but because life takes strange turns, her shoulders relaxing gave away her inner fear. On the way back to her apartment I asked her how the testing went.

She waved her hand dismissively and said, "Not much to it. I'm glad to be done and going home." She was tired and I helped her get settled before going to the business office to deliver their copy of the results and plan a search for memory care living.

I was given lists of foster homes for seniors and facilities for memory impaired adults. Some of it was out of date and not all of the listings accepted the government assistance that would be needed financially. I checked one foster home in the area. The house was nice. Her room would have a view of a stream and forest, and the woman running the place seemed pleasant but I saw her husband by the television and got immediate vibes that he was not happy with the strange assortments of guests living there. Not right for my mom. Other facilities I called or visited seemed cold or smelled bad or in some way would not work for my mom. But sometimes just a little bit of luck comes along, like the availability of her apartment when one was needed. It was like that when I called a memory facility about two miles from where I lived. When I asked if they had any openings, they wanted to hear about my mom. I told quite a bit about her and her current situation. They asked me to stop by and see the facility, telling me it sounded like they would be a good fit for her and were eager to meet her too.

I had such mixed feelings touring their facility. Their residents were truly suffering from various progressions of dementia. Some active and somewhat happy in appearance and some that didn't know where they were but knew it wasn't the home they used to know. Some were vegetative. I saw them getting very individualized care. There were no studio apartments, simply rooms with shared bathrooms. There was a lovely very secured garden area with benches and access for residents during daylight hours. The room that would be hers could still accommodate her bed, dresser and vanity plus a small chair. This facility had the same large day room area with a television for all, chairs at table in a dining area, and a circular floor plan like her current facility. It was both a relief and also a horror to realize the similarities were enough for her to move in with a sense that this was somewhat different but maybe not. By this time she was approaching her one hundredth birthday and the glimpses of the mother I had known were few.

This memory care facility accepted the government assisted payments. The staff seemed very engaged with the patients and the place was clean, smelled like a normal home and was secure. When they told me they had a nice room ready for my mom, I said yes and the paperwork began. They conspired with me, my daughter and her assisted living facility to bring my mom to her new home in the least stressful way possible. At any earlier point in her life this plan would have been deceitful, insulting and unfair. But now, we all agreed, if we could pull it off seamlessly, it would be the kindest thing to do.

My daughter picked my mom up on the designated morning right after breakfast. They visited at my daughter's house and eventually went for a nice long ride in the late spring sunshine. While this was going on, I frantically packed up everything she would be taking with her just as the movers I'd hired arrived. The furniture that would fit in her new space was delivered and placed in her new room. I unpacked and put away her belongings, hoping her new space had the same feel and key elements she still seemed to notice and appreciate. I think the truck had barely pulled out of the parking lot when my daughter showed up with my mom. My daughter kept my mom busy in conversation, and my mom was clearly tired from the busy morning. She wanted a nap. I greeted them in the day room of this new home and my mom looked confused. We held our breath. I walked with her to her room. She still looked confused. She waved us off and looked at the room closely, opening the closet, nodding with more comfort at her vanity and bench, pillow and art work. We walked with her as she slowly made the circle from her room through the dining area and back to the day area. You could tell she was thinking something is different about this. But she was unable to determine exactly what it was. She was ready for that nap and we sat with her until she fell asleep.

It was really hard for both my daughter and me to leave. When she woke up, would she be scared, upset, even notice the difference? Should I be there then, or bedtime, or the next morning? The staff advised me it would best to let her have at least two or three days to really acclimate and feel comfortable before starting visits. I took their word for it, worrying that stress about all this would affect her. There was good news. When I started visits again she wasn't sure who I was but knew I was an important person in her life and was happy to see me. She seemed pretty settled. This new location was close to my home, making it much easier to visit more often, which I did.

A few months later she celebrated her one hundredth birthday. A few longtime friends, staff from her assisted living community and our family attended her party. Other residents of the memory care were invited and staff that had been helping her joined us. We had a large cake. We all brought birthday cards and there was a card from the president of the United States with congratulations for turning one hundred. Everyone sang happy birthday to her. The staff had helped her put on a dress and she beamed. She was aware of all the admiring attention directed at her and she loved it. She nodded appreciatively at the President's card and singing. She managed a large piece of cake and accepted hugs. By the time the festivities were over she was clearly exhausted. It was easy to tell how the energy it took to be social was limited and she was blank and pale when we left.

In the year before leaving assisted living, her health had been failing and it was recommended to us that she should be on hospice. I was alarmed. I thought hospice meant someone was on the verge of dying. I learned this was often the case but sometimes the extra care was enough for the patient to add more time to their life. My mom was one of those who thrived on that extra level of nursing and started a pattern of getting well enough to be taken off hospice, only to lose the edge and need hospice again. But each time she needed hospice again, her level of fragility grew. The wonderful assistance of the hospice people continued for the rest of her life.

At one hundred and one, she needed to be fed and bathed. Every once in a while she would hum a little and play a little game with her hand with me she had done when I was a child. I think she saw me enough to know I played a role in her life. Her stomach bothered her and one day I was called because her doctor wanted her to come in for an exam which would include xrays and taking a diuretic to clean out her system. I called his office and talked to him. My mom hadn't left the facility for six months and was very fearful about leaving.

I explained to the doctor, "My mom has severe dementia, she is one hundred and one years old. She has severe arthritis and is bent over. It would be traumatic and painful for her to go through this procedure. If you found something wrong as a result of the tests, what would you do… a surgery?"

There was silence and when the doctor spoke he said, "No, she wouldn't survive a surgery and there wouldn't be much else we could do given her condition."

"So why," I asked, "would I take her in for this test?"

"Let's just not do this," he responded.

"Fine," was all I said and hung up. There was no way I would have put my mom through all that. It sent a shiver down my spine thinking of those people who have no one to look out for them like I was able to do.

A few weeks before her one hundred second birthday, I got a call from hospice. They felt the end was near. I was told I would receive a call from them when they thought I needed to be there and I assured them I had no plans to leave town. I would be available whatever the day or time. I called my daughter as well and she wanted to be there too. My son lived out of town and I let him know too. The call came mid-day, about ten days before her birthday. My daughter and I arrived at the same time, even though we had come from opposite directions. My mom lay in her bed, her breathing shallow and eyes closed. I left my daughter to sit with her while I finished signing a few papers.

When I came back, my teary eyed daughter said, "Mom, she opened her eyes and smiled at me. I know she knew who I was!"

She left the room as I sat down and at that moment my mom passed away. I had always thought she would go calmly with a smile on her face. But she had always been a very determined person and apparently was not ready to go that day. My last memory of her face was her look of shock, her lips mouthing, "Nooo!"

Her final moment haunted me for many years. Still, I was grateful her descent into the unraveling of dementia was over. It had been clearly difficult and frightening for her. The thing about that type of dementia is it takes the whole family along with the person afflicted. It was hard for my children to see her lose their names, who they were at all, and deal with the loss of her as the person they had grown up knowing. For me it was all of that as well as feelings of both grief and resentment. I needed to get counseling to deal with the grief of losing my mom, resentments for trying to keep my job while picking her up from doctor appointments, getting her prescriptions, being on call for every trip to the emergency room, or a care concern. There was resentment for all the random phone calls when she could still call and then grief for when they stopped. I've come to believe in quality rather than quantity of life.

Unwanted Journeys

Max and Rita

L iving in a big city, it's hard to imagine how two people could find each other and connect. Max was from a low income section on the city's eastern edge. Rita lived more prosperously on the west side. The city was Berlin, Germany. Max, his brother, sister and parents were poor, but avid readers with a family dream for Max to get a good education and help move the family into a better way of living. He was smart and open to a good challenge. Even tuberculosis couldn't keep him down for long. Rita, actually Margherita, was so named because it sounded Italian and Italy was one of her father's favorite places. Her family owned an antique store and they lived above it, as was common. She, her younger sister and parents were able to travel occasionally and had memorable times in trips to Italy and the seaside in summer. Max was the eldest, the adored son and big brother. He grew up with continuous family approval, optimism about the future, and a little too much interest in the horse races.

Rita's mother, Pauline, fell in love with a charming enigma her parents didn't approve of. Rita grew up on a roller coaster of trips and good fortune alternating with her father's deplorable behavior, mostly directed at her mother. Still, she grew up to be a vivacious and pretty young woman, and attended secretarial school. On completion of her education, she worked in a bank. Although she often thought of getting married, her father was never satisfied with any suitor. After turning twenty one, she grew impatient with his requirements and determined to meet someone on her own and make a decision with or without her father's approval. Eventually she met a charming man with visions of opening up a factory. He had designs drawn and a sense of purpose. He was fun to be with and had the most beautiful blue-grey eyes. This was Max. He was drawn to Rita's beauty, sense of adventure and uncommon "I won't take any BS" attitude. Before long he proposed. There was no fancy, formal wedding. First, neither was really religious and second, this was the decade of the 1930s.

Berlin was taking on a strange unsettling quality. Politically, elections had produced a government of blame and finger pointing. Life had been difficult for quite a while. On home turf, World War I took place and was soon followed by an economic worldwide depression. People were desperate, angry and it was easy to want to blame someone, any people would do. The government was happy to oblige and so groups of people became targeted. As the press and radio were taken over by the government, all one could hear was how the supposed creators and perpetuators of the problems needed to be removed so prosperous times could return. In this climate, Max and Rita got married in city hall. Neither family wanted the fact they had Jewish roots brought up in public.

Jews had become a targeted group. Fortunately, there were many organizations formed in other countries to assist in leaving Germany. Rita's sister, Margot, was able to contact a group helping young women. She married a Danish fisherman and moved to Denmark. These marriages were considered as a means to create a safe haven only. Many women moved on as planning allowed, while some stayed in Denmark.

It seemed each week brought new regulations and discriminatory laws that made being Jewish frightening. These new laws challenged many in the general non Jewish population in "how far below your former values will you go." Jewish citizens had to wear yellow stars of David (the stars with six points on them rather than the standard five) when they went out in public. The star now signified they were no longer considered citizens and were stripped of all rights. It was the law, and to be caught without it might involve being carted off by the police, perhaps not to be seen again. Checkpoints were set up in the cities and Jews had to check in and out. Margot had left for Denmark and the possibility of helping Max and Rita escape was in the works but to leave their families, their country, their home... it still felt so extreme.

One evening they were being checked by a guard on their way home from work. It was the same guard they saw every night. He never changed his expression, scanning the paperwork, but said quietly, "Don't go home tonight."

They passed through the checkpoint, barely breathing. They walked the streets all night. In the morning, they walked toward their apartment, only to discover all the Jewish tenants had been taken away during the night. Where they had been taken was unknown, but rumors abounded about trainloads of Jews being taken to prisons far away and what... beaten? Starved? Killed?

It wasn't long after, plans were made using Karl's fishing boat to haul them to at least temporary safety. Karl was the good natured Danish husband of Margot. By then, he realized she was not going to take the marriage as a temporary means to safety and was simply accepting he now had a wife and family responsibilities. Max and Rita were each allowed to bring two large suitcases, not too large for each of them to carry. But there was a larger burden to carry. They would be in hiding in Denmark while waiting for someone, somewhere to sponsor them to a country or find a country simply looking for any young hard-working people. They might be captured before that happened. It might be difficult to get two people allowed through the same documentations. This also meant accepting guilt and loss. Rita never forgot the look on her mother's face when she heard there was no way she could go along. Pauline had breast cancer and there were no doctors available to help treat her. She would die alone. Max's family, who so counted on him, would not be going along. And Rita often, in later years, looked at her daughter, almost seeing the older child that might have been born if there had been leeway for more than the two of them to leave.

They left at night and eventually arrived, tense and exhausted, at Karl and Margot's small farm. They moved into the loft in the barn. That winter they often woke with snow on their blanket as bitter cold swept through the drafty old barn. They had to be quiet and stay out of sight. Nazis were approaching Denmark and it wasn't easy to know who the Nazi sympathizers were. News still came through in Denmark as to where their possible new homes might be and how to apply for entry. They whispered in the evenings about possibilities. They considered El Salvador for a while. They had heard that country might be open to young hard-working people. They thought they might try farming. Yes, they were big city people and had never done such work before but the idea of being alive made most any endeavor sound appealing. Their best hope seemed to be the United States. A very distant relative of Max was located in New

York. The relative was open to sponsoring someone from the family in Germany. Sponsoring meant vouching for the immigrants. It meant saying they vouched for the immigrants' character and would help them get established. By the time approvals and all the details had been completed another snag appeared. By then, the Atlantic Ocean had been closed to all but wartime vessels. Max and Rita would somehow have to find their way to Japan, the allies of Germany. Once in Japan they would have to find their way to a specific ship which would carry them across the Pacific Ocean to Seattle, Washington instead of New York. They heard, just before embarking on the long trek to their ship, a Jewish couple in Seattle would be available to assist them on arrival. How to get to Japan and onto the ship safely?

It's not hard to imagine their quiet night conversations in the barn loft, sometimes centering on how in only a few years, their visions for the future had led to such a nightmare of options. Looking back from the early winter of 1940, Adolph Hitler had only been involved in politics since 1919 when he joined the army as an informer. By 1923 he was in jail and it was there that he wrote his book, *Mein Kampf* as a guideline to transform Germany into a dictatorship. Back then, Germany, the Weimer Republic, was a republic with a semi presidential system, including a parliament. Losses in World War I left an impoverished country and the following years of worldwide depression created a longing for any type of government that would return the economy to its previous standards. Hitle,r moving up in the government ranks, and his far right Nazi Party formed a coalition with another party creating the second largest political party in Germany. The party made promises of prosperity. Some didn't take him seriously. But as the old regime floundered, Hitler was listened to more and more and was empowered to ban the Communist Party and create some minor laws. This was unsettling news to many in February of 1933. Few people were prepared for the changes that came in the next five months. The enabling laws signed off on by the president allowed Hitler to be named dictator with full power to create new laws. Next came the Night of the Long Knives in which Hitler persuaded the president that army leaders were growing too powerful and were not loyal enough. Hitler was allowed to have over four hundred top army generals and leaders killed. In the election of March 5, 1933 the Nazis became the majority party and by mid-July, all other political parties had been banned. With the president's death, Hitler made himself president of Germany. 1934 found the military swearing an oath of unquestioning obedience to Hitler only, for the first time changing allegiance to one man instead of the country's constitution. Only one year later the Nuremberg laws were enacted, stripping Jews of citizenship and any rights. This law was later applied to Romanis and black people, and all three groups were called enemies of the state. The purpose of the law was touted to be only about protecting German blood and honor. The people of Germany were assured prosperity would soon return. This prosperity plan included expansion into other countries. In the autumn of 1939 Germany invaded Poland. Small wonder Max and Rita had to feel grateful to be in a leaking barn loft in Denmark. The unknown future in a new land couldn't be worse than the fate awaiting those unable to escape the steamroller of the Third Reich.

The timing to leave Denmark was a fortunate break. German forces seemed unstoppable and it was increasingly dangerous in Denmark and Norway as well as much of Europe. The idea of naming that government and its military forces the Third Reich came from a book by Arthur

Moeller Vandenbruck, a cultural historian in 1923, which called the Holy Roman Empire the First Reich and the German empire of 1871-1918 the Second Reich. Reich is German for realm and is not standardly used as part of historical terminology. It seems the author was inclined to a belief of superiority and inevitability of German domination. As Max and Rita prepared for their journey it must have felt like this Third Reich might be moving faster than even the train through Siberia.

The Trans Siberian Railway they would be traveling on was a system of railways connecting Moscow with the Far East and the section from Moscow to Vladivostok alone ran 5,772 miles and was the third longest railway in the world. By the time it arrived at the sea of Japan, it would pass through eight time zones. Little is known about the process of getting from the farm in Denmark to the ship in Japan. It is surmised all documentation and train tickets came from the organization connecting the refugees with sponsors.

Recollections, years later, from Rita, are as follows:

I could only bring a few small items that had family and childhood memories attached to them. These would be the touchstones to a life that no longer existed. I remember bringing some family photos and two small bronze figurines my mother gave me. There may have been some other things I'm not remembering now. The attentive bronze dog reminded me of our family dog and the petite girl was sitting as though she was leaning back, perhaps in a park, relaxing as though she had no worries or cares. The close up photo of my mother still creates an aching and I miss her. She was an angel. We had to remove some items we had brought from Germany for these irreplaceable items as well as for sausages, and a few other hard to find items that could be used for bribes as needed on our journey. I think we went to the train station on our own. It would have been risky for my sister or her husband to be seen with us in such a public place. We hoped we were blending in with the large assortment of travelers. The proof of this would be not getting arrested. We were given a paper with regulations for persons passing through the USSR with transit visas. It was written in Russian and English mostly reminding us to stay and do only what was on the transit visa and what would happen if we strayed from that format. The trip across Siberia was long and cold. Our itinerary showed we would be leaving Copenhagen April 8, 1941 and arriving in Japan May 3. I saved the itinerary and information about the journey for all these years. At first the time passed quickly with tension and fear in conjunction with the startling other worldly frozen terrain. That train ride lasted so long. In time, the landscape became monotonous and it was annoying to have to whisper all the time. We could speak only a few words of Danish and no Russian. We didn't want to draw attention to ourselves. Fortunately, the train conductors, who initially seemed inclined to view us with mistrust, became allies with no questions asked in exchanged for European sausages.

Rita remembered fear and alarm gripped both her and her husband as the scenery changed from endless snow to greenery and hills. Relief for an end to train travel was quickly replaced with the approaching train station in Japan. Would they be searched? Was their paperwork still valid? They could neither speak nor read Japanese. They had some general directions to find the harbor but were those directions still accurate and how would they find their specific ship?

Japan, in the 1920s and early 30s had been a democratic state with both parliament and constitution. Major cities had electricity, street cars and movie theatres. The country was progressive and there were voting rights. History professor Parks M. Coble, from the University of Nebraska-Lincoln, specializes in Eastern Asian history. He wrote in detail about the changes that occurred in Japan between 1937 and 1945. First, the world wide depression of the thirties caused poverty and the military increasingly obtained power with promises of expansion that would boost the economy and bring relief to all. The poor quality of living led to Japan as an authoritarian state. Press and radio came under government control with neighborhood surveillance of neighbor spying and reporting on neighbor. Most men were drafted into the military while women were encouraged to show their patriotism by sewing clothing and 'thousand stitch charms,' which soldiers wore for good luck. Western culture and westerners living in Japan during the later thirties were ostracized and even the slightest trace of western culture was treated with hostility. The United States turned down requests from the Japanese government for favors. Japan was invading eastern Asia. Germany was moving aggressively toward Russia. After the United States placed an embargo on Japan, it wasn't that difficult a decision for them to join forces with Germany and Italy.

It was into this maelstrom that Max and Rita's train arrived and left them to find their way. They had traveled through Denmark, Sweden, Finland and Russia. Now they were determined to get to the ship no matter how difficult. A room had been reserved for them at the Bund Hotel in Yokohama. They had already learned to be unassuming and quiet and polite. Along with their paperwork to gain entry onto the ship, were short and simple directions on how to get to the harbor from the hotel. But landmarks and quiet streets didn't seem to match the instructions. They took a chance, showing the directions to someone at the hotel. A nod of the head was followed by a small drawing of where to now turn down this street and that street instead. With suitcases in hand, they headed toward the harbor, hoping to look assured and purposeful. Eventually, the harbor and its ships came into view. It's hard to grasp the degree of relief they must have felt to hand their paperwork to the crew of the M.S. Hie Maru and be welcomed aboard.

The M.S. Hie Maru was a cruise ship and they had passage as just another couple of tourists or visitors returning home from the Far East.

Rita's eyes still sparkled years later when she described the voyage to the United States.

We didn't know how or where we would be housed on the ship, were only grateful to be headed to safety and a new home. It was an unimaginable gift to have a lovely stateroom, the freedom to wander through the ship and the option to attend all entertainment events. We were treated with courtesy and respect and the meals were all first class. A little booklet they gave us had information on activities and meal times. It listed all passengers by where they embarked and where they were landing and it was thrilling to see our names listed to arrive in Seattle, Washington. It was official and really happening. I could read English and speak a more British form of English I had learned in school and used at work, but Max hadn't learned to speak English yet. There was a section in the booklet to make notes or get information from fellow passengers. They were so nice and many of them wrote 'good luck' and some even left us their addresses. After living in fear so many nights in Berlin, sleeping in a leaky barn, and the long train ride, to have real beds and no fear of being arrested, well we could just breathe and relax. I saved a menu. On Friday May 9, 1941 we had a multicourse lunch with soup, fish, and choices in each of entrees, sweets, fruit and beverages. I remember thinking I couldn't remember when I had eaten so well. I still have a photo someone took of us as we arrived in Seattle. In the photo there are big smiles on our faces and our arms are raised up as in victory and welcoming to a new life.

Everyone was jubilant striding down the gangplank and eager to return to their homes and regular lives. Max and Rita were sobered with realizations they would be met by strangers who would help them navigate a new life. They hoped the photos sent of them had reached whoever that turned out to be. They had a copy of the affidavit of support, or sponsorship that allowed them to be here. A distant relative in New York had only, himself, arrived in 1938. He was a furrier with a wife and son. The reason given for the need to leave Germany was listed as "on account of political conditions." The paper implied the original intent that Max and Rita would be staying with him and his family. But, of course, they were in Seattle instead and no one seemed to be looking for them. Eventually someone appeared, apologizing profusely for the delay, speaking German.

Over the course of the next few years, they both learned American English, mostly by going to the movies, sometimes viewing the same ones often enough to recite the lines. A small group of friends emerged. They pulled out the design plans brought with them and started a small business. They bought a modest home, still in the city but next to an orchard in northeastern Seattle. They became naturalized citizens in November of 1946 and made the decision to join a Jewish temple. Information came to them about paths taken by Jews who had come to the U.S. About half of those escaping Nazi Germany determined they never wanted their future children to go through such a thing and changed religions. Half the people, like Max and Rita, determined that even though they had never been religious, they would undertake a reentry into their faith as a means of honoring those whose lives had been lost.

The toy factory they started soon had to hire people to make the large stuffed animals and aluminum jeeps, with a star on their hoods, just the right size for children to ride in. Patriotism and sentiment were high in the United States and these toys sold well. They had a daughter who spent her early years in the factory playing and testing the growing variety of stock. It would be lovely to say they fully realized the American dream of wealth and carefree living with antisemitism a thing of the past. What they got was an opportunity to stay alive, freedom to speak their minds, make mistakes, fail and get up and try something new.

They found antisemitism here too, but not to the horrifying degree they had experienced in their homeland.

Max would eventually say, "It was just that generation at that time. I wouldn't mind visiting Germany again, just to see the changes."

Rita vowed she would never go back and noted quite often, "If such things could happen in my home country, they could happen anywhere. Remember that you can't really trust anyone and there is no such thing as a safe place."

In spite of all they had been through, they determined to have lives well lived. Rita did office work, was a Girl Scout leader, and learned from the county extension service all kinds of things about gardening (although she set a fruit tree in their backyard on fire once trying to get rid of caterpillars). There were frequent trips to Vancouver BC in Canada and for Max, occasional visits to the horse races. As time passed, Max developed heart problems, passing away at the age of eighty-two. When Rita retired, she joined the local senior citizens center and assisted with welcoming people from other countries. She kept up her daily walks and worked hard to make every day as good a day as possible. Even while enduring a crippling disease, she fought to have as quality a life as possible right up until ten days before her 102 birthday when she ceased breathing.

Arriving in Seattle. Left to right: unknown traveler, Rita, Max

Patience

C alamitous illnesses, world war… a small quirk like lack of patience seems, at first glance, hardly worth including with them as part of one's unwanted journeys. But when my impatience literally brought me to my knees, it was because I finally started to understand the levels of unhealthiness underneath it and started to get a glimpse of the freedoms letting it go would allow me.

Since my late teens, I recall being more of an action-oriented person than someone who takes time and thought, waiting for the right moments. I was a quiet person, not because I was waiting my turn, but rather had discovered that being quiet and smiling pleasantly generally placed me in a position to not be scrutinized and therefore able to do as I pleased. When people would sit around talking about, "Wouldn't it be wild to do this?" or "We should try that," nobody got up to actually do any of those things. But I did. My motto was "why not?" I viewed my impatience to experience everything possible immediately as part of being an adventuress and so, the impatience a valued quality. I wanted my own way all the time and was willing to say and do whatever I would need to accomplish that. I had no time to wait on others. I moved through people's lives with little thought on my impact. Barely into my twenties, that path became a tangled mess. I was lucky to find a way which allowed me to grow emotionally and come to terms with living better, without the motion and escapism of always leaving and never facing myself or others.

I used a dictionary and literature a lot to look up meanings of words like happiness, success, solutions, and desirable traits... like the ability to really listen, to be a friend, to be honest, to be patient.

Over time, I improved in all these areas and gained clarity and ability to use the right words to describe what I was thinking and feeling. Still, I saw patience in the same light as lima beans... a vegetable that I disliked eating, but was good for me. It was a tool for getting what or where I wanted or needed. It became easier to live life comfortably and I could see a lot of progress in my ability to wait at traffic lights, in a grocery line, in a conversation that could have ended half an hour ago. So looking at my progress helped me see growth for my efforts, but also made it easy to not look at how far I still needed to go or the costs from this omission that were accruing.

There were days I waited patiently in the grocery lines, but just as many when, in frustration I simply left my groceries or found myself fuming to the point of barely being able to stand still. I heard lots of people groaning about the short-looking line only to find themselves behind that one person who brought a fist full of coupons, credit card that wasn't working, and arguments over the cost of an item. Lots of people found this frustrating, just like me. Likewise, there were days I was livid over slow drivers, particularly those puttering through the yellow light and being left to sit at the red. It all felt like I was being personally disrespected. Why should I have to put up with such things?! I recall raising my voice in a shop to the point where the owner physically escorted me out. It was really hard to not go right back in. He had quoted me a price for his services and yet at pick up time, the cost was higher. He just shooed me aside to wait on another customer. Was I going to put up with that? I had my rights. I'd also been in plenty of situations where men were listened to and women dismissed outright or interrupted. It wasn't easy to tell the difference when I was so often primed to take offense.

As a single mom, I assumed my children would feel safe if I spoke up often, making it clear as I moved through the world, one should claim their right to be treated with courtesy and respect. I found out later, I'd pushed way beyond that point and noticed my daughter flinching when I elbowed my way through a group of people to get the best camera shot or moved us from line to line to save a few of our valuable minutes.

I wasn't the public hazard this might sound like. Generally I was upbeat and pretty happy, getting along well with most people. It was only in looking back, trying to tell where my growth in gaining patience had slowed down to a crawl that some of these scenarios popped up as a slow but steady line leading to the automobile accident.

Mid December, one year, found me on a highway I had not traveled on before, on my way to an afternoon holiday party. I was running late and the driver ahead of me was driving quite slowly. Even though I knew no would mind if I was a little late, I wanted to be on time and could be, if the person in front of me would simply drive the speed limit. It was a two lane road and there was too much oncoming traffic to pass. I raised my speed a bit, getting close enough to that car that perhaps, I thought, the driver might notice and take the hint to drive faster. I was watching the car while looking at the directions on the seat next to me, and realizing there were side roads now accessible directly from the highway. The right hand turn

I needed to take, as indicated on my map, could actually be any of those streets. I also found, to my horror, there were stop signs on the highway and possibly traffic lights. As I looked forward, it was clear all the cars ahead of me had stopped suddenly including the car directly ahead of me. I was driving forty miles per hour. To my right was a ditch, to my left oncoming traffic. I hit my brakes knowing there was no way to avoid hitting the car in front of me and that's what happened. My airbag deployed with force and smoke, both scaring and injuring me. I smelled the smoke and thought the car might be on fire, so I climbed out of the car but found myself lying down in the road as it started to rain. I remembered lying there thinking, "How did I get into this mess, is the person I hit okay, and am I hurt bad?"

My car was totaled. The person I hit was not seriously injured. I was black and blue and swollen for a couple of weeks. I knew the accident was entirely my fault and a direct result of my willfulness and impatience. It was humbling and sobering. You would think that would have been enough for me to get serious about making whatever changes I needed so as not to find myself in such a situation again. And I certainly felt that way while recovering. But, turns out it wasn't that long before some minor changes felt like enough. It was five more years before the incident that dropped me to my knees.

That situation wasn't dramatic at all. I was at my granddaughter's middle school graduation. As students walked across the stage, relatives were waiting by the stairs to take photos. I was doing my best to be restrained, trying to get a good shot without pushing my way past anyone, but as I took a small step forward to get that best shot, I turned and saw my daughter's face.

The look on her face was sheer pain with me and exhaustion as she simply said, "Please don't do that." It hit me how she clearly had endured my impatient behavior over and over again in her growing up and into adulthood. It embarrassed her. It shook me hard. I knew in that moment this bad habit had become much more than that. It was becoming a real defect of character with an adrenaline rush as powerful as any addiction. Yet, on the way home, I almost convinced myself I was overreacting. I promised myself I would look up patience in the dictionary when I got home, sure that it would back me up as just being a bit too hard on myself.

My old American Heritage dictionary defines being patient in these three ways: Being patient is enduring trouble, hardship, annoyance, or delay without complaint or anger; Being patient is being tolerant and understanding; Being patient is having the capacity to bear delay and not be hasty. I had none of these.

I dropped to my knees and honestly admitted I needed help with my impatience and declared a willingness to do whatever I needed to do to get rid of it.

This began an interesting and illuminating journey that has walked me through hope for myself and compassion for others. I've been given the opportunity to be creative and learn the value and power of meditation. Once I was truly willing, with no stipulations, to be open to change, it occurred to me the best way to deal with such a big issue was one small bite at a time. I started with watching the car that slowly rolls through that yellow light leaving me to sit through an interminably long red. First, I asked myself how long I was really forced to wait. Repeatedly I timed the light and found I never had to wait more than two minutes.

Surely there was something I could do for two minutes. Sometimes I made a mental list of all the things I could be appreciative or grateful for that day. Sometimes I used the time to really look and see what was going on around me... the types of cars, people, trees, clouds... two minutes can move pretty quickly. Next I tackled grocery store lines. The easiest thing for me to do was shop at off hours when fewer people would be in line. One of the hardest acts of impatience for me to let go of was interrupting people in conversation. Even today, I find myself still doing so, just not as often. Eventually I was able to see my cutting off people before they were done with their share, as less a desire to share something pertinent before I forgot it, and more a simple matter of disrespect. I had to learn the difference between the give and take of conversation as opposed to situations where one person talks in a continuous stream leaving no possibility for responses. So it went with so many specific situations. Finally I realized using some of these situations to meditate might make my life easier and simpler. I had done some meditation in the past but it's really hard to meditate when you can't sit still and let your mind clear. Since I was open to change, I was willing to try attending a meditation center. This opened up a whole new way to connect to myself, the universe and to gain access to new concepts, concepts that were very liberating.

The heavy weight of negative emotions, anger, disdain, hyper-vigilance, has been mostly lifted, leaving space for peace, pleasure and better relationships. I've also gained the sense of continuing adventure. I know better than to assume impatience has been forever defeated. It is easy to become impatient on those days when I haven't had enough sleep and the upheavals of the world are riding on my shoulder. It feel like the impatience only needs the slightest opening to slide back in to color all my actions and short change me of peace of mind, my honesty and mess with healthy relationships.

My impatience led me to a gateway and the spacious journey of hope and compassion, and I am still in this adventure, knowing there is more to come. Today I see those difficult days as reminders to help me stay willing to grow in areas I would not of my own volition pursue, even though they are the areas that make me the person I can look at in the mirror and say, "I want to be her."

Pandemic of 2020

don't even remember which news source or the exact date in January, but it caught my eye with a statement that a virus was passed from an animal to a human at a live animal market in Wuhan, China. I'd been to Wuhan, most recently in 2014, and hoped all would be well for the citizens of this dynamic city. I thought of the SARS (Severe Acute Respiratory Syndrome) epidemic and knew there would be some ripple effect. Having traveled to India during the SARS outbreak, I avoided public transportation there and wore a silk scarf with a hepa filter in it. I encountered no problems and it seemed while many suffered, it was contained pretty well in a global sense.

Sitting here now, it's hard to know where we are in the world-encompassing cycle of this virus, currently called COVID-19. How ironic that I had just started writing the section of this book called unwanted travels. No one wants to have their livelihood, their ability to move outside their home, and their very existence challenged. We have all found ourselves held captive on a runaway train with no way off, headed on an unknown journey. We have no idea how long the ride will take, whether it is the end of the ride when the train stops, or merely a pause before we are forced to go even further. There is no guarantee as to who will eventually survive to arrive at the end of this ride and begin the hard work of gratitude and rebuilding our personal lives and our countries.

I am sharing my view and experiences of this unwanted journey as it progresses. I understand everyone's experience is their own and has equal relevance, but for the purposes of this book, I will share my version. My plan, mid-March, 2020, is to have this book completed and published by mid 2022. Wouldn't it be great if we are all looking at this experience in the past tense by then.

MARCH ENTRY

One of the first things I've noticed is how experiencing and managing my time has been changed by the speed of infection and impact. For the past few weeks I've felt so bombarded by information, disinformation, the need to change my everyday living drastically, plus grappling with how to regain the human connections and activities that are important to me. Emotionally and physically, is the added dimension of flight or fight brought on by fear of being ill, or dying, or what will happen to my family and friends. The spiral of all this, added to the concerns for city, state and country feels like they are all compacted into undoable sections of time with constantly changing demands. So the amount of what I'm normally asked to hear, process, think, feel and take action in the course of a week hits twice a day. I long for everything to slow down and am just now realizing my sense of emotional balance is not going to come from out there but requires me to find it as my personal path to create a new way of dealing with the world.

Today is the last day of March. Since I first started writing about the pandemic, I've found myself marveling at the heart people have in giving, sharing, helping, and the strength of active hope. I am intrigued by the ingenuity of people in how they stay connected, the way, in a big country like the United States, the communities within communities handle this with either large doses of fear, or by flaunting their perceived immunity, or by taking action to minimize the loss of people's lives. That new term in our vocabulary, flattening the curve, is a worldwide connective force.

Today, I am more comfortable in both my own skin and my community. I have a list taped to a kitchen cupboard with six essentials to try doing each day because I need some structure in my days to keep a sense of balance. My list contains some time in each day for meditation, at least thirty minutes of exercise, talking to at least two people each day, working on this book, some sort of work around the house, and some sort of self-care. Relying more on meditation has helped me to find a way to make my being hopeful an exercise in letting go of fear and making hope an action word. It has allowed my prayers for a reprieve from the Covid-19 onslaught to move from just myself, family and friends, to include all beings on the planet. I've become more creative in finding ways to exercise. I can't go to the gym or go on walks with friends, but I can view videos and rely on what I've learned to create my own routines from a patchwork of classes, gym work and physical therapy. The pleasure of walking with others is now replaced with a challenge to find interesting places to walk where few other people will be. Talking to people each day now has a broader scope. I live by myself and have to acknowledge this leaves an emotional space where family visits and hugs were available. Still, I am connecting with new conferencing groups to people I know in my family, my community and other parts of this country. I also count texting, phone calls, and chats with neighbors over the backyard fence, and across the street. Working on this book gives me a sense of purpose. The desire to complete it and share with you helps me keep the future as a goal of positivity. My version of self-care is pretty broad. It covers everything from getting dressed every day to taking a shower. Harder than I would have thought, well, if there is no one to know but me how clean I keep myself, it forces me to acknowledge my values and my own opinion of myself. I have become more linear and focused on things like noting the difference I feel in my wellbeing when I've had a good night sleep. I've learned taking a nap midday is fine on those nights sleep has been elusive. It's been strange to still feel there is no time to give myself a manicure, some beauty treatment for my skin or hair. I have plenty of time.

My most recent meditation session began with a focus on feeling safe and loved, but as I relaxed into those feelings they were covered over by a stronger deeper inner message calmly stating, "It's okay to breathe, it's okay to breathe" so I let myself submerge into the sensation that I was allowed to be okay, to breathe, to release the tension I didn't know was there.

It was a relief and surprising to me. Some grace became evident that I was worthy of breathing, even when others were struggling and dying unable to breathe. I felt somber with grief. It's okay for me to breathe. At least for today, I am breathing, safe in my home in suburbia and I think my family is safe too. It feels like such good fortune, a luxury and it's okay for me to be here with all this today and breathing. This morning has left me exhausted. I have soup, and sleep through the afternoon. I allow myself to relax, contact friends, do almost nothing for the rest of the day. Tomorrow I will take my grief for the world and its people turned upside down, and my awareness it's okay for me to be me here today breathing and doing what I can to make a positive difference.

But the thoughts and question remain: what can I do? There seem to be so many suggestions… again and again I run into the truth that I am in my mid-seventies with a slightly impaired immune system. I'm in that group that's supposed to be protected. I'm not supposed to go out to deliver supplies, clean store shelves, run errands for people. I'm on a fixed income and can't send much money right now to the many truly needy agencies and groups with their requests. I've not been sitting on a pile of masks, cleaning products or ventilators. My energy level doesn't even seem up to the many invitations to share in phone calls, conferencing, etc. I need to take some time to figure exactly what I can do. And then there is the rebellion. I want to go to the store. I want to pick up food to go and visit my friends.

APRIL ENTRY

All of my rebellion and ideas wound up on hold. The end of March also brought flowers in bloom and pollen producing allergies, which I held accountable for a scratchy sore throat. I woke up out of a deep sleep one night with intense pain in my bones and muscles. I had never had anything like that before. But within a couple of days that pain went away. It was quickly followed, in early April, by what felt like a quick case of the kind of flu that has you exhausted and wanting nothing but to sleep. It, too, left after a couple of days. My age and experiences made it easy to see this series of strange maladies as just the weirdness of the body as it adjusts to changes in the weather and who knows what else. But a week after this all started, I woke up one morning and couldn't catch my breath. After an hour of moving around, breathing was normal and I chalked it up to another strange physical happening. The next morning brought the same difficulty but took a little longer to return to normal. I was concerned. I hoped it, like the other symptoms, would be gone quickly. The third morning I again had trouble breathing. It was relentless and now I was scared. I tried deep breathing to stay calm but wasn't able to pull it off. I called my doctor's office. He was out and I spoke to another doctor at the clinic. I was already starting to wonder if there was some connection to the COVID-19 virus but felt I was just getting caught up in alarmist thinking. I answered all his questions about symptoms, when they started, details on the breathing issue.

He noted, "Sounds like your symptoms started about eight days ago, is that right?" When I replied that it was, he continued, "Around day eight is when breathing tends to become an issue with COVID-19. I think that's what you have."

It was one thing for my mind to play with the possibility, but a whole different thing to hear a doctor say it. I was feeling breathless and exhausted from talking but was able to continue the conversation. I think this is why he suggested we try to ease the breathing situation first with an inhaler. He sent a prescription to my pharmacy and told me I could use it every four hours.

His final comment was, "If you take it just before bed time and lie down without any relief in breathing, you need to go to the emergency room."

The virus... me? All too real for me to absorb.

I had to call my daughter to pick up the inhaler, since the doctor made a point of telling me I should be going nowhere. Catching her up brought it into reality. I hated to bother her but she picked it up for me with instructions since I'd never used an inhaler before. She knocked on my door and backed up. She had a mask on and so did I as I opened the door, picked up the bag and nodded at her. It felt awkward and I remember just shaking my head at how suddenly the world as I knew it had changed.

When my daughter got home she called her brother. As a school teacher in California, he was already teaching on-line and simply got in his car and ten hours later was here to assist. He stayed with friends, working from his sister's house during the day and visiting me in the afternoons. The weather was a sneak preview of summer so I sat on my front porch while he used a lawn chair perched at the far end of my front yard. Both he and my daughter took turns bringing me food I could heat up and it was helpful to all three of us to be sharing the situation together.

Over the next few days I experienced one day of strange sores that broke out on my arms, disappearing the next day, and one afternoon as I was standing by my dining room table, without pain or warning the floor and walls suddenly shifted upward leaving me in what felt like a slow motion fall. I was surprised to find myself lying on my back on the carpeted floor and simply lying there with great faith all surfaces would soon return to their proper locations. Within a few minutes, that happened. This was a one time occurrence. But every day I became more aware that I just wasn't myself. My thinking was fuzzy, I felt weak and dis-oriented. The doctor suggested I could go to a site where they were doing Covid-19 testing. But that brought up an ethical dilemma. I was not fit to drive myself across town and since it seemed most likely I had the virus, who did I know that would be deserving of probably catching it from me? Well, no one. Within a few days it became apparent the inhaler was not helping much any more. My son finally informed me it was time to go to the emergency room. I'd been watching too much television, seeing people being carted into emergency rooms, put on ventilators and never coming back out alive. I didn't want to go, but I also knew he was right. He convinced me the short drive could be done safely. I got in the back seat of his car with the window slightly open, wore a mask and a jacket with a hood so I could cover my face and my breathing as much as possible. My son wore a mask as well and we were on our way to whatever the visit would reveal.

My son wasn't allowed in the hospital. But I was greeted warmly, professionally, reassuringly. They only asked, "What are your symptoms, your name, address, and phone number. " I think it was the first time I've been someplace for medical assistance and not been asked for payment information. I was taken to a room within the emergency room and was asked to change into a hospital gown. Within minutes I was simultaneously given an EKG, had an incredibly long Q-tip shoved up my nose for the COVID-19 test, had blood taken to be tested, a finger in the oxygen level device, temperature checked, possibly an IV, my blood pressure taken and I was introduced to the doctor. There was a rap at the window to my room. The shade, that had been pulled shut, was now opened and there stood someone from the medical team with a machine.

The medical technician, who had been administering all the tests, told me, "We're going to take your chest x-ray through the window to avoid possible contamination, and I'm going to assist." He ended while holding up an x-ray plate which he immediately shoved down my back. I felt like a car being parked. The technician with the machine kept motioning a little to the right, now up, no now to the left as the plate was moved along my back. Finally there was

353

an okay sign. He opened the door to the room and told me to hold my breath, quickly followed by another okay sign. There was nothing left to do but wait.

I remembered the doctor telling me, "While we're waiting for the blood work, we'll also get an x-ray of your lungs," and me telling him about the time frame of my being ill, he had continued "We'll have the results of the Covid test within forty-eight hours and someone will let you know. I think you've had the COVID-19 virus but are far enough along the test will show negative. We will send you home unless the tests or x-ray show major issues. Please stay home and do as little as possible. I think you are having the rolling symptoms we are seeing in some patients. Your symptoms will keep coming back, just more lightly for a while. And you may not be contagious any more."

"When will the rolling symptoms stop?" I wanted to know.

He shrugged his shoulder and said, "We don't know... maybe quite a while. If your breathing gets worse, come back to the emergency room, otherwise just check with your regular doctor and be patient."

I thanked him and felt relieved. Now, as I focused less on me, I noticed how tired and worn down the doctor looked. His mask was frayed and he had on what looked like a yellow plastic bag over his scrubs for protection. It was very humbling. The lack of most basic supplies for the medical workers wasn't just happening in big cities far away but in my home town too.

Essentially, I lost the month of April and it wasn't until mid-May that I truly started to feel like myself again. I did have the rolling symptoms, but knowing what they were and knowing there would be an end to it made a huge difference in accepting the situation. I was also grateful to be retired, with no job to be concerned about, and the ability to make my house payment each month, all a better situation than many were going through, and are still suffering through.

JUNE ENTRY

Now, the beginning of June, the virus continues to work its way through the world. Worldwide there are over six million confirmed cases and nearly 370,000 deaths. In the United States the death toll is almost 104,000. I realize the confirmed cases are only those who have been tested and of those, found to have a positive reading. What about all the people who were asymptomatic, or simply stayed home until they felt better, or people like me who didn't get tested until later in the progression so there was a negative reading. The effect, physically, economically, and educationally of the virus and how each country deals with it, will continue and its scars will last for decades.

While we are dealing with COVID-19, another older virus, one of a more human made basis has been slowly simmering and breaks through. Racial hatred in my country is video recorded and the world is repulsed to see the deliberate killing of a man, done for no reason other than the ability to do so… again… again… again. The COVID-19 has taken its toll on patience and endurance. There is nothing of that left to swallow or allow this, again and so blatantly. Streets across the country and the world erupt in protests and in this country it is followed by violence.

I follow the news as peaceful protest marches occur in my town. The first night they are followed by mass destruction of much of the downtown area buildings. It is alarming but it was not until the morning of this writing that

I felt shattered. All the triggers from my family's history were set off. Here, in this country, we have allowed such inequality and hatred to flourish that now has to be time to reset… whatever that takes. It feels to me, that reaping what we have sown worldwide, but especially here is bringing us to the precipice of a viral pandemic, destruction of livability on this beautiful planet, perhaps destruction of the entire planet and, from the inside out, an ugliness of fear and hatred that threatens to destroy us. Isn't there some way we can simply be respectful of one another? I remember writing about this in the fun adventure section of this book. "All people are entitled and have an inner need to be valued and respected."

What set this all off was a phone call from a friend who lives in an apartment in the core of the city's downtown. I was glad she had called. I was wondering if the protests and rioting had affected her. She needed to talk… to hear herself talk through options, someone to listen and let her know if they thought her thinking process was sound. She was traumatized. She lived in a building with many seniors and people with disabilities. The fear and reminders of other times had many of them with packed bags and the inner instinct to somehow flee to safety. But there really was no one to come get them and no safe place to go. The morning after the first march and riots she walked through the downtown area to see for herself how much damage was done.

Her words were, "I've never seen so many buildings so damaged, so marked with ugly graffiti. The press wasn't going for drama and ratings. The actuality was much worse than what I saw on the news."

She had heard from her family members in the area and across the country. They were concerned. She hadn't told them about the helicopters with megaphones during the night or the water hoses. Tear gas was being used and there was a concern it might somehow get into the building. What if the looters broke down the doors and entered, or set a fire like they had done elsewhere? The later it got, the more the crowd turned into the thugs and the white supremacists with baseball bats she had been seeing off and on in the city. She recognized some of them. This was definitely not the crowd seen earlier with signs for justice. How long would this last, would it get worse? Should she make arrangements to leave? What about her cat? She decided to stay where she was, for now. No decision needed to be made as a final decision. I told her I would pick her up any time to get away. I told her she could stay with me for a while if she wanted to. I think she just needed assurance there were options. Just needed to accept the plans for her future, so carefully and reasonable laid out might need to be flexible... a good reminder that plans are not outcomes. This is the world we are in and there are no guarantees or long-term road maps out of here. We are in our own wilderness and will have to find or create the path.

AUGUST ENTRY

The last full week in August is usually a big gulp and protest from children, upon realizing in a week or so they'll be back in the classrooms. Not this year. School in my area will start mid-September and be on- line for at least the first nine weeks. School shopping does not need to involve new shoes, jackets or lunch pails. Many businesses declare employees will be working from home through at least year end. Some businesses have been incredibly creative and are still operational. Just as many businesses simply cannot survive in the crush of COVID-19 prevention and the prevalent stress in our communities.

My health is finally almost normal. Strangely, my breathing stamina has not completely returned and I cannot do a full yawn. I never realized a yawn has two parts to it. The first part is the body asking for more breath via the start of a yawn. The second part is that final deep breath that tells you the yawn has been completed. I can't do the second part. After a little experimentation, I realized my body only needs the first part. While it feels uncomfortable, the second part is not mandatory. This is just another reminder of how much we can take for granted in the course of everyday living.

The downtown streets continue to have evenings and nights filled with protestors. Federal troops appeared in July and remain. Their presence and activities created a firestorm of civil outrage as moms and dads, reporters, and peaceful protesters were attacked with tear gas and rubber bullets. There are looters and people who insist on acts of violence and vandalism. It seems strange that the array of trained enforcers seem unable to separate those few doing damage from the many who are peaceful. My friend, who lives downtown, tells me they have gotten used to the noise and tend to sleep through it. Her routine has changed and she only goes out in the mornings, a time she can still claim the city as her home base.

There has been a loosening of the quarantine in my area. Social distancing plus masks is creating opportunities for more socialization. My family and I felt giddy and celebratory the first time we got together for lunch at a restaurant. With summer weather, it has been easier to host a few friends to visit in the back yards or public parks. It feels like a necessity, not the current luxury it is. The malaise of not having life as we knew it, coupled with a major election year and its divisiveness, plus no way to divine what the future holds for longer than the day itself, has even the most upbeat of my friends struggling. There are still risks but the need for deeper connection with others is hard to deny.

To have a balanced day increasingly involves a more intentional mix of doing productive activities, taking good care of myself, tending relationships with others and some positive time for reflection, at least for me. I think of this in terms of pie. Partially because I'm a big fan of pies… fruits, creams, even those that slide savory, like quiches. I visualize everyone receiving a pie made of energy and time each morning. It doesn't have to be earned or merited, or gifted. Everyone gets a new one each day, no exceptions. All the pies are the same size for everyone every day. Everyone gets only one pie each day. At some point most of us realize there are days the pie doesn't last all day and it's in our best interest to figure out why that is. I've learned when I am physically ill, or mired-down with heavy emotions, the energy is sucked up very quickly. Apparently, healing and feeling require massive amounts of energy and seem to skim it off the front end of available time. I was used to thinking of energy in a more physical sense and now needed to also allow emotional space if I hoped to still have enough energy to thrive in the later parts of my day. These days, a larger piece of the pie is allotted to fill with things like finding gratefulness as a scavenger hunt each day, time to sit in my backyard just being with the plants, birds and occasional squirrel. I make a point of interacting with people I come across whether at the grocery store, on a walk, or a Zoom activity. I'm still grateful for a book to be working on as a sign I can recognize, of productivity.

We recently went to the beach for a few days. Perched in a condo with a deck, huge windows and breathtaking views of the ocean, we had gone with no plans. We accomplished nothing, said little, laughed more than usual. We took turns with random walks on the beach and eating at odd hours. The entertainment center was never turned on as the sound of the ocean filled us up. I came back with a shift toward more calmness. The world hadn't righted itself and many of life's difficulties continue their roller coaster ride through my gut, but the sound and feel of the ocean still remains with me and I strive to provide the energy to keep it contained in my psyche.

SEPTEMBER ENTRY

I hadn't planned to write again until October or November but here I am, hunched over my computer with a fan running to move the smell and tiny particles of smoke away from me. Without the fan, I have a headache, runny nose, scratchy throat and cough. My lungs are working hard. Ten days ago the Labor Day weekend was coming to an end with blue skies, light breezes and sunshine. Attention was moving toward upcoming school starts, and whether to start taking down the backyards' summer trappings of lawn chairs and plants going to seed. The main undercurrent of restlessness came from the continued but necessary restrictions on social distancing and what appears to be a long-term need for wearing masks. I noted my concerns about what would happen to the protests as we moved to cooler and wetter weather, what had actually been accomplished, what comes next.

Ten days ago, in the afternoon, I noticed a sudden shift in the wind and humidity. We, who normally have comfortable amounts of humidity, were starting to experience a rapid drop to the single digits along with the kind of Santa Ana winds associated with California. Weather forecasters sent out alarms of a most unusual wind storm of hot air and we scrambled to move items indoors, shelter plants and wait for this to pass. But the wind continued. Watching many of my plants turn as brown as if they had just been flash dried, I briefly wondered what effect this might have on the lush landscapes that contribute to Oregon's beauty. The next morning started with frantic notices filling the air waves with news of vegetation, trees, crops ready for harvest all drying out like tinder and warnings to not do anything that might spark a fire. In fact, some fires were being reported. It was the strangest thing. From my neighborhood I could look north and see nothing but blue skies. But looking west and south, the skies were ominous shades of grey. Any other time this would have meant a rain storm was about to occur, but the winds were hot and there was no moisture to produce rain clouds. I got a prescription filled and bought extra groceries. I didn't know what was happening but it felt unfamiliar and scary. It wasn't long before the blue skies turned gray and bright orange, in the middle of the day. The orange was fire, the grey was smoke. Day and night became differentiated by lighter or darker shades of orange and gray.

The unthinkable: all over the local news, parts of Oregon that had never been at high risk of fire were burning. The forests, always at risk, were burning. The state divided into zones of evacuation notices, with green, "begin to pay attention and locate your important papers and mementos," then yellow, "get everything you might want to take ready to go," and finally, a red for "go now." The ever changing winds blew fire in every direction. Fire and smoke occupied the south quadrant of the state while winds blew fire northward, eastward, even west making the coastline barely visible and rolling smoke far out into the Pacific Ocean.

My blinds and curtains have been closed for over a week. Towels have been shoved into every window, door or crevice to prevent the campfire smell and particles from entering my home. Both the skies and the news tell me fire approaches my neighborhood most closely from the south, east and southwest. It doesn't seem any of them is closer than twenty miles away, but that isn't much if the winds pick up. "It's okay," I remind myself." I still have a home to complain in. There are people who live on the streets and never have a home. I am not among those who are barely escaping with what they can fit into their car, hopefully their family pet too. There are also people who can't just hunker down waiting for respite. Their jobs are deemed essential and demand they show up, making their way to work or working in the thick layers of smoke and disarray. I sit here and count on the linesmen, fire fighters and police to be brave and focused on saving lives and all that stands between the fires and me."

Tantalizing stories come from weather forecasters of rain clouds forming off the coast. Rain is coming. We have no idea how much, but any would have us more than excited. This is so strange for us, who generally are forced to embrace infinite varieties of rain and our favorite color, gray. Rain is headed to the coast and will work its way inland for sure. Maybe tomorrow, or the next day, or the day after that.

I sit here this afternoon, thirteen days since first noticing the shift in wind and humidity, blinds open after rain has scoured most of the smoke from my area. I felt like calling everyone I know to tell them I actually saw a patch of blue skies with white clouds out my window an hour ago. My daughter calls and we decide to go out to dinner to celebrate the blue skies. With all that has been happening, we have not gone out together for a really nice dinner or spent an evening downtown in at least seven months. It was a quiet Saturday evening. We thanked the restaurant wait staff for their good service and didn't care that the menu was limited. Nothing about the freedom of that evening was being taken for granted.

Many of the fires are still burning. Some families still don't know if they have a home to come home to. There are towns that have simply disappeared. I factor in all this as I read the headlines of this morning's newspaper about the loss of Supreme Court Justice Ruth Bader Ginsberg, on September 18th, her immense contributions to the betterment of our country, and the implications of what comes next.

Like the impartial forces of fire and wind, 2020 continues to assail us and bring out the best and worst in how we respond.

2020 ELECTION NIGHT AND AFTERMATH

There is no Santa Claus. I felt like a child realizing, for the first time, a chunk of their perceived reality had just crumbled. As an adult last night, it was the sinking feeling in my gut as I realized there was no big blue wave coming to impressively declare beyond any doubt we are, as a majority in this country, more than a collection of selfish, compassionless people.

I switched from the news to the back-to-back trio of *The Hunger Games* movies on my TV and finished up the leftover Halloween candy. In between I gingerly checked for local election results. I watched *The Daily Show* pull off a gutsy hour commentary with just the right amount and type of humor. I finished the evening watching a cooking competition on TV. Actually, by then it was early the next morning. When I slept, it was a solid deep sleep filled with dreams of funerals; planning, attending, crying, some real and most random references.

This morning, it took me a couple of hours to get a sense of how I feel and what to do with the day. Facebook is generally such a mess of help, camaraderie and strangeness. But this morning it brought sobering relief and the ability to allow myself to weep. Today will be a day of coming to terms, aided by time with friends, and reaffirming the also reality of those things that have not changed, at least not right now. I'll take a walk through the crunch of autumn leaves and spend time watching squirrels and birds go about the necessary business of preparing for winter. I will wear my mask and social distance. I can do my part in curbing the virus that continues to take and disable lives. What will develop is a knowing that there is more to this planet than any one country's struggles, and actions count more than expectations.

I had planned to end my pandemic journal the end of December, but the events and tone that followed the election, in addition to a new strain of COVID-19 appearing, convinced me there would be no tidy wrap up of 2020. The spillage slopped over into the new January like a stone gathering only momentum and coming to land against an embankment of directional change.

THE LAST ENTRY IN MY JOURNAL OF PANDEMIC 2020

I've started this last post on January 20, 2021, having just watched the inauguration ceremonies of our 46th president and new vice president, realizing I am finally able to stop holding my breath. Back in November of 2020, just a few weeks after the election, a large body of people were convinced the election was a fraud and there might be no limits on what they would do to change the results. I clipped an article from the newspaper with the timeline of constitutionally defined dates and events that happen before an inauguration. It explained what happens at those events and how our democratic process is spread out. As each date came up I held my breath a little tighter until that day had passed and the process was still intact. I visualized it as a large tapestry. We step back and see the overall design, but every thread of the fabric is important and necessary to preserve the integrity of the design and its value. So it is with the dance between protesters, the process and the role everyone plays. The voters, the poll counters, the certifiers, government officials, judges, the ethics of the electorate right up through the three federal branches of our government. As each date passed, I felt relief, but not enough to just relax and breathe. I was waiting for the day congress would certify the election as valid and the ensuing inauguration later that month. I was not assuming anything.

January 6, 2021: carnage, democracy on a tipping point... jackals- the politicians at all levels who have lied to promote their own pocketbooks and careers, peaceful protesters fearing the loss of democracy, foreign and domestic interests whose agents used manipulations and violence while promoting and taking part in terrorism to increase their influence.

The lack of both masks and safe distancing added a whole extra dimension of danger for not only those in attendance that day, but to all they would come into contact with. It was a day of deliberate vandalism of the peoples' building, thefts, threats, looting, loud pronouncements of taking back rights and freedom by demolishing democracy, shouts to hunt down and execute non-helpful members of congress. But worst of all there were deaths, dying while attempting to overthrow the government, and others dying to defend it… all while elected officials were attempting to certify the results of an election that had already been checked and double-checked for its veracity. It's always shocking when we discover something we thought was so strong it could be taken for granted, isn't. Yet the fragile democracy and the Constitution still remain. The inauguration took place and with it comes a shift in tone, style and content.

The actual pandemic turned out to be dual in content. One is the medical, physical one and the other a malignancy of deep bigotry and hatred that finally erupted for all to see and come to know. Medically, mutations in the COVID-19 virus have been found around the world with at least one of them having the ability to infect much more easily than the original strain. Within weeks of the notice, new waves of infection are springing up everywhere. The good news worldwide is creation and approval of vaccines. The caveat is production, dispersal and actual inoculations of so many millions of people worldwide. Newer strains might show up resistant to these vaccines. We all become the trial participants as only time and cases can provide answers to the questions of efficacy; if you are vaccinated how long is it effective; and if you don't get sick can you still pass it on to others not vaccinated… also the scary vision of our children as guinea pigs for effect on the young.

But today, even though there are active elements still working to overturn the promised change of direction for this country, I can stop holding my breath. Today it seems possible to focus on common direction and unity to help my country return its children back to their classrooms, for businesses and employees in redefining and building the economy that actually affects and can help most Americans. Today feels a little hopeful. Let's see what the next week brings.

MOVING FORWARD

At the end of January 2020 a news source made me aware of a virus In Wuhan China, where it seemed, the virus had jumped from an animal to a human and now was spreading. As I wrote of starting a pandemic journal, there was no way to know what would transpire in that year. I'm glad I didn't know. I'm glad I wrote the introduction and these seven entries as events were happening. It's important to always retain the ability to find things to be grateful for, to strive to maintain the best of us in all times. But I hope all that made up the year 2020, especially the worst of it, will be heeded and used to avoid being caught in a year like this again. I hope the resolutions and solutions lead us in the direction of peaceful national and global alliances to protect and heal the planet, our ability to attain and maintain good mental and physical health for all, and both find and utilize equality and equity for all. That is my prayer. In the meantime I find I've once again had expectations I didn't know I had. I know that by my disappointment and frustration over the chronic political discord in my country. I somehow thought in the days following the inauguration there would be a noticeable dissipation of threats and undercurrents of violence. I've gone back to watching only limited amounts of the news. I'm giving myself the dubious luxury of just breathing and doing Covid-19 normal things. The turmoil of both pandemics continues and I will soon step back into the fray to be a positive presence again… but not today.

The Epilogue
(I wasn't planning to write)

Thank you, Amanda Gorman. *Fugue,* the poem you shared on the CBS Morning Show on Dec. 7, 2021, moved me from my prior last entry on taking action again "but not today." I felt the emotional impact of the possibilities you offered. In my initial comprehension of hearing you, you asked us what we can believe in, what must we believe in. I found myself saying "Yes, today I will stand up and believe that today and in every coming day I can bring the spirit of kindness, grace and hope. Why? Not because life is better or worse with these components, but because life is all of that."

The Interviews

Introduction to Interviews

When I think about all the events that happen, making life so interesting, it isn't hard to come up with difficult and unwanted journeys that cause heartache. The kinds of things most of us, a loved one, coworker or neighbor we know, has gone through.

I decided to conduct five interviews with people touching on those kinds of unwanted journeys. I originally wished that I could meet with each of them and have conversations, simply taking notes as we talked. I visualized how seeing faces and body language would make the experience more pleasant and insightful for them and me. Instead, because of the pandemic, I asked them questions over the phone. Two interviews are on the same subject and I asked them the same questions. The other three are each a separate subject. In order to capture their words, the tone, pauses and tensions, I needed to focus completely on listening. No space for thinking of anything else, what I might want to say, what was going on around me... simply listening and keying in as quickly as I could. Sometimes I had to ask them to pause so my keyboarding could catch up. I sent them each a copy of what I wrote and asked them to correct or add whatever needed to be done to have an accurate accounting of what they were willing to share with me for this book. I asked them to determine how they wanted to be identified... full name, initials only, or whatever would be most comfortable for them. I needed to convey my respect for their willingness to open up about difficult subjects and I wanted them to be comfortable with the results. It's one thing to think about a difficult subject and totally different to actually talk to someone about it. To then see it in print is a whole other experience. The consensus: it was helpful to them to see their words on paper. For some, it clarified and simplified where they were and what needed to come next. For some it was a relief and a way of sharing to help others. I read one interviewee's interview out loud to them and was told it was a welcome and intense experience.

I feel privileged to have had this experience, to realize the profound difference and value of truly listening, and to feel the intensity in a very clear and expressive way of others dealing with the difficulties life presents. I feel fortunate to know these quality people who make up the following interview section.

Interview with Drew

QUESTIONS

1. What was the situation or the action that created an unwanted journey for you?

   The unwanted part of my journey was my journey into full blown alcoholism. I was overtaken, like being on a train you can't stop. I felt utterly alone and isolated and beaten down till I was thinking about killing myself... no one action caused it, maybe genetic and born with it, maybe predisposed. I just didn't know how else to deal with things.

2. What is your definition of an alcoholic?

> Reaching a point where I no longer wanted to drink but had to drink... it wasn't even an option. Never even considered not drinking... only how was I going to be able to drink today and hide it.

3. How old were you when you started drinking?

> I was seventeen years old and a junior in high school drinking and smoking marijuana. The marijuana was easier to get than alcohol... all an escape. I tried lots of stuff at least twice but eventually set down marijuana and all the other stuff, turning to drinking only.

4. How old were you when this path became a problem and tell me about your journey.

> By the time I turned forty one, I needed to drink. I was drinking anything, lying about drinking, and hiding my drinking until sobering up at fifty one years. If you haven't had this kind of experience, it's hard to describe what it did for me... it helped me hide from my feelings and who I was. In my family, behaviorally, I grew up with the understanding that if you look good on the outside all is well. I wasn't able to pay attention to what was happening on the inside. I used that as a guide to tell myself there was no drinking problem. I did this to the best of my ability for a while and then it became a battle with wanting to tell people how I felt but wasn't able... couldn't face losing my "look good." It became unsustainable. I was so physically sick at the end... there were hangovers, shaking, headaches. Every morning began with me

throwing up with dry heaves while brushing teeth. While throwing up, I would think about how to pull off the day's drinking. Even more brutal was the hard work it took every day with family and job to keep it up. I barely hung on to job, house and car, but used those to say I can't be that bad. Didn't realize I was killing myself.

5. Where are you in this journey now and how long have you been sober?

I've been sober since October 2012. It still feels like a journey but rather than the unwanted journey, it is now the unexpected journey. Today I am comfortable in own skin, okay with who I am and able to share who I am with others without being afraid, even when outward appearances aren't so perfect. It is an indescribable relief, to not feel like I am being judged. 1,000 pounds has been lifted off my shoulders. I had never shared with anyone that I am bisexual before I got sober. The fear of day to day living, of being found out, the booze wouldn't fix it anymore… to discover it's okay to be who I am and that I can still be accepted, rather than being ridiculed and shamed if I was honest with anyone. All I have is my story and if this helps just one person, it's worth sharing. I can talk about who I am and what I feel, specifically on this issue. As a good athlete, even getting scholarships still didn't help me feel like I fit in with that group in high school. Events eventually caused me to feel terrified of being outed against my wishes. This was happening near the beginning of my heavy daily drinking. My secrets were going to kill me and alcohol was the vehicle. I'm thinking now of the sense of relief that came in sobriety… when I was able to finally tell this secret… the weight of the world had been lifted. I finally thought, "maybe it's going to be okay… maybe all the dire consequences aren't going to come to pass. Maybe there is a solution." Today I can tell, when it feels appropriate, to share my story if it can be helpful to someone

---

Interview with Mary

QUESTIONS:

1. What was the situation or the action that created an unwanted journey for you?

    It's not the typical answer for someone in a 12 step program… but emotional neglect as a kid set me up for alcoholism. I was in a family where my dad had already gotten sober but had unrelated bipolar disease, so living with him as a kid was volatile and scary. When I drank for the first time I felt a comfort and an ease I had never experienced in my life. Did I have a chronic fatal condition? Yes, I was unable to not start drinking, even when I knew it would eventually kill me.

2. What is your definition of an alcoholic?

    Someone who is unable to stop drinking once they start no matter the consequences and someone who can't not start drinking, no matter how bad it was the last time they drank.

3. How old were you when you started drinking?

I drank when I was probably twelve years old but I was terrified because my mother talked to me about alcoholism a lot after dealing with my dad and my three older brothers, who all had drinking problems. So the first time I drank, I only had a little out of fear. At fifteen I started drinking and it became my solution to my fear, anxiety, worry and feeling apart from. I drowned out everything I already knew about alcoholism because I simply just wanted to drink. I had blackouts, I lost periods of time where I had no idea of what I had done or where I had been. I began to obsess about if there would be enough to drink once I started and when I could drink again once I stopped.

4. How old were you when this path became a problem and tell me about your journey.

Problems started in high school, and at fifteen years I already had a problem. I did things when I was drinking that hurt other people and that I was terribly ashamed of. From the outside I looked happy, but inside the shame of drinking was already there and I wanted to hide how much I was drinking and how afraid I was of being an alcoholic. But I already knew I had a problem and I barely graduated from high school, partly because of drinking, but also because I was an emotional mess. My family life was scary and dysfunctional, gave me no structure or direction. I was lost. I knew there was something really wrong with me and I believed I was broken in a way no one else would understand and I was sure it wasn't fixable. I worried I would be like my dad,

who by then was unable to work, reduced to sleeping or pacing with paranoia. I went to college and
just drank. I skipped classes, and found the people
who drank like me. By this time, my capacity to
drink was massive, so much more than others. I was
kicked out of college during my sophomore year.
When I got home, my mother made me get a job. So
I was a bartender for the next four-five years. All my
time was spent with people who worked the same
and drank the same. I stopped being with friends
from the past because of my shame and feeling less
than. There was one period when I got an office job,
thinking the problem was working in a bar. I tried
to control my drinking and it worked for a couple
of months. But I was so miserable wanting to drink
every day. Eventually I found the people at my office
who drank like I did and happy hour became a daily
routine. I never understood why people left early
to go home to families rather than stay and drink.
At end of my drinking I found places to drink all
night and then went directly to work sometimes in
the same clothes from the day before. At the end of
my drinking I started using cocaine and that was a
really fast downhill to my bottom. Coming down
from cocaine, I was as close to being suicidal as I
had ever been. I ended up with a very small world
that included a drug dealer boyfriend and my last
real friend who finally said it was too painful to
watch me and had to stay away. My last night drinking was in a basement and I had a moment of clarity
where I had a thought of, "I can't do this for another
minute." I got up and walked out. It was a beautiful

day. As I was driving down the street I saw people living normal lives, walking dogs, having coffee and all I could think was, "I just want to be normal. Why can't I live a normal Saturday morning like the people I see?" I was filled with despair, sadness, fear, and hopelessness. I knew I was an alcoholic and drug addict but this felt bigger than just that. I felt too broken for any solution. I went to my mom's house and felt like I was going to tell her the truth for the first time.

My mom just looked at me and said, "Are you ready?"

And I said, "Yes."

She called one of my brothers, who took me to a 12 step meeting and I have been sober ever since.

5. Where are you in this journey now and how long have you been sober?

Now I know the problem... alcoholism and drug addiction. I've had so much hope since my first sober day because there is a solution that works no matter what the problem is. I've now been sober for thirty two years. I no longer feel broken and I found a God more powerful than any fear or hopelessness. Today I can be proud of the person I am. It's taken time and work, including some professional therapy. But today, no matter where I am, my insides match my outsides. That is with family, work, my 12 step program... always my authentic self. I'm married now to a man who has been sober for 27 years and I have two stepsons, and we have healthy and close relationships. I feel at home, I feel safe, and I feel loved and loveable. I finished college and graduate school in sobriety and I have a successful career that allows me to be of service in a most fulfilling way. I stay in the middle of my 12 step program, where I can help other women who have been in those same broken shoes find the same hope, joy and faith that I have found in my program. I feel grateful and blessed for the life I get to live today.

Interview with Steve B.

QUESTIONS:

1. What was your unwanted journey?

   My unwanted journey was losing my home after having lived there for 12 years and was given only six weeks to move out.

2. When and how did it happen?

   Living in the house were myself and two house mates. We were all on good terms with the owner. When one of my house mates left for a while it turned out the other housemate didn't want her to return at all. She started talking to the owner and before we knew it, the owner decided it would simply be easier and less stressful to get rid of all of us and probably sell the house. This all happened the summer of 2020.

3. What and who were affected and how?

   I was deeply affected. It felt like this was my home

not just a house. The neighborhood and one of my housemates created a core group of friendship together so it was like losing family... very traumatic. This also impacted the owner who had to look at her life's priorities. The roommate who had been away was looking forward to returning to what she felt was her home. The neighbors were greatly impacted because we were all close like Mayberry RFD neighborhoods... celebrating holidays and our lives together. The house was located in a special part of town overlooking both river and wildlife area. Gardening, one of my great interests, meant I had lovingly placed and tended to all sorts of plants and gardens on the property. Loss of bonding and relationships on so many levels.

4. How are you and where are you in this journey now?

I'm still in the beginning of getting settled. Going through the normal grieving stages of initial shock, and speed to which the move happened. It felt like dealing with a death but now has moved on to anger and I still can't communicate with the roommate who instigated the event... that connection is no longer there. But I am also at beginning of gratitude for a new home with a friend and that is a positive situation of respect and rebuilding. As a single person at my age, it's not so easy to find a positive situation. Life is very challenging but there is also comfort and support from friends. It's a mixed bag of feeling of so much new and letting go without having wanted to... like shopping at a new store when you knew where everything was at the old store. This will get more comfortable. The old house will go on sale, the owner prefers to sell it versus having it torn down, but will have to see which buyers appear. For me… both reassuring and disturbing. That house was like an old friend to me and I would hate to see it torn down and replaced with something new and out of place with the neighborhood. It seems to be tied to my own mortality, which I had been avoiding. I know others have had to leave a beloved home with even more years at residence, a sign often of aging.

5. What prompted you to share your journey with me and this book?

   When you asked if you could interview me, it woke up my imagination as a way to process what was going on with me… a healing opportunity.

Interview—Anonymous

QUESTIONS:

1. What was your unwanted journey?

   The end of my marriage-a long path around a mountain, neither climbing nor falling.

2. How long were you married and any children?

   I was married for 40 years. Yes, 2 adult daughters and 4 grandchildren

3. Tell me about that path

   The difficult part of my marriage began 20 years ago when I intuited something was wrong, that my

husband was not an honest person. I did the best
I could by modeling honesty and kindness. But
that led to him being resentful, angry. I look back
with my wise 20/20 eyes and wish we had gone
to counseling then! Twenty years of looking away,
but finally I now know he was, over many years,
unfaithful.

Suggesting we go to therapy was a scary call-I
knew that to go forward into an authentic life meant
everything had to be laid out on the table. Ultimately,
therapy laid out the body of our marriage for burial.
Now I realize we were dragging a dead marriage for
several years. His being unfaithful and my inability
to face the possibility were symptoms, the stink of a
rotting corpse that he knew about and I suspected
but denied. I just couldn't see it before, because of
the deep dishonesty and gaslighting on his side, and
my inability to accept that he could do such a thing. I
resisted the impulse to look more closely.

The divorce was a release of my expectations
of where I thought my life would go and how he
and I would be. It was a mechanism to free us
both from the predicament of a marriage that was
over. Gravity won out.

4. Where are you now in this journey?

Living by myself, especially during a pandemic,
has had its challenges, but on the whole I can say
I am happy with my life and how I am living it.
Sometimes, circumstances come up that I would
have shared with my ex, leaned on him about; but
today I have even deeper friendship, a medita-

tion practice and new ways to deal with life. It is clear to me that the comfort of allowing myself to stay - for the luxury of turning to him for comfort, for familiarity – was too high a price to pay for the emotional freedom I now enjoy. The fears and discomforts I face are resolved each time with a feeling of growing strength and confidence. My relationship with my children was initially strained but now more complex and so much richer: better than it ever has been, because we have endured some heartache and growing pains that have made our ties stronger. Our new configuration has rendered us more able to individualize our attention and had deepened perspectives and appreciation for one another. My relationship with my ex is calmer and more productive, and we have found a way to be family-and to put family ahead of our individual needs and comforts, for the most part.

5. What did you gain from this journey?

I have regained a sense of self and reunited with my younger self while exploring who I am as an older woman. The compare and contrast work is deep and fulfilling. There is sense, at times of giddy anticipation for what comes next. The path is being made as I walk it… versus my past prospects in a marriage where expectations often set the path. I feel more like who I was as a kid, and am profoundly grateful.

6. What did you lose from this journey?

I'm not sure I lost anything irretrievably; for a while, at the end of marriage, I lost my self assurance because of my gas-lit predicament and inability to understand what was going on. When we rely deeply on another's honesty and it fails us, it makes us doubt our own judgement, our ability to see clearly, to walk steadily in any direction. But I am no longer lost. I did lose the illusion about what marriage is, about what permanence is, about, what happiness is; and all those illusions, once broken, now have facets that reflect both sunny and dark perspectives. I am like the poor scientists across the world after Galileo and Newton. Hard truth about gravity and the universe, but new knowledge, and a feeling of joining my future as a bright and bumbling collaborator instead of enduring it as a predestined passenger, fractious and sleeping, by turns.

7. Any final thoughts to share?

Just that when I think about an unwanted journey I think about resistance and that has its place for me as a marker. When I am resisting something, often it's because of misapprehension or fear about it. But resistance is a call to arms: the flag inviting my attention to something I must lean into, be curious about and possibly surrender to.

Personal honesty is a core principle that helps me see clearly what I fear. Courage is what I have to muster when I feel the urge to look away. Faith in myself is what fuels that courage, and experience is what tells me I have done it before and can do it again- and that each time I move forward-to new landscapes, new possibilities.

Interview with Amy S.

QUESTIONS:

1. What was your unwanted journey?

   Losing my hearing- I loved music and the sound of people laughing. The audial progression… It was devastating. The awareness came about twelve years ago. It probably started slowly before that… just not hearing the low range of sounds. I tried joking about it in the beginning, but soon was not able to pull that off. People took not being heard personally and unhappily.

2. Tell me about this journey?

   I had gone to a large store that had a department for hearing aids and did testing. I had heard good things about them in terms of their testing, products, service and low pricing. The pricing was important because most insurances don't pay for adults hearing aids. They told me I was suffering from profound hearing loss. They wanted to know medical history but because my parents died without disclosing any of this info to me I was unable to give them any genetic history on hearing issue. I remember asking the audiologist if she knew a possible cause, would that fix it? "No," she said, but it could help with genetic info for my kids. I simply trusted the audiologist, the free testing and recommended hearing aids for both ears. My left ear was worse, and the testing couldn't tell if the loss was progressive. She said I would need a head scan for that. This meant I needed to go to my regular doctor to get a referral to a specialist. I got a team of people and was tested again to validate followed by the head scan. It was tricky finding the best pricing for the best product for my specific needs. I'd urge anyone in this position to be sure to investigate needs, quality of product and pricing and service because they vary to a surprising degree. Hearing aids are like buying a car... soon as you buy, a new better version becomes available and the whole process needs to happen again. Continuing service is extremely important, as the software for the hardware (hearing aids) is updated constantly. Once I had the hearing aids, I discovered I had to get used to the assault of real noise again... like even the rustle of paper, click of cars turn indicator. Hearing aids amplify sound. At that time I didn't know my cochlea was damaged... This created loss that was profound and progressive. After a while, I couldn't catch speech consistently. I started to avoid places where I could hear a sound but not make out words and life got much smaller. Also began a great deal of thinking about acoustics, for example, wooden floors and walls don't carry sounds well. I was getting too exhausted in trying to listen. It was a heart breaking situation for an extroverted person like me. Conversations became too difficult to try any more. It was hard to advocate for myself and I felt broken. I didn't understand hearing aids couldn't really help with cochlea problems (those are the little hairs deep in the ear and they carry the sound back to the brain to process). This became clear after my second pair of updated hearing aids. It took me about 1 ½ years to make the decision after a second set of hearing aids. It was then I was told about the progressive nature of the damage and that no hearing aid would help with this. At that time I heard about cochlear implants. I went back to my doctor, now becoming assertive with questions to get the answers I needed for my options… which seemed to include a bone implant (which doesn't help people with damaged cochlea), medical grade hearing aids a little while longer or the cochlear implants. Of course, another round of hearing tests was necessary to qualify for implants. Then came research for what that is and how it affects you. I learned from cochlear specialists that my hearing loss was not only profound, but aggressive, especially in my right ear. In addition, having the procedures has caused some people to lose the rest of their natural hearing. That was terrifying… what a choice… continue to lose my hearing ability slowly or take a risk on trading it for hearing now with a cochlear implant but possibly losing what I naturally had left immediately. In the process, I went to concerts and realized most of what I thought I was hearing was really my memory of what the music sounded like. Praying for willingness to be willing to look and learn, letting go of grief and trying to move into gratitude for years prior of having been able to hear. I sought to accept current reality and be grateful for options. I needed to stand up for myself and accept I deserved the ability to hear. I joined an online cochlear implant support group after seeing three different audiologists, who all verified prognosis and said a cochlear implant was the only option that would work. The online group was helpful. I didn't bare my soul, but tuned in periodically and talking to real people and their experiences was even more valuable than the literature I was given. Between the people and the literature, I learned tips for keeping further damage from happening and what I was getting into.

3. What is a cochlear implant and how is it compared to regular hearing or hearing aids?

A receiver and mic that transmits to a processor are implanted in the skull with a wire that follows the hearing nerve. Usually the worst hearing ear is done and a hearing aid specifically designed to work with the implant is used in the other ear. The implant ear connection to the brain needs to learn to hear from a whole new place which requires time and training.

4. Where are you now on this path?

Speech in the implant side (my left ear) sounds like a drunken fly with a tracheotomy. I have an implant in the left ear only and got a new hearing aid for my right ear that would interface with the implant. After I got the implant, I was given time to acclimate and then it was turned on. It's designed to patch the sound that has been missing… like high pitch noise, and is slightly different for each person. Finally I heard a sound that was birds chirping. It works at a different frequency than regular hearing aids. I have to learn what sound sounds like now, rather than before. Having had hearing before, I know the cadence and pitch of sounds and have memory of what the sounds would correlate to. A hearing aid amplifies, but an implant bypasses that process and digitizes. This brings a whole other level of grief... hearing is there, but will never be the same. There is still so much adjusting.. building up a muscle in my brain that is not usually used. Activation was overwhelming... headaches, minimized sound, exhausting... I need to periodically take out the hearing aid to focus on the implant... so many levels and time... I can no longer just listen. My exercise consists of taking the hearing aid out and having someone speak with hands in front of their mouth so I am relying on hearing only with no sight to assist. I still have some normal hearing in my right ear but not much so I try to watch subtitles on TV, and use audio books-starting with ones I'm familiar with. There are also several apps for hearing therapy available for most smart phones. For speech comprehension, the sub titles verify what I'm hearing. I try to hear music with implant only... some adjustments will allow more music in. Speech is easier in the way it comes into the brain. Different frequencies come in at different speeds as well as noise variations... there are differences between regular sounds and electronic... I hear treble in my implant ear and bass and mid sounds in my right ear. There is also a difference between regular and electronic sounds. There are more games to play that will help me arrive at the best possible hearing for me and it is much more of a journey than I had imagined.

5. What are your thoughts and hope for the future?

> The implant was done about two months ago. Right now, I ask for willingness and courage to do the therapy. It requires work and effort and I'm still dealing with sadness... feeling overwhelmed. My left ear's hearing on its own, it's gone. It is a loss even though I knew it could happen. I really have to go forward with the therapy to be able to hear... more and more relying on the implant. It's hard because the hearing aid made it so much easier... but in the long run it would have failed me... thus, the reason for the implant. I'm hoping all the therapy and work will lead to a new normal that allows me to really hear again. And I've found, in this journey, hearing loss is really common... but people don't want to talk about it.

Jack's Story

On Being Better:
My Greatest Journey Yet

By Jack Kauppila

I saved Jack's story to be read at the end of the fourth type of journey because of how he shares a spiraled slice of his life. Jack has a magical way of zig zagging from today to times past and what comes next that is grounded in both hard reality and stream of consciousness. His story is a circle that encompasses all four sections of this book. There is a coming to know that each adventure brings part of the old circle with it as it continues on as a new circle. We get the realization, the sense that having arrived is less a final destination than a point of being, filling up, acknowledging, and accepting. You may, like me, need a moment to reflect and then, like a giant Anaconda snake, having devoured its prey whole, or in large gulps, pauses to digest.

y greatest journey yet, I'm still on. It began a couple years ago with a completely impromptu trip to a small town in the coastal range of Oregon. But it really began the year before that with a cross country trip to move my son to Philadelphia.

And that wouldn't have happened without an eye surgery gone terribly, terribly wrong.

But, actually, it began 30 years before that with the car wreck that led me to get the surgery, so many years after.

And the 27 years before that were filled with travels, and journey, and searches within and without that led to a horrible night that ended with me hanging upside down in my truck on the edge of a cliff beside the tide flats in Tacoma, Washington.

Phew...

It may not sound like it yet, but this story is one of healing, redemption grace, forgiveness. It has some pain, because what would we have to heal from if we didn't get hurt? And, while the healing process sort of sucks, let's be honest, being healed, the state of having healed, feeling better, being better, well that feels pretty awesome.

This essay is about Being Better, because being better might just be the whole damn point.

———

MY SWEET MARY AND I HAVE DISCOVERED WE ARE really good at road trips. Thank God! Because, before we discovered this, we volunteered to move our son Nelson to Philadelphia, PA! Six thousand miles there and back is a long way to go in an over-packed car if you're not really good at road trips.

It's a long way to go even if you're good at it. There are so many things that have to go just right. And it's not the engine, or the tires, or the luggage. Or even the roads and the motels and the Waffle Houses-although we did have a minor kerfuffle at a Waffle House after a long day on the road.

What has to go just right? It's all in the packing:

<u>Must Haves:</u>

- Toiletries
- Underwear
- Willingness
- Shoes
- Jackets
- Acceptance
- Forgiveness
- Phone chargers
- Gratitude
- More phone chargers
- Love and Tolerance
- Books
- Medications
- Grace
- Trust
- Snacks

Must Leave Behind

- At least half of the shoes you packed above
- All but two of the jackets
- Expectations
- Assumptions
- Any weapons-loaded or un
- The past-including what happened when you realized you had to leave half your shoes behind
- Fear

Actually, if you leave the Fear behind, everything else, the toiletries and shoes and books (even the phone chargers!) is probably going to be just fine. Hide $20 in your shoe and find a Big Box or a Gas'n Sip.

Our trip came preloaded with some big fear-factor triggers. Derailers. Things that put us immediately into fight or flight mode and can send the whole trip into a ditch. One was the Rocky Mountains-pretty hard to cross the Continental Divide without being on high, narrow, curvy mountain roads. So we found the lowest mountain pass for our return trip and one fear dissolved before us-thanks AAA!

The second obstacle was that the entire northwest USA was on fire! Wildfires blocked the highways and freeways in Washington, Oregon, Idaho, Montana. AAA couldn't quite find us a way through the Inferno, so I pulled on my daddy-pants and found us a route across the south side of Mt. Ranier in Washington and took us through eastern Washington and southern Idaho, avoiding most of the hot spots. We had a couple of glowing red evenings as we made our way across Montana, but the freeway wasn't blocked and we just kept moving forward, fearless.

Funny how fearless and delusional look alike sometimes.

Our other derailers were a little more subtle.

Now, I'm Pacific Northwest, born and raised. I grew up making midnight runs back and forth across the Cascade Mountains, escaping whatever nightmare my mother, sisters and I currently found ourselves in. That's what road trips (had always) meant to me-being forced out of wherever we lived, with no idea where we were going or what we'd do when we got there.

Wildfires, mudslides, volcanoes, floods, these things had nothing on me! Coming home from school to find out we didn't live there anymore, that kept me in a constant state of fear as a kid.

Guilt, shame, and resentment, fear's ugly cousins, should all be on the Do Not Pack list; they all have the power to trigger that 'fight or flight' instinct and derail your journey at any point. None of them came with us on our cross country trek. Instead, when we drove through Spokane I was able to think, 'Yup, this is where Mom got arrested when we lived in the park...' and it had no hook, no weight, just a funny little tickle acknowledging that it happened.

I left out the violent, suicide bits when I told my kid and just focused on the terrain. I was able to point out the state park in Montana where we lived for a while. And the abandoned copper mine we holed up in (punny!). And the general direction of the hunting shacks we 'borrowed' to get out of the cold.

But the stories weren't filled with all the blame and shame and misery they'd carried in the past to justify whatever crappy thing I felt or did. They were just funny little anecdotes to keep the car entertained as we made or way East. And soon, I ran out of them, as Montana turned to Wyoming, and Wyoming turned to South Dakota. We filled the car with funny new stories about the giant elk burger Nelson ate (giant burger, not sure about the size of the elk), or the great flour I found at Wheat Montana! (their exclamation point).

And then Mt. Rushmore, where we rescued a couple of Taiwanese damsels in distress from getting eaten by bears-at least that's where the story ended up by the time we hit Wrigley Field.

But first, Foreshadowing on the Mississippi...

This is where I absolutely fail my Junior High Geography quiz: Who knew the Mississippi River flows by Wisconsin?!?! If I remember right, Huck and Jim never mentioned escaping up that grand ol' river to Wisconsin? It's beer and cheese, right, Wisconsin? Not beignets and chicory coffee like the Mississippi River I met in Louisiana.

It was the end of a long day of driving and I was in no mood to defend my Junior High geography or my literature degree. We followed the corkscrews off the dark highway and swirled our way into another 'Overnight Express' type of hotel. It promised a free, hot breakfast, but that seemed a lifetime away and we were BIP-STB (pronounced bipstub it means Back in Pajamas-Straight to Bed).

Standing there on its banks, in Wisconsin of all places, with my Sweet Sweet Mary and my baby boy, I felt part of something even greater, more majestic and loaded with such great power. I was so happy to share that with my son like we'd just shared something that would change us forever.

"Can we get breakfast?" Nelly asked...

We snapped the necessary pictures to prove to whomever that we'd been there, and made our way to the dining room.

Our eyes were pretty glazed-over by the time we'd arrived the night before, but in daylight the place looked clean and well-cared for. The dining room looked like it had been frozen in time during an Orthodontist convention in 1978. And there we met Mr. Bentley and his famous Bentley Eggs.

We knew a thing or two about Complimentary Continental Breakfasts by this point in our lives and current journey: Make a pancake in a machine; somebody eats a boiled egg; everybody's disappointed; get out quick.

Mr. Bentley was having none of that! He led us to the perfect table in the empty hall and then walked us over to what he'd prepared for us that day. It felt just like that, like he'd prepared all that stuff for us, specifically, and he was so happy to make sure we had everything we needed.

He introduced us to his scrambled eggs. Now, they weren't what the hotel wanted him to make, he told us in confidence, but he just couldn't see fit to make bland, boring hotel scrambled eggs. Mr. Bentley mixed his eggs with a little cream and seasoned them with his own blend of seasonings. The eggs came out fluffy, soft, and filled with flavor.

This part's about grace. It's about love and service.

We had a wonderful breakfast there on the Mississippi in Wisconsin. Mr. Bentley stayed close, asking us questions about our trip and telling us stories about his own journey up and down that river. He cocked a fuzzy eyebrow at the thought of us delivering Nelson to Philadelphia, but assured us that'd be okay if he stayed close to the college. This worried Sweet Sweet Mary a bit, but I and Nelson were undaunted and we had somewhere to be. Not the same 'somewhere', but...

LISTEN

The first thing I did in planning our trip was to buy home game tickets to a Cubs game. Actually, the first thing I did was map every major league ballpark on the way and cross-reference their schedules with our timeframe. There were spreadsheets involved. Through the same misguided geography that got us to the Mississippi River in Wisconsin, I had us seeing the Colorado Rockies, the St. Louis Cardinals, the Cubs, Twins, Brewers, Tigers, Indians, Reds both NY teams and of course the Phillies. I was saving Boston for a trip of its own, I'm not crazy!

And that was just getting there-you should have seen the trip home.

While most of the schedule required some pretty clever refolding of the map to make the mileage work, some of it actually required time travel. Since I couldn't quite get the spreadsheet formulas to work on a quantum level, when I saw that the Cubs were playing the Mets in Wrigley Field I pounced.

Chicago was only a couple hours way from our Wisconsin breakfast. We checked into our hipster hotel-a bed, a couch, and a closet with a toilet in it-right beside the "L" (when the trains went by it was like we were livin' in the movies!). The hotel clerk assured us we were walking distance to Wrigley Field and so we wandered out to see the neighborhood and find some great Chicago pizza on our way to the game.

Let's talk about 'Walking Distance...'

———————————

SEE, I'VE BEEN HOBBLING AROUND FOR THE LAST 30 OR so years, since that dark dark night in Tacoma I mentioned at the beginning of our journey. It was 3 a.m., a drunk me, a sober tree, and a truck upside down on the edge of a cliff with me hanging from a seat belt.

It was a month of being in a coma and many more months learning to walk and talk and think on my own again. It was a deep, dark bottom that I kept digging deeper for the next two years.

And then, recovery. Let the healing begin! I had suffered a traumatic brain injury that affected the left side of my body, so I walked like a drunken sailor. I had one good eye and a blind one that wandered off on its own, so nobody was ever quite sure who I was talking to. And I was sober.

For the next twenty years I practiced the principals of my recovery program, started a career, got married and had two beautiful boys. Got divorced. I met and married my Sweet Sweet Mary, and we do our best to live each day in love and service to each other, our family, and the people around us.

… And some days it rains…

After all those years of living with my disability, I was still bothered by the most glaring example of my injury-my droopy, blind, yet still wandering eye.

Through a strange, cosmic alignment of an Ophthalmologist, a surgeon friend of hers, and an insurance plan with a great deductible, it turned out I could have my wayward eye fixed for the cost of a copay. I would still be blind in that eye, but at least it would be looking at you when we spoke!

OH THE HUMANITY

It was Christmas (Happy Christmas to me!) and I scheduled the surgery for the first Thursday in February.

Since that day, about eight years ago now, the eye has been in constant, show-stopping pain. I was back at the doctor the Saturday after the surgery, the Tuesday after that, and about every other week for the next three years.

This unending pain shortly developed into Complex Regional Pain Syndrome, which has hijacked the pain centers of my brain to send debilitating pain signals throughout my body, all day, every day.

Wait, that sounds ridiculous! I thought we were going to a baseball game!

Stick with me-remember, this is about healing.

For the next three years I became increasingly unable to function. I lost my career, my volunteer activities; I couldn't cook for my family or spend time with my boys and my Sweet Sweet Mary. I grew ever-increasingly disappointed by doctors and the medical community. Doctor after doctor quite literally threw their hands in the air and asked, "What do you want me to do for you?" As if telling me I had a syndrome were enough.

And then I was done. I was done fighting; done feeling like a victim; done looking outside for an answer to what was going on inside. I returned to my meditation practice, and came back to the breath. Each breath brings me back to the present moment, right now as it is. As each pain arose I welcomed it like an old friend-not all friends are pleasant when they arrive, but I welcome them warmly: "Hello my little friend... how are you? What can I do for you today?" It's a practice, and practice isn't perfect. Some moments are still met with despair and disbelief. Yet, I'm still breathing. I go back to the breath and watch how each pain, no matter how severe, has the same characteristics of beginning, persisting for a time, then passing.

I stopped saying, "I can't," and started saying, "I'll try." The more I tried, the more I found I could do, and "I'll try," became "Yes, I can." So, when my son said he was moving to

Philly, I said, "Can I take you?" And he said, "Yes," and Sweet Sweet Mary said, "I wanna go!" And our road trip was born.

WE MADE IT TO THE FIELD JUST AT GAME TIME. THAT grand old stadium, so much larger than life! That big red sign announcing "Wrigley Field Home of Chicago Cubs" and the matchup-Mets 0, Cubs 0, Top 1. I was absolutely dumb – struck - part of me still doesn't believe I was there. And then the real walk began.

One of things I love about baseball is that you can still find really cheap seats for most games. I outdid myself at Wrigley. We entered through the front gate, found our section, and began our ascent. We climbed and climbed those awkward, vertical, mini-steps carved in concrete. Then we climbed some more, crawled over some other super fans and worked our way to find the highest row of seats in the stadium.

We were high enough to feel a constant blast of wind off of Lake Michigan. Embarrassingly, I must admit that at one point I wondered why they didn't turn off the damn air conditioner! Then I realized, "Oh, yeah, 'The Windy City,' Nevermind… "

It was a great game. It was the sound of a 100 mile an hour fastball hitting the catcher's glove; the crack of the bat; the turn of a double play. The Mets took an early lead with a solo home run, but Chicago came right back and led the game 7 to 2 by the time we left at the bottom of the 7th. I was getting anxious about making it back down those steps, and honestly, my enthusiastic rendition of 'Take Me Out to the Ball Game" has prompted my family to rename that part of the game "The 7th Inning Screech," and we were all ready for me to leave at this point.

By the time we hit terra firma on the hard streets of Chicago I was a jiggling, pain filled wreck. The breath was hard to find and a nasty old tape started playing over the screaming pain in my head and limbs. It told me I was disappointing my son, burdening my sweet sweet wife, and ruining our night in Chicago.

It told me that I was a disabled wreck of a human being and nobody could love me.

The entire trip hung in the balance as we stood in the glow of that big red Wrigley sign. If I listened to that tape all would be lost - I would shut down, wrap myself up in pain and suffering and lash out at anyone who tried to break in.

I found a breath. In that brief moment of space that the breath provides, I was able to tell my wife and son that I was really done and couldn't make the walk back to the hotel.

"Well," my Sweet Sweet Mary smiled, "let's take one of these pedi-cabs!"

Pedi-cabs! They were everywhere! Sure they're a tourist trap, but we were tourists! And it wasn't that far to the hotel, so how bad could it be?

We told our skinny little hipster on the pedals what hotel we were at and settled in for a long, traffic-dodging trip through the north side of Chicago. It was perfect! We turned a 15 minute walk I couldn't do, into a forty-minute terror ride we wouldn't have traded for anything!

This is where all the willingness, acceptance, love and tolerance, gratitude and grace from our Must-Haves packing list come in. I was honest about my condition and we gave ourselves permission to change our plans and try something new and unexpected.

Maybe this is where traveling is at its best. In those unexpected, undeserved moments of grace that could never be put in our travel plans, but that make the entire trip meaningful.

FOR SOME...

It was at this point in our journey that Nelly began asking "Why are we here?" This was his version of *Are we there yet?* Sprinkled with a little *OMG, why didn't I just fly!?!?* Elk burgers and baseball games aside, he had an apartment to move into and a new life to begin in Philadelphia. We picked up the pace, slowing only to snap pictures as the Welcome signs for each state whizzed on by.

We found our way to Philly and wound our way up historical avenues of beautifully restored buildings interspersed with streets of boarded up housing, abandoned lots, inner-city poverty and ethnic division. I began to ask my own version of, "Why are we here!?!?"

The area was sketchy. This was definitely the dodgy end of the block. This was the Philadelphia that had caused Mr. Bentley to raise a fuzzy little eyebrow.

OH, MY...

We found Nelly's basement apartment two blocks from the ivy-covered halls of his friend's university and right across the street from, "Oh, hell no! I never gave permission for this!"

To be fair, we had done our research: the neighborhood was safe according to all the police reports; his roommate had been in the area for a year without incident; and, finally, Sweet Sweet Mary had a friend in Philadelphia married to a cop, in addition to a fierce contingent of northeastern family only a couple hours away. Nelly had all the phone numbers and all the confidence that twenty-something brings, but, as the three of us stood in that empty, dingy-grey basement, we realized we weren't quite ready for this next phase of our road trip.

"Howbout a cheesesteak!?!?" I diffused the tension with food (judge me later!) and we made a hasty exit for a Philadelphia landmark.

Then we found a Big Box downtown and stocked up with bathroom items, kitchen organizers and cleaning supplies. A plunger. We still weren't ready to go back.

I wasn't ready to let go; not yet.

But, as we drove around the city, Nelson began telling us some of things he'd been learning about his new town. We saw beautiful murals painted on old brick buildings and he told us about programs that offer artists the chance to do projects like this around town.

He told us about his plans to explore his artistic expression and groups he could be a part of on campus with his roommate. I began to breathe again.

And in that space the breath brings, we were able to come up with a plan: Nelson would stay the night with us in our hotel and tomorrow we'd get him set up in his new apartment. Whew, what a relief it is to have a plan!

We slept like babies.

The next day we found a warehouse store with all the furniture-in-a-box we needed to keep Nelly off the floor and his clothes in a drawer. We had to fold the kid up like origami to get him back in the car amidst his new furnishings. We still laugh ourselves to tears when we think of our mad, bouncy trek back to the 'hood'.

Remember how sometimes fearless looks a lot like delusional?

Technically, we still had one more night in Philly planned. We had a cute little B&B scheduled, and the Phillies were playing baseball the next day, so we could have had one more family day together. But I was ready to go!

This part of trip seemed complete - we got Nelly to Philadelphia. He was set with hours of cartoon furniture assembly instructions and allen wrenches, so it felt like time to go. I'm not sure I communicated this with my Sweet Sweet Mary all that well, I don't think I understood it myself - I was just ready for this part to be over. She took my hand and said, "Okay, let's go."

Our trip through the south was peaceful and beautiful. I blew it in Nashville, though, where for some reason I talked my Sweet Sweet Mary out of some adorable cowboy boots that she really should have gotten. I made it up to her by not making her go to the Graceland strip mall in Memphis. It was enough to say we drove by.

In the sense of full disclosure, I should mention that we called Nelson every hundred miles or so to see how his furniture was going together, and if he'd changed his mind and wanted to come home - I was ready to turn that car around in a heartbeat!

We visited a presidential library, the Oklahoma City National Memorial, and I got snack-shamed by some locals when I tried to figure out boiled peanuts at a gas station (seriously, people, we don't have those here in the Upper Left, USA). We snuck our way across the Grand Canyon and up through southern Utah. There were some exciting moments in a snowstorm on a windy mountain pass, the very conditions this route was designed to avoid (Kids! Listen to your geography teacher!), but we made it through to Salt Lake City. Then it was up, up, up to Idaho and all the way down the Columbia River in Oregon to our beautiful hometown.

It was this journey that prepared us for everything that came next. It was nothing but faith, hope, trust, willingness and grace that got me off the couch to even try a crazy trip like this. It was an equal or greater dose of all the same that let Sweet Sweet Mary believe I could do it, and that she could do it with me. And, whatever it was that allowed Nelson to say yes to being trapped in a car with his dad and step mom for a week, well, that's a gift I will forever be repaying.

See, I told you it was about healing. It's about being better. Despite physical limitations, pain, more pain, a past filled with trauma that could derail us at any moment, fear, poor geography, boiled peanuts (seriously!)... despite all the things that could have derailed our journey, we stayed in the moment, breath by breath, and it made us better.

And it led us to our next great adventure! That little road trip to the coastal range I mentioned at the beginning was the actual beginning of my new life as a small town baker. It was the perfect next step for me in learning to live with my pain condition and still live a life of service. The pain hasn't changed, but saying 'yes' to life has allowed me to find joy in my days and I've begun to consider my condition an attribute, rather than a limitation.

Being better is a decision I get to make each day. It's a journey, and the journey continues as I practice saying yes to what's next. And, while I'm not sure where this journey is taking us, I am sure that we will arrive safe and sound, and better for it, as long as we keep the Must Haves with us and the Leave Behinds behind us. It's all in the packing!

Returning from the Adventure— with a Side Trip

efore going on, a reminder this book is nonfiction. What I have written is my actual experience and I take the word of the guest authors that their writings are accurate as well. My goal in writing this book was to take you on a series of adventures with me, including some not often covered or viewed as part of traveling. If you picked out those sections that spoke to you, I hope you found them a worthwhile read. Hopefully, if you've read through the four types of travel and journeys, you noticed in the process we've created a whole separate travel adventure together.

My travels through the six continents may have awakened a desire to explore our beautiful planet. The equally interesting inward journey may also have caused an introspective look at your similar practices or what you might consider in adding to your life activities. All of us are in the journey of aging and maybe you felt the same sense of camaraderie I did with the survey participants, even the toddlers. Perhaps the variety of unwanted travels was uncomfortable, easy to identify with or foreboding.

I started with the largest section covering some of my world travels. People read about traveling for all kinds of reasons but the question does get asked: "Why travel?" Perhaps to see life as a series of adventures? And why find fulfillment from experiences more greatly than accumulation of things? I've found the lens you use to define and experience life becomes the perspective used in processing and determining further experiences.

I remember being at one workplace where I was sharing my photos from a trip. One of my coworkers waited until everyone else had left and then said, "I hope you don't mind me asking, but what did that trip cost you?" I told her and she looked at me with a totally shocked expression saying, "But you could have bought a dining room set for that amount of money!"

I remember responding with equal bewilderment, "Why would I do that?"

We just stared at each other for a few minutes. It was then I realized, because most people have to make tough decisions about large purchases, they tend to be either havers or doers. You either get your satisfaction from possessions or experiences.

If you're going to travel, it's good to have an idea of what you hope to attain from the experience, where that might happen, and what it would entail. It's also good to know how well you handle risks, disappointments and changes to plans. The goal is to arrive back home feeling the trip was successful. The goal of some trips is relaxation, no worries. Other trips involve action and challenges. I suggest not waiting until everything is perfect. The trip you take at thirty will be very different from the trip you take when you retire. Find the balance for you of due diligence and enjoying life.

As I related in the bridge stories to inner travels, I had never really considered traveling to be other than out there in the world. It took the possibility of me not having that option to be open to examining that large internal and mostly unknown place. For me the internal view provided a truly unexpected adventure. Some days it is a narrow pathway too rocky to go into and yet other times find me moving, jaw agape, as I take into my heart and mind a new clarity and depth of emotion, thoughts and directions. It was pleasing for me to read the guest authors' varying ways of connecting to that space and the power found within. I learned a lot about subjects not that familiar to me. The Mandalas and their purpose are a good example, especially the creativity involved.

I included the prayer I put together and use daily to take the temperature of my wellbeing because it is a practical tool, keeping me in awareness of the largeness beyond my everyday thinking. And while all this feels intensely personal, it is universal in the same way we both yearn for and require water, food, shelter and light.

Looking at the way we move through our lives and the viewpoints that shift or become entrenched through aging, could easily become a book of its own. The survey was designed to have no real capacity for extensive data analysis. I resisted any urges to simplify or dehumanize the results, using the human experience to define capsules of life at so many ages. One thing I have since wondered about is the impact on the high school students who graduated into the Covid-19 pandemic and so many other areas of volatility. I hope each of them was able to find their way through a year that demanded we acknowledge the future always has the capacity to redefine plans and expectations.

The bridging story of my mom's journey into dementia was very difficult to write. The relationship wasn't always warm, but the older both of us got, the more we were able to accept the differences and similarities, both jarring at times. I've found the relationship is still there, even ten-plus years after her death. It is more subtle and reveals itself in different ways. Also, love expresses itself in such a variety of ways. I wish I had known and been able to translate them better. It was hard, but I felt it important to share with honesty and caring the slow motion travel taken not only by my mom but her family and people who cared along with her. It is, unfortunately, a situation many families have to face. I remember my mom, in a point of just being confused, not yet into the deeper end... I would take her to a doctor appointment or the store and people would chat with her, asking her secret for being her age and still so vivacious... she always told them she had a piece of good dark chocolate every day and advised them to do so as well. There often ensued earnest conversations on the merits of various brands of chocolate she enjoyed. Those little memories helped mitigate the loss of those kinds of moments later on.

The interview section of unwanted travels was hard to determine because there are so many different directions this could go. I hope at least one of these situations presented struck a chord with you-something you've been through or felt, or perhaps reminding you of someone you know, or caused you to consider the plight of a situation not normally in your scope.

As to our journey together, I know I am not the same person for having experienced these travels, working with the guest authors and interviewees, and feeling your presence as this adventure unfolded. I hope the experience has been as powerful, informative and varied, and in the end, a positive experience for you as it has been for me.

But the book doesn't quite end here. Like so many travels, just as we think our adventure is over, we see a sign at the side of the road beckoning us to take just one more narrow path up some hill for a slice of opportunity. So, following is a section titled "The Notes." I didn't want to interrupt the flow of each section so I didn't insert extra observations, additional facts or even footnotes. Instead, this final section has information in the order of related stories with their page numbers as they appear in the book. For example, more information about the Anaconda snakes of the Amazon Basin, data on the massive dam I visited in China, a detailed visualization journey you can take, information I recently discovered relevant to Max and Rita's story, famous quotes that have gotten me through strange times and more. Enjoy.

The Notes

p. 62: My first trip to mainland China: the poet Li Bao

The poem I wrote in Greenland seemed to be eerily
similar to the poem recited to me as being written
in China centuries before by the famous poet Li Bao.
I have since, looked up the characters on the scroll
and in adding them to what our guide said it seems
his poem is speaking about "water sky color, endless
wind moon, without edges or end."

p. 98: My third trip to mainland China: The Three Gorges Dam

Just for a sense of the scope of this project, I'm
quoting some stats from the book "Three Gorges
Project in China" by The China Travel and Tourism
Press. The idea of controlling this river had been
floated since 1919. The Yangtze River is the longest
river in China, 6,300 kilometers, starting in the
Qinghai-Tibetan Plateau and running from west
to east, eventually finding its way to Shanghai and
out into East China Sea. The three phase project
was officially announced to the world in 1994. The
plan was to have all phases completed by 2013. The
goal entailed relocating almost one million people
from the flood prone areas, to provide flood con-

trol, improve navigation, provide more power, and enhance tourism. The grounds around the dam area include a building housing all sorts of information on the process and parks for the people's enjoyment. The locks are numerous and while I was there, a new lock was in the process of being built.

p. 140: From India: new insights on the ladies in saris.

One of my beta readers is originally from India. After reading the book, she gave me her thoughts on why the ladies might have withheld their smiles. She reminded me first, I did not know what the driver had actually told them. Also, in India, as in so many places, there are cultural norms for women. Emotional displays, including smiling, would not be considered appropriate to be shared with strangers. Thus, we don't know whether my original theory is correct, or whether they were pleased to get the ride and happy to comply with the photo request.

p. 154: From Brazil: More about Anacondas.

On rereading my notes of the morning in the jungle when we saw the giant Anaconda break through the dock, I wondered if I had been exaggerating but in researching, I found from many sources, including LifeScience.com, Anacondas can indeed be over thirty feet long and weigh as much as 150 lbs. They are common in the rivers of Brazil. They are preda-tors that can eat a deer of 120 lbs. and first restrain their prey with sharp curved teeth, then usually drag them under water, with constricting as their killing technique. I don't know what caused it to break through the dock but there is no doubt the workers must have felt they were battling for their lives in that moment.

p. 199: How the Money Appeared for my Trip to South Africa and Dubai

The great opportunity for this long dreamed of trip had one big caveat. The price was certainly a great deal, but I had no budget for a trip of this size. What to do? I remember sitting at my dining room table drooling over the specifics of this adventure and possibly said out loud, "If only I had the money!" Within minutes, the doorbell rang. I wasn't expecting anyone. On my porch was an express mail envelope and the delivery service driver was waving at me as he drove off. I thought it was most likely for one of my neighbors, but my name was on the envelope. I went inside and opened it up. It seems an employer I had many years ago had a pension fund for employees, and I had been enrolled in it. In reading the letter, I found out I had just turned old enough to start collecting the pension. It stated how much I would get each month and when it would start. I only needed to confirm the information they had on me. I would have enough to pay for the trip. I danced around the room looking up, laughing and saying, "Thank you, thank you."

INNER LANDSCAPES:

p. 257: The prayer I shared in *Taking My Temperature* had suggestions on how to use it. In case you prefer the prayer without the extra comments, here it is:

Thank you God for letting me be me, here today.

Thank you for the _____, _____, _____ and sanity I have today.

Please help me to maintain and grow in these areas.

Thank you for the awareness of your presence and knowing from my own experience, you always have my back and really all of me… which is the best place to be.

Thank you for the quality of life I have today, the quality people in it and the more quality person I have become and yet am still growing into. And that's okay.

Please help those who are suffering in any way to find relief and guidance through you.

I ask for your goodness and light to do its work for me and all those concerned.

I ask to be open and clear to catch your intuitive thought or intention for me, and when I have it, to take the right action today.

Please help me to be a positive presence and bring my patience: on the road and with myself

Please help me to not cut off people in conversation or on the road but if I do, help me to make amends and stop doing it.

Thank you for my family

Please, extra-large portions of your grace, your guidance, your blessings, your mercy, your joy, your safety and good health-both physical and mental for _____.

Please, your grace and guidance for this very extended family as well.

Please help me to be a good _____, _____ and a good
friend to them all including myself.

I ask for strength to endure, to last, to be.

The power to heal and the wisdom to learn.

How will I do that? Please help me to bring my honesty, my
open mindedness and my willingness into the day.

Please help me to use the gifts and talents you've given me
well and be of service today.

Thank you

Amen

p. 261: Two brief visualizations to bring peace and relaxation
to your day

1. thirty seconds visualization to relief stress and anger

I've used this at work often: Close your eyes;
visualize, in slow motion, taking your coffee cup
full of coffee or tea and throwing it as hard as you
can against the wall or cubicle partition. The cup
shatters and coffee is slowly in the air, running
down the wall as pieces of the cup float and land
on the floor, the desk,... ; you turn your head and
see people looking shocked, moving away, talking
without any sound; you don't care. You lean back
in your chair, put your feet up on your desk, relax,
smile and say, "Aah." Thirty seconds well spent.

2. one to four minutes to relax and refresh visualization

Sit comfortably and close your eyes. We will be
at the beach, but you could use the mountains, or
any other place that you enjoy. Breathe in and out
slowly a few times. The sun is warm and there is a
slight breeze. Note that you can feel warm, crunchy

sand between your toes. Wiggle and stretch your feet and toes. Continue to breathe in and out slowly, letting yourself feel the sensations of sand, sun and breeze. Let your body relax. Imagine glimpsing a kite flying. Note the colors of the kite and see the clouds. Are the clouds puffy or do they have shapes like ships, faces or whatever. Take your time. Still breathing slowly, notice the sound of the ocean. The regular sound of waves rolling into the shore is almost hypnotic. Take a few moments to focus on the sound of the ocean, the feeling of the sun and sand. Breathe in and out. Slowly open your eyes and notice how relaxed you feel.

UNWANTED TRAVELS:

p. 325: Max and Rita-additional notes from Rita

Just before finishing this book, I came across a small notebook from Rita. One page had directions for use of a new thermostat. The next was a recipe. The following pages were her remembrances as random notes on their times from 1932 in Berlin until leaving Copenhagen for the train station. I've pulled out comments that I think will add depth to the Max and Rita saga.

We married September 17, 1932 and both had good jobs. Still, we struggled financially to help support our parents. We had a small apartment that was cozy and comfortable. We were at the movies January, 1933 when over the intercom came the news that Hitler won the election. We were speechless. We were not alone, but about half the people there were jubilant. Most people thought he wouldn't last longer than a year, we belonged to this group.

Lots of our friends left the country as soon as they could, especially those with a lot of money. After a few years we realized we should also leave, but Mac didn't want to leave without his parents and both were very old. We sent entry forms to the Dominican Republic and Australia; both refused, they were looking for professional people or those sturdy enough to be farmers.

Rita's mother saw the ad for opportunities for single Jewish women to marry Danes, and that is how Margot escaped Germany, which ultimately led to Max and Rita's escape. There were many close calls in the transit from Germany to shores of Denmark. Shortly after the saving words of the guard who told them to not go home that night, there was a sharp knock on their door. Rita said they both thought it was Hitler's people to pick them up and take them away. It was Margot and her husband. Margot told them they had to be ready to leave by the next evening. Margot and Carl had rented a large boat, not fancy but large enough to take Max and Rita. They were to meet in the warehouse area of a harbor at midnight. There was only time for quick goodbyes.

We piled on layers of clothing. We had to take a bus to the railway station and walk to the harbor. The boat had both a large sail and an outboard motor. We hid in a disguised toilet area while Nazi inspectors came on board. Carl invited them to have drinks and a bite to eat while inspecting. They were actually so close to us and it seemed to take forever, but perhaps kept the search from being too thorough. Then came a storm. The sail broke, the motor sputtered and then died. We drifted the rest of the day. Eventually, we ran into the shores of Denmark. Carl worked for the government and could not be a part of our arrival. We were instructed to take a train to Aalberg and go to the police department and report we were illegal arrivals. We told them we had walked across the border through a wooded area and that a friendly man with a wagon had given us a ride. Clearly the police didn't believe us and teased us a bit but never bothered us again, as we made our way to Margot and Carl's home. One morning I woke up to a roaring sound. I jumped out of bed and ran outside. As far as you could see the sky was covered with formations of airplanes. Max was up too and said they were probably Swedish. But when we looked closely they were German planes. We told Carl. He laughed. He said that wasn't possible. The Danes would go to war with the Germans before they allowed Germany to invade Denmark. He had a leisurely breakfast and went off to work. He was back ten minutes later, angry and frustrated: he had to cross a bridge to go to work and on the bridge were Germans. They didn't let him cross to get to work. Carl actually cried. He was so ashamed and frustrated that nobody was fighting the Germans. A few days later, a German officer went from house to house to find out how many bedrooms each house had and how many people lived there.

It was time to leave Margot and Carl. Max's sister, Elsie, had sent a large wooden box to Margot's with warm clothing for us and some of Max's patterns. We took these with us to Copenhagen. We had met a lovely and anti-German couple who then invited us stay with them in the country. It looked very plain from the outside but inside it looked like something out of a fairytale. It was so elegant, with oriental rugs, original oil paintings, a table set with the finest of china. We stayed there briefly. It was from there, we finally headed to the Trans-Siberian Railway and our futures.

(You may have noticed in these notes, written many years after they arrived in the United States, Rita referred to Max as Mac. In order to feel and appear more 'American,' Max had his first name legally changed to Mac. I don't know if, in later years, he still thought it was a great idea to change his name, but the name stuck and Rita fondly called him "Macki.")

WRAP-UP

Here are a few additional suggestions to put the odds for a successful trip in your favor:

1. Basics-Money and time:

   How much money do you have available for all the expenditures of your trip? This includes the large basics of travel to and from your destinations, meals, housing, and entertainment. Also, consider the smaller basics- unexpected expenses like illness or injury, souvenirs and gifts, anything unique to your situation.

How much time do you have for your vacation? If you have constraints like a job, or health issues, it's wise to leave a little extra time after the trip to allow for heavy traffic, plane schedule changes or just breathing space before jumping back into your regular routine.

2. Location:

    Do you have one place specifically in mind, or is it more a matter of what fits the desired activities? If you are traveling with others, each person in your group could describe their version of what this vacation would be like and where it could be. This helps avoid disappointment and arguments during the trip.

3. Comfort and safety:

    Are you traveling to areas that might be dangerous? Do you hate the idea of having to arrange and set up everything, or is it part of the excitement of the trip for you? Your answers will help determine whether to go through a travel agency, go with a tour group or set out on your own.

4. Cruises if the sea is calling you:

    Some things to consider when planning a cruise- Do you want a large ship with lots of entertainment, dressing up for meals, athletic facilities or do you want a smaller ship with fewer formalities and on board options? Do you want a ship that caters to families, adults only, or no particular focus? How important to you is all-inclusive for tours, wi-fi, meals and beverages versus basics included and paying extra for those other amenities you want.

5. Trip reminiscing:

> While I hope you won't see your whole vacation through your camera lens, taking photos, keeping a journal, considering a playlist, DYI videos, or scrapbooking are all great ways to keep your vacation memories fresh as time goes by. Pick those ideas or others you come up with that work for you. Most everyone thinks they'll remember events, that amazing sunset, the name of the couple that you went on the tours with. But they don't and then it's too late.

6. To maximize your trip, remember there are three parts to your adventure:

- The pre-trip is a time for planning and anticipation
- The trip is living the actual trip
- The post-trip is sharing the trip with others and remembering your experiences

MISCELLANY:

Useful Quotes-Here are a few of the quotes I use to add savvy and perspective.

"When I am out of red, I use blue," by Pablo Picasso. I think when a volatile and talented painter such as Picasso runs out of the color he wants to use, surely he would throw a temper tantrum… but no. He simply turns to another option and goes on with his painting. My path is smoother when I do that too.

"When you come to a fork in the road, take it," by Yogi Berra. I take this to mean: be flexible, remember you have options and keep your sense of humor.

"To live is so startling, it leaves little time for anything else," by Emily Dickinson, reminds me to really experience where I am right now.

When I am in a really annoying situation, I ask myself, "If I saw this in an *I Love Lucy* rerun, would I laugh?" Usually I would, and knowing that calms me down and reminds me of Rule #62. I don't know who first thought of this rule but it is a reminder to not take myself too seriously.

"And suddenly you know: It's time to start something new and trust the magic of beginnings," by Meister Eckhart.

Acknowledgement

I'll start with gratitude for having discovered that for me, journeys are improved when shared with others; especially when the sharing can have a positive effect on people. I learned that first in writing about the painful spinal peril I endured and shared in *My life as a Metal Sculpture: Navigating Through Medical Adversity* in 2013, and the related workbook in 2014.

More recently, I had a desire to create a different kind of book, one that would highlight some of my most memorable travels but also explore other ways in which we move through life. I wanted the book to feel conversational and wondered how I could share these travels around the world and connect them with journeys more textured, and varied.

Without the help of the following people, *Traveling Beyond the Surface* would have contained more awkwardness and less clarity, more unneeded words and less character. The writers group I belonged to during the writing of my first book had disbanded. I was without any such group for several years. Just as I seriously committed to writing this book, I discovered The Embracery-a small writers group that gave me just the right amount of honest feedback, TLC, and encouragement. I felt very fragile about my writing at that time and without Steve, Nancy, David, Tara, Jani, Peter, Daniel, Greg, Duncan and several others who attended occasionally, I'm not sure I would have finished the book I am now proud to have written.

Thanks to my first reader/editor, Tina Meier-Nowell for her bluntness, creativity, thoroughness, expertise and enthusiasm. I expected to be making many changes but held my breath waiting to see if I had pulled off the overview of my book's goal. Her "yes" made next steps so much easier.

My thanks are also joined with much enjoyment at the variety of responses from my six beta readers-Nick, April, Saaz, Clara, Dennis and Shelley. I felt, instinctively, that they would provide the feedback needed to move closer to publication. Each brought their special set of evaluations and skills, leaving me comfortable with what the next rounds of edits needed to be.

Thanks to Price Luber and Nancy Hoffman Bieber for their eagle eyes, and willingness to proof the just before going to the publisher manuscript and the just before book printing.

There was no question of who I wanted to publish the book. Luminare Press published my first two books and they made the process easy for me. I also appreciate their integrity and working with a woman owned local company. I am happy to report Luminare Press, which was a newly formed company by Patricia Marshall only a couple of years before our first venture together, is now larger, thriving and with its own office, staff and connections. Once again, thanks to Patricia and Luminare Press for turning pages, designs, ideas and a desire to get it all out to the public shaped into a reality.

I needed to come up to speed with marketing, distribution, and social media. Thanks to the *Nonfiction Authors Association* under the guidance of Stephanie Chandler. I attended their virtual conference in the spring of 2021. The cost of the conference was reasonable and all the seminars I attended helped me develop knowledge and confidence that were critical. The Willamette Valley Conference, attended earlier gave me a good foundation. Seminars from Alessandra Torre of Inkers Con, as well as Sue Campbell of Pages and Platforms have also helped bring me up to speed.

How much less in value my book would have been without input from the guest authors, interviewees, and respondents to the surveys. Special thanks to my granddaughter, Kyra, for her assistance both as a participant and in viewpoints regarding the survey.

Support, encouragement and honest appraisal from my son and daughter were critically important to me. Thank you.

Finally, "Thank you" to a few famous people who don't know me but have inspired me specifically in creating and completing this book:

Amanda Gorman for sharing her tremendous gift of inspiring with hope and clarity as well as her own story of persevering to use her voice to achieve her dreams.

Trevor Noah, for showing how well balance can be done with multiple disciplines and talents. He does this in a way that preserves who he is while employing humor, truths, and by giving opportunities to many voices and organizations that deserve a chance to be heard.

Ibram X. Kendi, in his book *How To Be An Antiracist,* gives lessons on how to share incredible amounts of information, definitions, and history through sharing his story of heart felt living. I also appreciated being able to read and get into the book because he left the necessary notes for the back of the book instead of on every page. Although I am not the writer he is, I borrowed this concept of note use for the back of my book too. I have also gained from being exposed to his ability to take the complex and both organize and display it.

Stacey Abrams is an amazing model for being centered enough to simply do what she intends to do. Family, politics, writing books and more. No fanfare, justifications, adulations, or permissions seem to be required. This is being a grown-up woman.

And I give thanks for the opportunity to be a part of the connectivity that flows through all of us.

Made in the USA
Middletown, DE
04 August 2022

70433667R00245